Ships of the High Seas

In 1895 the steamship *Ruatehu* and the sailing ship *Turakina* were following the same course through the 'Roaring Forties'. In the unofficial race that followed, sail—surprisingly—beat steam.

Ships of the High Seas

by Erik Abranson

with 20 paintings by
Edward Mortelmans

Peter Lowe
2–4 Queens Drive London, W3 0HA

Acknowledgements

Erik Abranson: pp. 17 (bottom), 40 (bottom), 62, 70, 71, 79, 90 (bottom)
Alphabet & Image: p. 80 (bottom right)
Bergens Sjofartsmuseum: p. 25 (bottom)
Bethlehem Steel Corporation: p. 109 (left)
Brunel University: pp. 81 (bottom), 85 (bottom right)
Central Press Photos: p. 106 (left)
Cutty Sark Society: pp. 88–9
Druppel: pp. 104, 105
Mary Evans Picture Library: p. 69 (bottom)
Globtik Tankers Ltd: p. 121 (left)
Imperial War Museum: pp. 106 (right), 107
Michael Lennon: pp. 109 (bottom), 116
The Mansell Collection: pp. 28 (centre), 32 (left), 33 (top), 36 (top & bottom), 40 (top right), 41 (bottom), 48 (top), 52, 53, 61 (top & bottom), 80 (bottom left), 82–3 (top), 88 (top right), 89 (top right), 90 (top), 91 (top), 93 (centre), 97 (top), 97 (bottom left), 101 (bottom right), endpapers
Colin Mudie: p. 61 (bottom)
Musée de la Marine: pp. 56, 72 (bottom right)
National Maritime Museum: pp. 31 (top), 32 (right), 37, 40 (top left), 48 (bottom), 49, 57, 60, 65, 68 (bottom), 73 (bottom), 77, 88 (top left), 89 (top left), 93 (top), 96, 109 (top)
Pictor: pp. 11, 14, 31 (bottom right)
Popperphoto: p. 85 (top)
Radio Times Hulton Picture Library: pp. 20, 72 (bottom left), 81 (top), 84, 85 (bottom left), 97 (bottom right), 101 (centre), 101 (bottom left)
Science Museum: pp. 41 (top), 72 (top), 73 (top), 76, 100–101, 121 (top)
Seaphot: p. 22
Schleswig Holstein Landesmuseum: p. 25
Ronald Sheridan: pp. 23, 24, 30
Shipping World and Ship Builder: pp. 117, 121 (right), 121 (centre)
Swedish Maritime Museum and Warship Wasa: pp. 42, 44, 45, 46, 47
Town Docks Museum Hull: pp. 80 (top), 80 (centre)
Universitetets Oldsaksamling Oslo: pp. 21, 25, 28 (bottom), 28 (top), 29
US Government Printing Office: p. 71
US Navy: pp. 112–113
All diagrams, in colour and line, are by Ray Woodward.
The diagram on p. 93 is from a plan by Harold A Underhill, published by Bassett-Lowke Ltd.

Far right: One of the last of the square riggers, the three-masted steel bark *Penang*, remained in commercial use until she was sunk by an Italian submarine in 1941.

Captions by Brian and Eileen Horton

ISBN 0 85654 019 6

Printed in England by W. S. Cowell

Contents

Foreword

Ships have played an important role in the history of mankind and his civilization. They made world-wide exploration possible; they were at the origin of new nations such as the United States; they made the wealth of maritime leagues such as the Hanseatic League and Venice and of maritime empires such as that of Great Britain; they brought other empires, such as those of Mexico and Peru to an end. Perhaps most significantly of all, they were both cause and effect of international trade and until recently they were the only means by which large quantities of heavy goods could be transported. Even today, despite competition from railways, trucks and aircraft, they carry the greatest part of world trade.

This book explains the history of ships by describing nineteen ships, chosen for their historical or technological significance. The different ships are treated informally with the emphasis adapted to each one. In some chapters it may be the technical achievements the ship represented that were her chief claim to fame and made her typical of her class or of her times. In others it may be the history of the ship herself which is most important. Again, the men who built or manned a ship may have a larger nautical significance and their story is in these cases linked with that of the ship herself. Whatever the emphasis, however, there are comprehensive technical details of the individual ships.

Seen in sequence, the nineteen different ships show the gradual evolution from early Viking longships to the giant supertankers of the present day. To start with the Vikings, however, would be like starting a novel half way through and before the chapters on individual ships there is therefore a brief summary of earlier sea-going vessels.

The introduction forms a general background to the chapters that follow, with details of hull shapes, the principles of sail, sail plans and rigs and the development of mechanical propulsion. There is also a section on the relatively new science of nautical archaeology, without which many of the facts contained here would never have been known.

Erik Abranson

Introduction

The Hull

A hull, regardless of its method of propulsion, must have the following qualities: seaworthiness, capacity and speed. Unfortunately the features promoting these qualities often conflict with one another and hull design is a matter of compromise. Different hull designs have the desired qualities in varying proportions and an order of priorities must be established before designing a new vessel.

The most important element in ship design is the length/beam ratio. High ratios produce long ships which are fast but have less carrying capacity than hulls of the same length and greater beam. The Oseberg ship, the *Cutty Sark* and the *Queen Mary* are 'long ships'. Low ratios produce capacious but slower vessels. The big Roman grain ships of antiquity were typical round ships. Although they do not represent extremes in low ratios, the *Victoria,* the Liberty ships and the *Globtik Tokyo* were or are 'round ships' in comparison, respectively, to caravels, the *Queen Mary* and the USS *Enterprise.*

The use of plans in ship design has only become generalized since the end of the nineteenth century. Before then vessels were built by experience, rule of thumb or by using hull models. Many of the famous clippers first came into being as half-hull models. Since a hull is symmetrical, models need only show one half of the hull. Modern line drawings show the hull in section, plan and elevation.

On the section drawing, different transversal sections are projected on the plane of the widest section. Only one side needs to be drawn as both are symmetrical and, conventionally, the forward sections are shown on the right hand side of the centreline and the after sections are projected on the left hand side. The midship section of a hull shows the maximum beam and the shape of the bottom or bilges and of the sides or walls.

The simplest hull shape has a flat bottom; it provides a roomy hull at the expense of speed and seaworthiness. Examples of flat bottom vessels are the *Globtik Tokyo* and all river and coastal barges, including the Thames barges.

The next simplest shape is the V-shaped bottom which can have varying amounts of deadrise, as the angle of the 'V' is called. The *Oseberg* ship and the *Constitution* belong to this class; both are rounded where the bilge meets the side (the chine) whereas many modern power boats have angular or 'hard' chines. Some of these modern hulls are meant to lift partially out of the water at speed, thus reducing the displacement and resistance. Such hulls have a pronounced deadrise forward which flattens out to a flat bottom at the stern. V-shaped hulls are faster than flat-bottom ones but they do not allow so much internal space; they are also not as seaworthy as round-bottomed hulls.

Round-bottomed hulls are the most common design for sailing ships, being seaworthy, stable and a good compromise between speed and hull capacity. The whaler *Charles W. Morgan* illustrates the round-bottom ship. In practice few ships have pure or extreme types of section, but are a blend of the different shapes.

The sides or walls of the hull can be vertical, they can curve gently towards the vertical—a common modern yacht feature called 'flam'—or they may slope inboard, tumblehome. Sailing men-o'-war and most of the pre-nineteenth-century vessels had tumblehome; it reduced weight above the waterline and was a good protection against boarders who would have to jump over a big gap. The clippers and many modern vessels have 'flare' at the bows. Flare is shown by concave sections.

The plan describes the hull seen from above and the contours at different horizontal levels, known as waterlines. In plan, the hulls can show either sharp or bluff entrances. The former improve speed, the latter allow more cargo space. The *Cutty Sark* provides an example of sharp entry, the *Globtik Tokyo,* one of bluff entry. In plan, small vessels tend to have continuously curved waterline and deck edge. Until the clippers, the favoured position for the maximum beam was forward of amidships, producing the characteristic 'cod's head and mackerel tail' hulls. Modern sailing yachts have their maximum beam amidships or even further aft. Larger vessels, sail or power, often have sides running parallel to one another for an appreciable part of the hull's length. When these straight-sided walls are also vertical they produce 'slab-sided' vessels, a feature of roomy hulls of large size. Ships and boats designed to carry as much cargo as possible, such as Thames barges and the *Globtik Tokyo,* are slab-sided.

The elevation shows the profile of the hull and the buttocks, the longitudinal sections running parallel to the centreline. The profiles of the bows vary according to usage and custom. The traditional design is spoon-shaped, although the shape was often hidden by the cutwater and figurehead assembly. The profile of the clipper bow is concave and its merits and comparison with traditional bows are discussed in the chapter on the *Cutty Sark*. Straight stems became popular with power vessels; they can be either raking (inclined) or plumb. Raked bows have more reserve buoyancy in head sea conditions. Plumb stems, which were also found on sailing smacks and pilot cutters are now old-fashioned. A new type of bow which is becoming a standard feature on all large, powered ships is the bulb bow. Basically a torpedo-head shaped bulb is added under the waterline; this makes the water flow in such a way as to reduce the power-consuming bow wave. The *Globtik Tokyo* has a bulb bow.

Sterns come in even more shapes than bows and the vessels described in the following chapters show a fair variety. Double-ended vessels, with pointed sterns, are generally more seaworthy than the other types; flat transom sterns are the least seaworthy, being vulnerable to following seas. The main drawback of double-ended sterns is the considerable loss of internal space. The Oseberg ship is the only double-ender described in detail here. The *Victoria, Mayflower, Wasa* and *Zeven Provincien* show examples of transom stern; the *Victory, Constitution* and *Savannah* also have flat transom sterns but below the waterline they have 'round tucks' which do not create such a turbulence (hence drag) as 'dipping' transoms. Later, elliptical sterns such as those on the *Cutty Sark* and *France II* came into fashion. These lack the charm of the sweep of windows lighting the great cabin but they produce much cleaner lines on the underbody, reducing eddies to a minimum, and they are more

Extremes of hull design: the flat hull of a Brazilian log boat (right) is built for sailing in shallow waters and needs no special adaptations for speed. The V-shaped hull of the steamer is more seaworthy and, with reduced resistance through the water, can move much faster.

seaworthy. Modern vessels have elliptical sterns, cruiser sterns and cut-off transom sterns above the waterline.

The sheerline is the profile of the upper deck. Mediaeval and Renaissance vessels had a pronounced sheer or curvature; by the nineteenth century many sailing ships, particularly naval vessels, had straight, horizontal sheerlines. The *Constitution* and the *Charles W. Morgan* have no sheer but the *France II* had a strong sheer forward. Small North Sea trawlers of today still have a considerable sheer which keeps the bows dry while giving a low freeboard amidships for easy net-handling, an important design consideration.

Hull design used to be an art but it has now become a science. The first tank-testing of models was done as early as 1670 but the systematic testing of new designs is very recent. Computers are now also extensively used, not only to assist in the drawing of the actual lines but to predict their hydrodynamic performance with greater accuracy.

SHIPBUILDING

Until the last century all ships' hulls were made of wood. Hides, reeds, pottery and bark were only used for small boats. The early method of shipbuilding, both in the Mediterranean and in northern Europe, was to assemble the planking first and to place the reinforcing frames afterwards. The Mediterranean people knew the saw and they could saw planks with neat edges that could be fitted edge-to-edge, carvel-fashion. However, they only had short lengths of timber to work on and they devised an ingenious method of fitting or tenoning the hulls together. The north Europeans had plenty of long timber but they worked with adzes and in the early days they could only produce rough edges. They found it more convenient to overlap the planks or strakes—lapstrake or clinker fashion. This method has survived to the present day for small boats.

Some time between the seventh and the twelfth centuries, in the Mediterranean, the modern practice of frame-first building appeared. By the seventeenth century this method was used throughout Europe for large vessels. Improved woodworking and shipwrightry techniques allowed vessels to grow steadily in size and the introduction of diagonal bracing in the early nineteenth century made it possible to build ships bigger than ever before. However there is a limit to the size of a wooden ship beyond which the hull becomes too elastic, hogs (sags on the keel) and breaks up. The largest wooden vessel ever built was the American six-masted schooner *Wyoming,* launched in 1909. She was 120 m long and had a beam of 18 m.

The first iron ships were built in the 1830s. At first iron simply replaced timber shape for shape but soon specialized designs were produced which were better adapted to iron and took full advantage of the new material. For instance the *Great Eastern* (1859) already made use of a double bottom which prevented her from flooding and probably sinking when she struck a reef. Shipowners were slow to adopt iron and there was a period of compromise when many ships were composite built, with iron keel, frames and beams which were conventionally planked and decked with wood. The *Cutty Sark* (1869) is composite-built.

Steel was first used in shipbuilding around 1870, and is now the universal material for all large vessels. In steel ships the keel is no longer the only longitudinal girder; the sides and decks have similar girders, so the whole structure is very rigid. Steel is an ideal material for double-skinned hulls, water-ballast tanks, and watertight bulkheads. It also allows huge hulls to be built—the *Globtik London,* the largest ship in the world at the time of writing, is by no means the technological limit in steel ships; there are plans for tankers of over one million tonnes deadweight.

One of the big advances in steel construction was the application of electrical welding to replace riveting. All-welded ships were first built in the 1930s (*Graf Spee*; *Queen Mary*) and they have become the rule since the Second World War. Prefabrication, which was pioneered for the Liberty ships, has also become the rule for building all large ships. Whole ship sections are made separately, and assembled later on the stocks. Plates are now often cut automatically under computer control.

Small craft, particularly pleasure craft, use a variety of materials, including plywood, moulded veneering, alloys, stainless steel and rubber. Two other materials, fibreglass and ferrocement are sometimes used for commercial or even naval craft under about 36 m. Fibreglass (glass fibre in epoxy resin) came into use in the 1950s and has since almost completely replaced traditional wooden boat building; it has the advantage of durability and it requires little maintenance. Ferrocement (fine concrete plastered on a web of wire mesh) has the same advantages as fibreglass and is also cheap. It became widely known in the late sixties although the method was pioneered over a century ago.

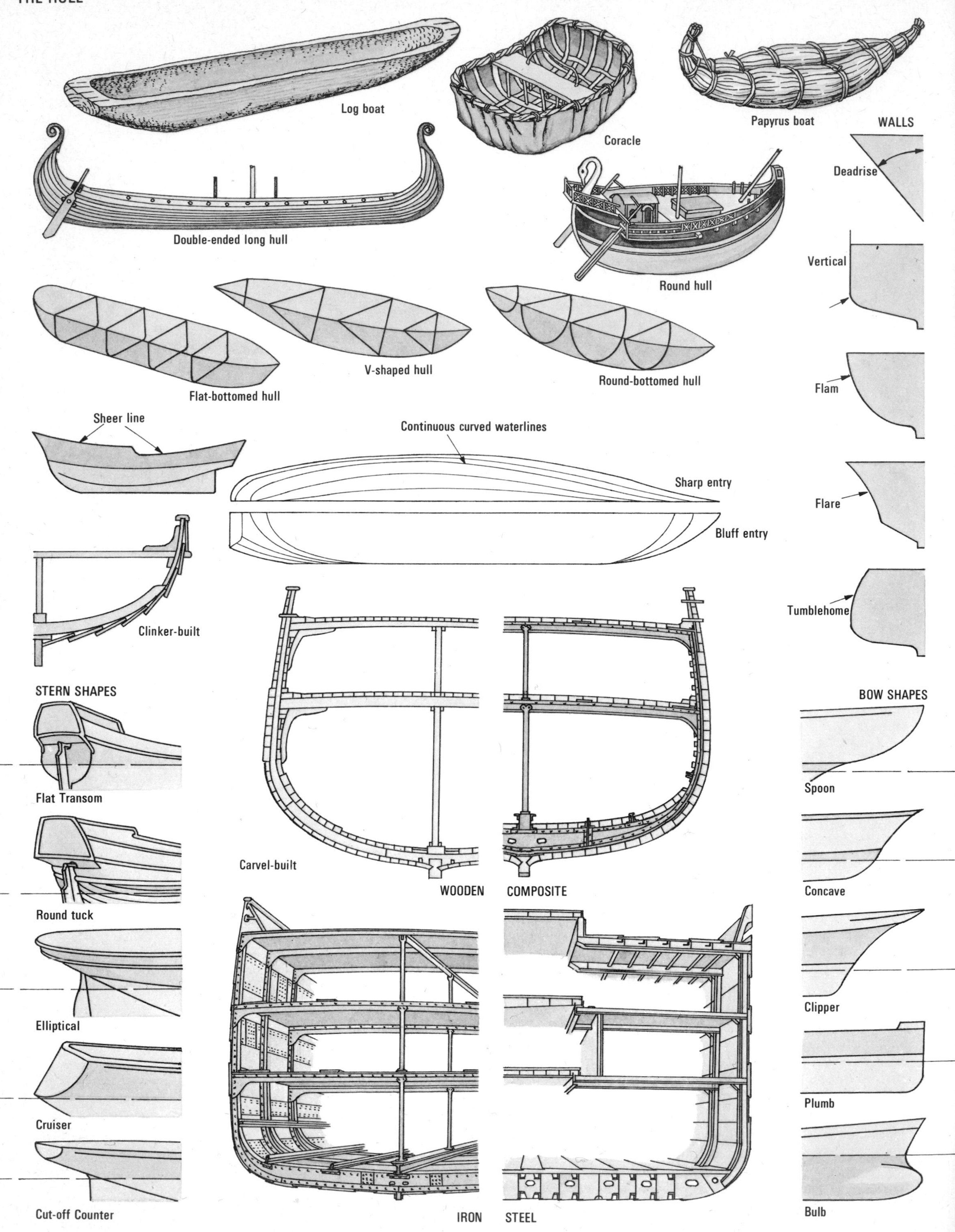
Log boat
Coracle
Papyrus boat
WALLS
Deadrise
Double-ended long hull
Round hull
Vertical
V-shaped hull
Round-bottomed hull
Flat-bottomed hull
Flam
Sheer line
Continuous curved waterlines
Sharp entry
Flare
Bluff entry
Tumblehome
Clinker-built
STERN SHAPES
BOW SHAPES
Flat Transom
Spoon
Round tuck
Carvel-built
WOODEN
COMPOSITE
Concave
Elliptical
Clipper
Cruiser
Plumb
Cut-off Counter
IRON
STEEL
Bulb

Left: Hulls can be divided into 'round' hulls, which have large carrying capacity but low speeds, and 'long' hulls, which are fast but can carry less cargo. Varying shapes of bows and stern affect a ship's performance differently.

Sails and Rigs

The major part of this book is devoted to sailing ships. This is not the result of a bias in favour of sail over power but is unavoidable in a book dealing with the history of ships. The era of sail lasted from the days of ancient Egypt until our own century and a thousand years separate the Oseberg Viking ship from the *France II* alone. In comparison, the whole history of powered ships is easily contained within the last two hundred years. All the major maritime geographical discoveries were made in wooden ships crewed by men who knew how to use the winds and who learned how to navigate the high seas and find their way back home. The world as we know it and nearly all the international trade routes owe their existence to sail.

While commercial sail is still within living memory, the whole technology of sail is almost forgotten and to write about sailing ships is like talking about motor cars and the internal combustion engine to New Guinea tribesmen who have never seen a road. Before discussing specific sailing ships, it will therefore be helpful to explain the principles of sailing and some of the complexities of sails, rigging and rigs.

HOW SAILS WORK

Although sails have been used for centuries, the principle that makes them work was only explained in a scientific way as a result of aerodynamic studies on aircraft. Sails and wings are both aerofoils and work in much the same way. The wind flowing around a sail is disturbed so that a low pressure occurs on the lee (downwind) side of the sail. The sail is thus *pulled* rather than *pushed* by the wind. The downwind force applied to a sail can be resolved into two forces at right-angle: the drag, which is parallel to the main plane of the sail and which causes the vessel to heel, and the lift, which is perpendicular to the main plane. This lift force can be in turn resolved into two components, one directed forward, which causes the vessel to advance, and the other directed sideways, causing the vessel to drift sideways—to make leeway. As a sail is progressively turned closer to the wind, the lift decreases and becomes more oriented sideways so that its forward component decreases at an even faster rate: no sail can be made to work dead to windward.

The hull plays an important part. A raft with no steering rudder or centreboard can do nothing but drift downwind, regardless of the type of sail. Hulls are so designed as to have a minimum resistance to forward motion and a maximum resistance to side motion. Thus the forward pull, even though it may be much smaller than the sideways force, will make the vessel advance on its heading. At the same time the sideways pull cannot be entirely suppressed and all sailing vessels, when sailing on any point other than downwind will make some leeway, having a crabwise motion. This is why the compass heading of a vessel—the direction in which it points—is different from the course—the direction in which it is advancing through the water.

To perform, sails are controlled by a variety of ropes known as running rigging. Halyards are used to hoist the sails and downhauls are used for the opposite manoeuvre. The leading edge or luff of a sail must be kept taut and while the head of the sail is kept aloft by the halyard, the lower end of the luff, the tack, is bowsed down by a rope also known as the tack. The trailing edge or leech is controlled at the clew (the lower corner) by a rope called the sheet.

On an ordinary triangular sail this arrangement of halyard, downhaul, tack and sheet is generally sufficient. Such a sail, known as a Bermudian sail (hoisted along a mast) or a staysail (hoisted along a stay), is a fore-and-aft sail because it can be set along the fore-and-aft direction of the vessel. The gaff sail is another type of fore-and-aft sail but the gaff (the upper spar holding the head) calls for two halyards to keep it at the correct angle. Lateen sails, which have a long inclined yard along the luff, lug sails and junk sails are other types of fore-and-aft sails. All these sails always have the same side acting as luff and they can work with the wind on either face, depending on which side of the vessel the wind is blowing.

Square sails are different. They are called square not because of their shape (which is seldom square and can even be triangular) but because they can be set square to the fore-and-aft direction. They are symmetrical and, depending from which side the wind blows, their luff can become the leech and vice versa; they will only work with the wind blowing on the side facing the mast. Their running rigging is more complicated than that of a Bermudian sail. The halyard is fixed to the centre of the yard on which the sail is bent or tied. The sides of the sail, which are interchangeably luff and leech, are called leeches (weather- and lee-leeches). The lower corners, which are interchangeably clew and tack, are called clews and each clew has a sheet which draws it down to the yardarm or extremity of the yard of the sail below. The weather sheet acts as a tack; the lee sheet just keeps the clew against the yard below. The sail is trimmed by turning the yards in the horizontal plane by means of braces—one brace to each yardarm. The yards can also be trimmed in the vertical plane by means of topping lifts that lead from the yardarms to a block on the mast above and then down to the deck.

A square sail is furled by being folded on its yard. The yard is usually lowered first, the sheets let go and the sail gathered up to the yard by clewlines (acting on the clews), buntlines (bent to the foot of the sail) and leechlines (bent to the leeches). The sail is then hanging in loose folds below the yard and the men 'lay aloft', climbing up the ratlines and sliding along the yards with their feet on footropes. They then proceed to fold the sail in tighter folds and lash it on top of the yard with gaskets.

Sails carry reinforcing ropes sewn along their sides—the boltropes. In the days before wire rope was used, the boltropes would stretch and the weather leeches would sag and flutter when sailing to windward. To prevent this, ropes known as bowlines were fixed to the leeches and hauled forward to stiffen the weather leeches. Other running rigging include reefing tackles. When a square sail has to be reefed or shortened, a horizontal row of reef points (short lengths of rope dangling from the canvas) is tied over the yard, gathering away the area of the sail above it. As the wind pressure on the sail makes it impossible to draw the first reef points

Right: Masts and sails can be arranged in a great many combinations, known as rigs. Rig names were standardized in the nineteenth century and are still used today. The windjammer (left) has square sails, set square to the fore-and-aft direction of the ship. Junks on the River Po (below) have triangular or Bermudian staysails, fore-and-aft sails which can be set along the fore-and-aft direction. Running rigging for Bermudian sails is less complicated than that for square sails.

up to the yard, a reefing tackle bent to the leech is used, to apply more power.

Standing rigging is the generic term for the fixed ropes which maintain the masts in position. Stays, leading forward, support a mast backwards; shrouds support a mast laterally and backstays prevent the mast from falling forward. Square riggers usually have masts in three sections, the lower, top and topgallant masts, each with stays and backstays, and the two first masts also with shrouds. The topmast shrouds lead to the top (the platform at the foot of the topmast) and the lifting strain on the top's rim is taken by reverse shrouds, the futtock shrouds, which lead to a band around the lower mast.

The arrangements and names of sails on square riggers are most easily seen in the illustrations. The sails are usually called after the mast on which they are set: main topmast staysail, mizzen topgallant sail, etc. Square riggers with a pretension for speed carried skysails above the royals (the royal mast is an upward continuation, in one piece, of the topgallant mast) and a few extreme vessels carried up to three sails above the skysail. These were very small and not worth the extra weight of rigging.

RIG TYPES

Masts and sails can be arranged in a great number of combinations known as rigs. Most of the rig names came into use during the nineteenth century; before then vessels were usually described by their local names or by their trade such as cat barks (North Sea colliers, usually rigged as ships), frigates, galleasses etc.

A sloop is a single-masted vessel with a single staysail; a cutter is similar but carries more than one staysail. Ketches are two-masted vessels with a tall fore mast (the main mast) and a smaller after mast (the mizzen); nowadays cutters and ketches are always fore-and-aft rigged but two hundred years ago cutters could carry one or two square sails as well as their gaff main sail and staysails, and ketches could be entirely square-rigged. Yawls are similar to ketches but the mizzen is of very small proportions.

Schooners are two-masted fore-and-aft riggers where the fore mast is either smaller or equal in height to the main mast. Some schooners carry square topsails but the rig always remains predominantly fore-and-aft. Vessels with between three and seven masts carrying schooner-type (fore-and-aft) sails are also called schooners, with a prefix denoting the number of masts (i.e. five-masted schooner). A brig is the square-rigged counterpart of a (two-masted) schooner and if its mainsail or brigsail is bent to a small auxiliary mast just abaft the main lower mast, it is

Ketch

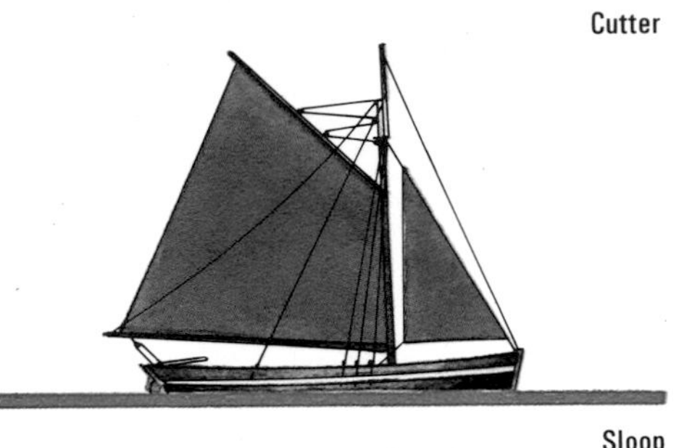

Cutter

Sloop

Lugger

Junk

Lateen

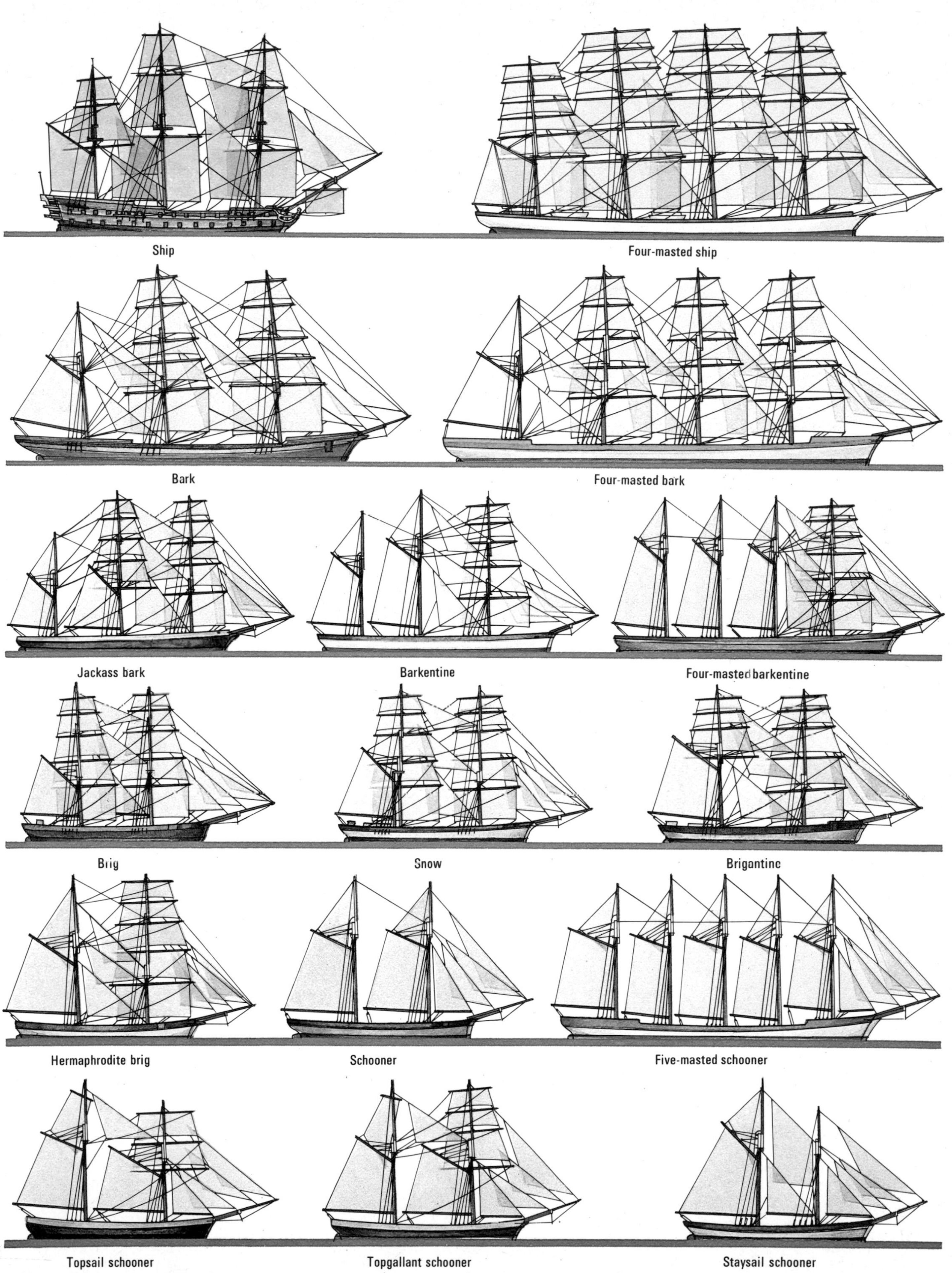

Ship
Four-masted ship
Bark
Four-masted bark
Jackass bark
Barkentine
Four-masted barkentine
Brig
Snow
Brigantine
Hermaphrodite brig
Schooner
Five-masted schooner
Topsail schooner
Topgallant schooner
Staysail schooner

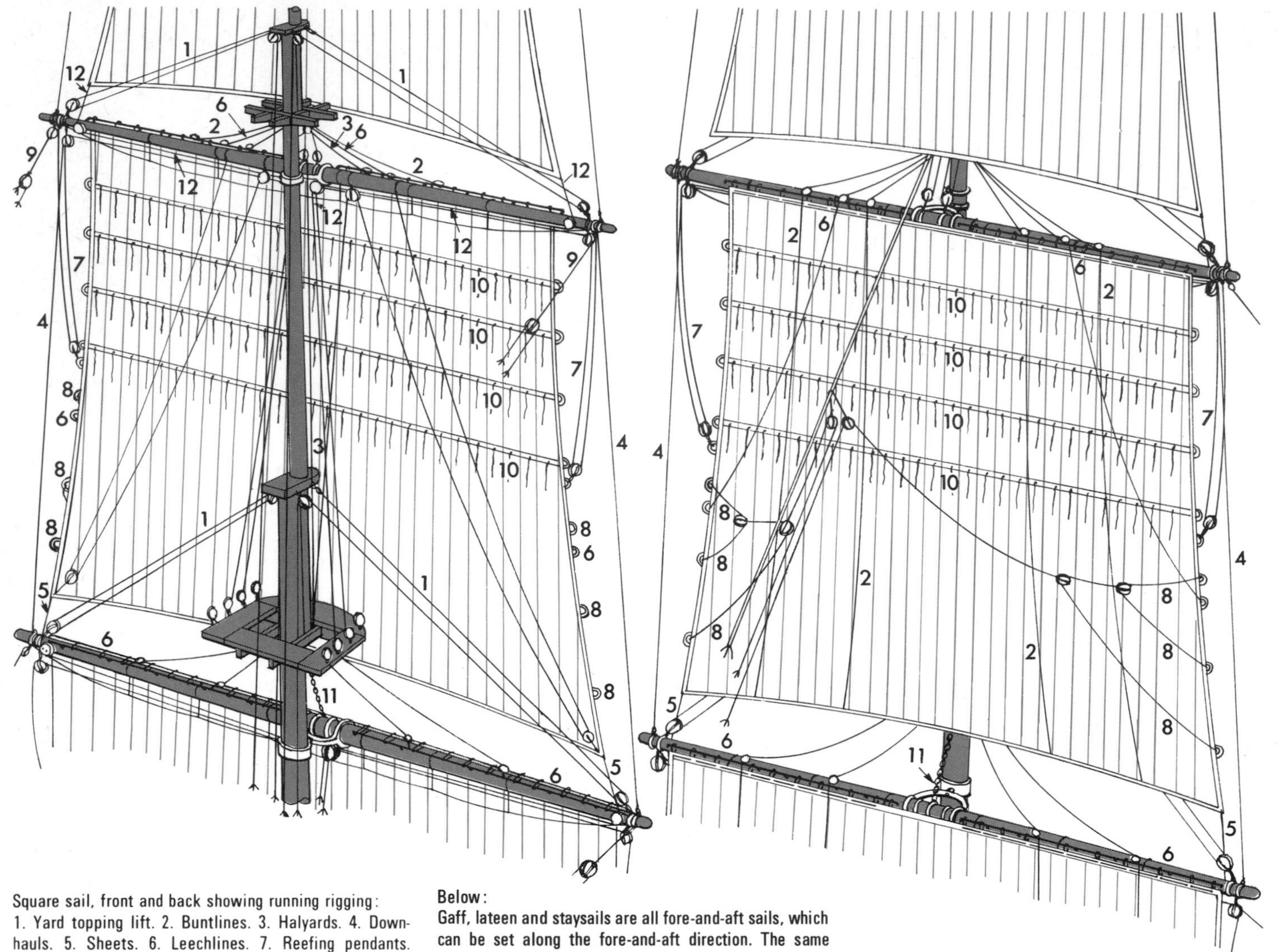

Square sail, front and back showing running rigging:
1. Yard topping lift. 2. Buntlines. 3. Halyards. 4. Downhauls. 5. Sheets. 6. Leechlines. 7. Reefing pendants. 8. Bowlines. 9. Braces. 10. Reefing points. 11. Sling. 12. Topgallant sheets.

Below:
Gaff, lateen and staysails are all fore-and-aft sails, which can be set along the fore-and-aft direction. The same side of the sail always acts as the luff or leading edge and they can work with the wind on either face.

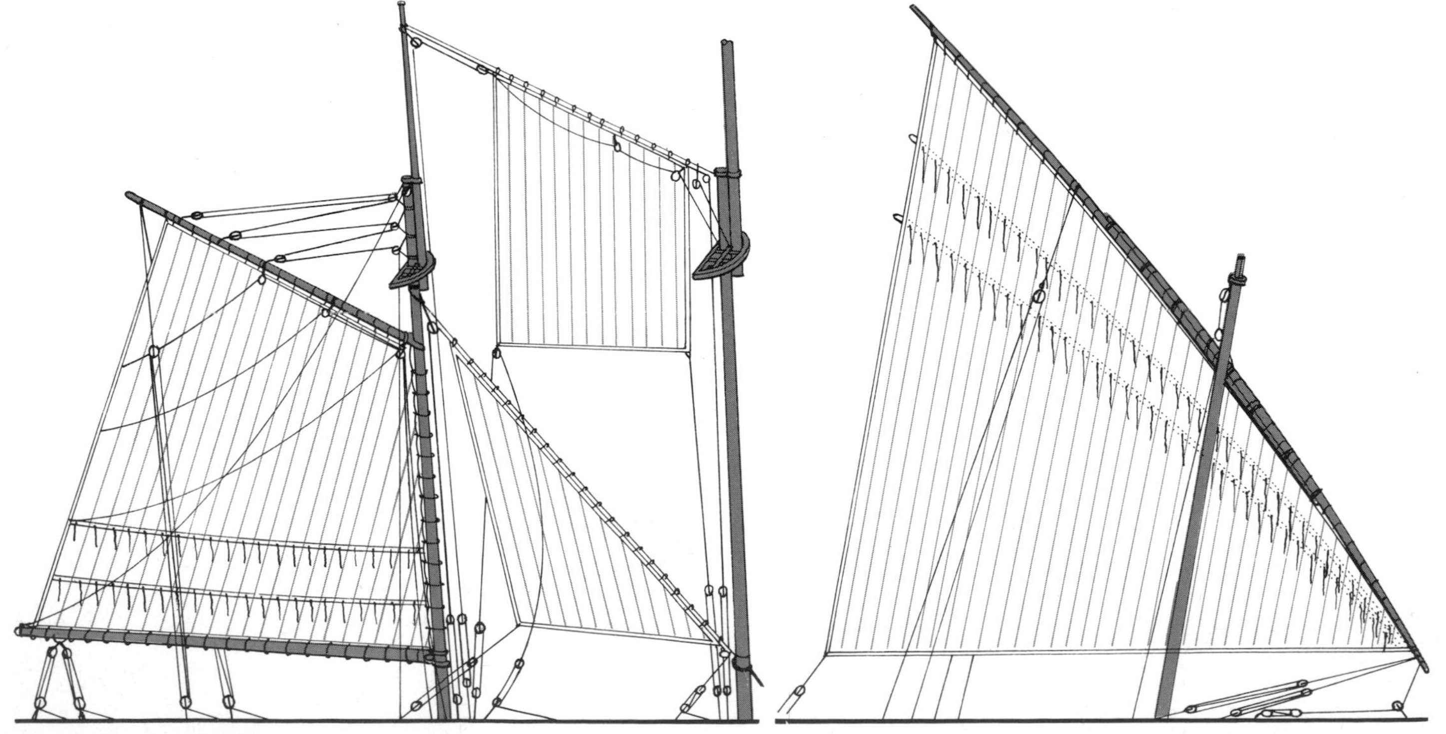

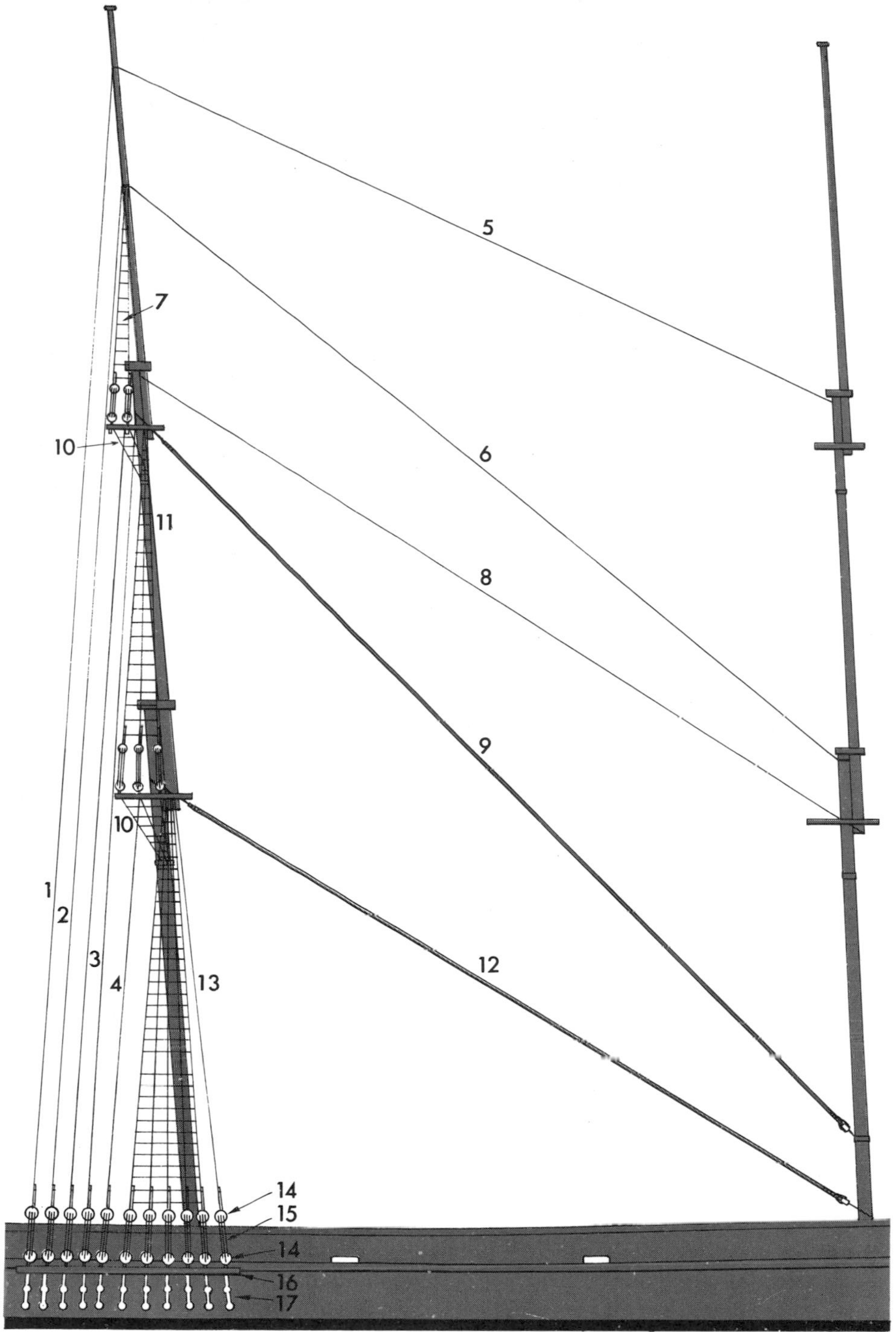

Main square mast with standing rigging:
1. Main royal-backstay. 2. Main topgallant-backstay. 3. Main topmast-backstays. 4. Main backstay. 5. Main royal-stay. 6. Main topgallant-stay. 7. Main topgallant-shrouds. 8. Middle staysail-stay. 9. Main topmast-stay. 10. Futtock-shrouds. 11. Main topmast-shrouds. 12. Main-stay. 13. Main lower-shrouds. 14. Deadeyes. 15. Lanyards. 16. Channel. 17. Chainplates.

Right: Detail of the rigging, or shrouds, with their ratlines, on the starboard main chainplate of the U.S.S. *Constitution*. The circular blocks of wood are dead-eyes: the three holes are for the lanyards of rigging to reeve through, without sheaves; the groove is for an iron strap.

called a snow. A hermaphrodite brig has the fore mast of a brig and the main mast of a schooner and is commonly called a brigantine although the true brigantine carries one or more square sails above the schooner-type mainsail.

A ship or fully-rigged ship has three to five masts all completely square-rigged whereas in a bark (or barque) the aftermost mast is schooner-rigged. A barkentine (or barquentine) has three to six masts all of the schooner type except the fore mast which is entirely square-rigged. A few vessels have rigs half way between a barkentine and a bark and these are called jackass barks.

All these square rigs have now almost vanished from the seas although a few are preserved as museum ships and a few others still work as sail-training vessels. Every even year many of the last square riggers and large schooners gather for a 'Tall Ships' Race' and onlookers can catch a fleeting glimpse of a forest of yards and rigging which recalls a glorious era of seafaring when function and beauty were synonymous.

Ropes and Tackles

Ropes remain an essential feature of ships although few modern sailors have the proficiency in rope work possessed by their elders. In modern vessels wire or synthetic fibre ropes are used for mooring and docking lines, steel wires are used for loading booms and derricks and other ropes still find their place in boat davits and a thousand-and-one jobs aboard. Ropework is still an important and detailed part of the curriculum of boatswains and quarter-masters.

Traditional or natural fibre ropes are made of hemp, manila, linen flax, coir, sisal and cotton, which have different properties and therefore different uses. They are prone to mildew and rot and are sometimes tarred for protection. Recently a variety of synthetic, non-rotting ropes have come into use, the main types being nylon, terylene, and polypropylene. Stiff and flexible wire ropes (plough steel, mild galvanized steel, stainless) are also available and are mainly used for standing rigging and some running rigging such as halyards. There are some composite ropes, wire sheathed in braided fibre, for uses where strength must be combined with comfort in handling. Chains have replaced ropes for some uses since the mid 1800s, for instance for bobstays (the stay beneath the bowsprit), for square sail sheets (where they reeve through blocks) and, more importantly, for anchor cables.

Some ropes are braided but most are stranded, with three or four strands. In stranded ropes, the fibres are twisted together counter-clockwise to form 'right-handed' spun yarn. These yarns are then twisted clockwise to form 'left-handed' strands. Three or four strands are twisted together counter-clockwise to form a right-handed 'hawser laid' rope: the common rope. Three hawser laid ropes may be in turn twisted clockwise to produce the large 'cable-laid', left-handed 'rope' which was used for anchor cables before the introduction of chain.

A sailor never 'ties' a knot. Instead, he may make a knot, take a hitch, bend two ropes together, clap on a lashing, a seizing or a stopping, put on a whipping or put in a splice. Knots are used to form loops, such as the bowline, or to form knobs, such as the star knot. Hitches such as the clove hitch are used to make ropes fast to another object and bends, such as the carrick bend, are used to fasten two ropes together. Lashings secure two objects together with ropes or small stuff (there is no 'string' on a ship), seizings bind ropes together or to other objects and stoppings are temporary seizings. Whippings are turns of small stuff around a rope to prevent it from fraying. Splices join two ropes together by tucking the strands under one another.

Until the invention of engines or motors, tackles, windlasses and capstans were the only mechanical aids at sea. Tackles are combinations of two or more blocks with one or more ropes reeving through them. They multiply the effort applied to the moving block by a factor equal to the number of strands leading from it (although friction loses some of this theoretical purchase). Many different types of tackles were used on the old windships and a certain number are still found on powered vessels, for instance on boat davits and derricks.

Power

The mechanical propulsion of boats is of great antiquity but, of course, the power was originally supplied by muscles. Oars and hand paddles are forms of human-powered mechanical propulsion that were never successfully adapted to engines but even the paddle-wheel is an ancient invention. Roman bas-reliefs show paddle-wheel boats powered by oxen which were used by Claudius Caudex for his invasion of Sicily. The same principle was also used in Byzantium and the Chinese had multiple paddle-wheel boats, operated by treadmills, as early as the eighth century A.D. Compared to oars and even hand paddles, paddle-wheels and Archimedean screws were not efficient when operated by muscle power. It was not until the steam engine was invented that they came into their own.

The power of steam had also been recognized for a considerable length of time but no practical means of harnessing it was devised before Denis Papin, who lived from 1647 to 1714, showed how steam could lift a weight placed on the lid of a pot—a very crude piston. He also invented the safety valve, based on the same principle. He is known to have built and sailed a paddle boat but it was hand- and not muscle-powered.

Captain Thomas Savery, an English soldier, patented the first working steam engine to pump the water out of mines. It relied on the condensation of steam which, by creating a partial vacuum, would draw up the water from below. Thomas Newcomen (1663–1729), a Devon blacksmith, was called to repair one of Savery's 'fire engines' and he became interested in them. In 1705 he perfected a piston and cylinder engine for pumping water. Newcomen's engine used the steam to lift a piston and as the steam condensed inside the piston, the atmospheric pressure pushed the piston down. This engine proved too inefficient for use on boats, as Jonathan Hull found out in 1737 when his experimental stern-paddler failed.

James Watt (1736–1819) was the first person to conceive a steam engine where the power was produced by the direct pressure of steam pushing the piston. This was unlike the atmospheric engines where the partial vacuum caused by condensation had pulled the piston. Watt also invented the external condenser and the double-acting cylinder, where the steam is allowed in alternately on both sides of the piston, providing a push and a pull of equal force. This was the answer to the proper conversion of linear mechanical motion to a circular motion. Watt's engines were efficient enough to be adapted to steamboats with success.

Most of the early steamboats were fitted with beam engines on which the piston rod was linked to the end of a centre-pivoted rocker beam, the other end of the beam being linked to the crankshaft. The story of the early steamboats is summarized in the chapter on the PS *Savannah* (pp. 72–75).

The early paddle-wheel had fixed floats but soon a system of cams was devised that kept the floats vertical throughout their passage under water. As early as 1770 the Frenchman Daniel Bernouilli had proposed using both Archimedean and windmill-type screws for the propulsion of steamboats. However, screws needed faster revolving shafts than paddle-wheels and it was not until 1836 that an Englishman, E. P. Smith, fitted an Archimedean screw to a boat. It broke during tests leaving only a stump resembling a modern screw—which considerably increased the speed of the boat!

Propellers were still inefficient in design and, more seriously, the contemporary engines were too slow acting. The first large screw ship, Brunel's *Great Britain* (launched in 1843) had increasing gears. Brunel's giant, the *Great Eastern* (1859) had both paddle-wheels and a screw. The superiority of the propeller was finally demonstrated by the famous tug-of-war between the identically-powered sister ships, HMS *Rattler* (propellor-driven) and HMS *Alecto* (paddle-driven).

The first boilers were extraordinarily inefficient and they consumed enormous quantities of fuel (coal or firewood) for every horsepower delivered. They were of the pot type, with an external firebox and they could not withstand much pressure. They developed into boilers with internal fireboxes and then into fire tube boilers (Scotch boilers) around 1900. These greatly increased the heating surface by having the heat flow

Steam power was first successfully harnessed at sea in the late eighteenth century and is still used today. Diesel engines and gas turbines function without a heavy boiler; a ship's nuclear reactor, however, is simply a very much more efficient way of producing steam.

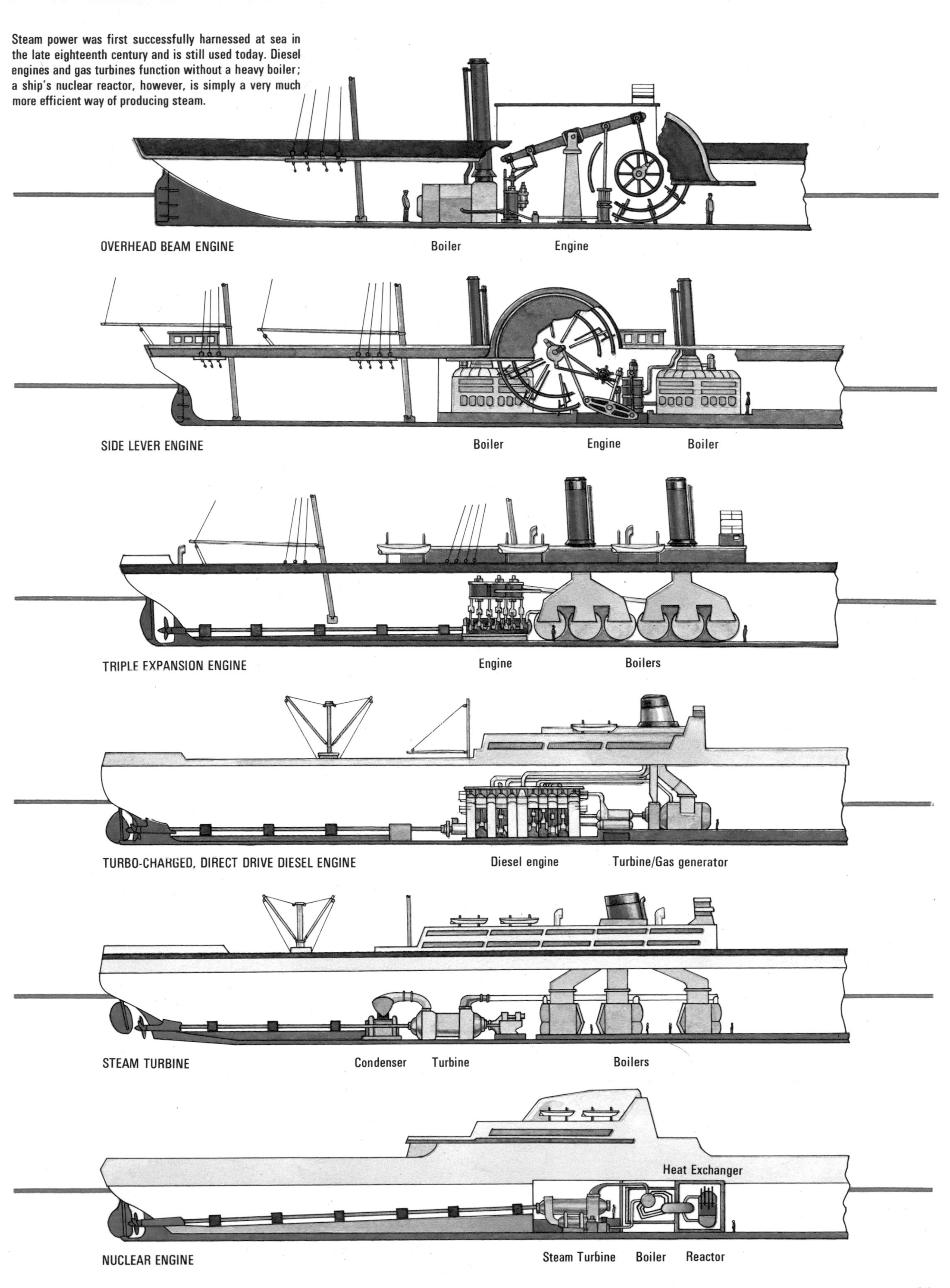

In 1845 the *Rattler*, with a 200 h.p. steam engine and two-bladed screw, took part in a tug-o-war with the *Alecto*, a steam sloop of equal size and power but paddle-driven. With apparent ease the *Rattler* towed the *Alecto* along at 2·8 knots, proving the superiority of screw to the more cumbersome paddle.

through tubes inside the boilers. A further and more recent improvement are the water tube boilers where the boiler consists of a series of tubes passing through the firebox. They are capable of raising steam faster than fire tube boilers. Ancillary improvements consisted in superheaters, forced draughts and preheaters for the water.

Engines themselves were also improving, with direct acting underfoot crankshaft engines, followed by triple (and even quadruple) expansion engines, where the steam flows through high, medium and low pressure cylinders as every ounce of remaining pressure is tapped. The triple expansion engine with coal-fired Scotch boilers (used on the *Ocean* standard emergency freighters of the Second World War) or diesel-fired water tube boilers (used on the Liberty ships) was the most common merchant navy engine during the first half of this century.

The principle of the steam turbine had been known for almost two thousand years when it was first used by the American John Stevens to propel a boat—with moderate success—around 1800. Stevens' turbine had only two blades, but basically a steam turbine is a multi-bladed rotor on which jets of steam are released. The steam drives the rotor which, in turn, drives the propeller shaft. Steam turbines require steam at high pressure if they are to be efficient, and because it was not possible to produce this at the time, turbines were not at first developed. However, in 1894, an Englishman, Sir Charles Parsons, built the steam yacht *Turbinia* (now preserved at Newcastle-upon-Tyne). At first the high propeller speeds caused some problems but the *Turbinia* soon achieved the unheard-of speed of 34 knots. The Admiralty were not impressed, however, so Sir Charles invited himself and his boat to the naval review at Spithead in 1897, where he sailed rings round the fast patrol boat sent to stop him. The turbine ship HMS *Viper* was the result.

Turbine engines are vibration-free and require less space for the same power than expansion engines. They were soon adopted for naval and passenger ships such as the famous battleship *Dreadnaught,* the *Queen Mary* and the USS *Enterprise.* The supertanker *Globtik Tokyo* is powered by a 45,000 shaft horsepower turbine. A recent development in turbines has been the use of gas where steam is replaced by combustion gases. This increases efficiency by cutting out the boiler stage. This development has only been made possible by the discovery of alloys resistant to high temperatures.

The German Rudolf Diesel (1858–1913) invented in 1893 the engine that bears his name. Fuel (diesel) and air are drawn into a cylinder as the piston moves out. As the piston moves back the gas mixture is compressed to spontaneous ignition and the gases produced by the combustion push the piston out again (power stroke). The piston then moves back, expelling the spent gases through an exhaust valve and the cycle starts over again. Compared to the two-step energy conversion of boiler and expansion engine, the diesel motor has the advantage of converting the energy of burning fuel directly into mechanical movement. The relative ratios of fuel energy conversion are 35 per cent to 15 per cent in favour of the diesel engine. However, diesels had considerable mechanical problems at first. The five-masted bark *France II* was originally fitted with auxiliary diesels in 1913 but these later had to be discarded as being too unreliable. By the time the German pocket battleships such as the *Graf Spee* were built, diesel motors were quite satisfactory and since the Second World War they have been used in the vast majority of vessels, now known as motor vessels (MV) to distinguish them from steamships (SS). Diesel motors are not suited, however, for very large or very fast ships, for which steam turbines are still preferred.

NUCLEAR POWER

The steam engine, the steam or gas turbine and the diesel motor are all basically different engines, conventionally powered by solid or liquid fuels. Nuclear 'engines', however, are merely steam turbines with a boiler heated by nuclear fission. The nuclear reactor itself has no moving parts; it just generates heat. The amount of heat produced is controlled by the withdrawal or plunging of the fuel bars in a graphite moderator that slows the neutrons produced by radioactive decay to speeds where they can be 'caught' by fissionable atoms. These atoms then split, emitting new neutrons and starting a chain reaction. The core is cooled by a closed circuit coolant that transfers the heat via a heat exchanger to water which is converted to steam. This steam drives a conventional turbine and is then condensed and returned to the heat exchanger.

The energy content of a kilo of enriched uranium fuel is two million times that of a kilo of fuel oil. Nuclear fuel is, however, very expensive and so are the reactor and its maintenance. Furthermore a very heavy shielding is required to prevent the radiation from escaping and this takes up much valuable deadweightage in a ship: the first nuclear merchant ship, the American NS *Savannah* has a shielding weighing 1,930 tonnes. Few other nuclear merchant vessels have been built: West Germany has one and the Russians have two nuclear ice breakers. There are several surface nuclear ships in the US Navy (aircraft carriers such as the USS *Enterprise,* cruisers and frigates) but so far nuclear power has been used at sea mainly for submarines in the Russian, American, French and British navies. The advantages for submarines of a power plant that consumes no oxygen and that can keep going for years without refuelling are obvious.

The price of fossil fuel is bound to increase dramatically as the reserves become depleted in the not too distant future and it is possible that nuclear power will become more commonplace. Its use on a large scale would pose serious problems as it could greatly increase the probability of a nuclear shipwreck or other disaster, with catastrophic ecological consequences. The alternative would be a return to sail and experiments are now being carried out with computer-controlled sails which would be able to take the maximum advantage of sophisticated meteorological techniques.

Marine Archaeology

Much of what is known about the evolution of ships and of the history of shipbuilding is owed to marine or nautical archaeology, a field so new that each year brings new discoveries, new knowledge and often fundamental revisions to previously held ideas. Artistic representations are more often than not inaccurate and need careful interpretation which can usually only be substantiated or disproved by studies of the remains of real ships. The oldest known accurate models date from the mid-seventeenth century and shipwright's plans from the eighteenth, but even these frequently do not show many important details. The study of actual, preserved ships, is therefore of enormous interest. Two of the chapters in this book, those on the Oseberg Viking ship and on the seventeenth-century warship *Wasa* are entirely based on marine archaeology and many details of other ships are known because of the work of marine archaeologists.

Marine archaeology can be said to have started in the late nineteenth century when Viking ship tombs were unearthed in Scandinavia. The ships had been preserved by the particular quality of the soil in which they had been buried. Wooden ships are rarely preserved. Some have decayed, or been broken up for re-usable parts and firewood when they became unserviceable. Those ships which escaped the scrapheap have usually done so by shipwreck —and wrecks are hidden under water. It is only since the 1940s that the perfecting of aqualung SCUBA diving has allowed submarine exploration to expand and many wrecks have since been located.

A good example of underwater marine archaeology is provided by the salvage of a seventeen-metre Greek merchant vessel which sank in about 300 BC off the coast of Cyprus, near Kyrenia. She is the oldest sea-going ship to have been found and studied. In 1965 a sponge diver, Andreas Cariolou, using aqualung gear, discovered a pile of amphoras at a depth of nearly thirty-three metres. Two years later he showed the spot to Michael Katzev and other archaeologists from the University of Pennsylvania Museum. Only about a hundred jars were on the sea floor's surface: there was nothing to show that this mound hid a full-sized merchant *holkas* ('hulk'). A cord grid was staked out on the bottom to map the area for a preliminary survey and divers with metal sounding rods felt that the wreckage extended below the sand over a distance of 23 by 12 m. A further survey with a metal detector and a proton magnetometer indicated metal concentrations and revealed the hidden position of the wreck.

The prow of the Oseberg Viking ship, dated A.D. 800. The oak timbers, with their carved animals, were particularly well preserved because of the quality of soil in which the ship had been buried.

The next summer the salvage work began, using air lifts (underwater vacuum cleaners) to remove the unwanted sand and silt. The divers dug with spatulas, with their hands and they even used brushes for the delicate work, just as land archaeologists do. It was, however, a more time-consuming operation than a land 'dig' because not only is working in water more awkward, but the depth of thirty-three metres meant that a lot of diving time had to be spent in decompression ascents to avoid the danger of the bends.

The Kyrenia ship, a Greek merchant vessel which sank off the coast of Cyprus around A.D. 300, is a fine example of the way in which SCUBA diving has allowed submarine exploration to expand. The hull of the wreck was dismantled by divers and re-assembled ashore.

A permanent reference grid of plastic pipes was used to note the exact position of each find and twice a day the whole site was covered by a series of stereo photographs to record and map the three-dimensional structure of the wreck—a necessary precaution for future reconstitution and interpretation.

By August 1969 all the cargo had been raised and a remarkably well preserved hull had been uncovered. The hull was of much greater interest than the amphoras, millstones, coins and other artefacts, which were of well known types. The cargo and artefacts are interesting, however, for the story they tell us about the ship. Some of the amphoras at the bottom of the pile had been loaded at Samos, the probable port of departure for the ship's last voyage. They probably contained wine. Some millstones were picked up, perhaps at Kos, and most of them were sold, perhaps at Rhodes where more wine in amphoras was loaded. A few reject millstones were retained as ballast, on the ship's floors. There were other amphoras which may have contained olive oil and foodstuffs, and sacks of almonds. The sacks and the kernels have long since disappeared but the shells have been preserved. Then the ship set a course for Cyprus and she must have been overwhelmed by a squall off Kyrenia: she sank in deep water.

Tableware for four was found, indicating the size of her crew. Perhaps they managed to escape in a boat, for there is evidence that the ship had been abandoned in an orderly manner. Only a few bronze coins were found and these indicate that the wreck did not occur before 306 B.C. Drinking cups were found in the forepeak. In today's Greek caiques water is still kept there: how old is the tradition?

More than half the hull was found on the sea floor, but it was in such a state that it was not possible to lift the wreck up bodily. It had to be carefully mapped and dismantled and was re-assembled ashore, in Kyrenia's Crusaders' castle. Before the jigsaw puzzle (with its many missing pieces) could be put together, the wood had to be treated by long immersion in polyethylene glycol. The method is described in the chapter on the *Wasa* (pp. 42–47). A full size midsection replica and a sailing model were made to test various hypotheses. Radiocarbon datings of the timbers indicate that the ship was about eighty years old when she sunk and there is evidence of several repairs done during her career. The bow planking had been covered with a veneer of pine as reinforcement when she had passed her prime. An interesting feature was the use of lead sheathing as a protection against teredos (marine borers); copper sheathing was applied for the same reason on wooden ships from the late eighteenth century onwards. The mast and sail had disappeared but there is the intriguing possibility (deduced from the position of the mast step) that the Kyrenia ship was fore-and-aft rigged.

The Kyrenia ship is just one example of the way marine archaeologists work. Treasure seekers have eagerly adopted SCUBA diving techniques and many more wrecks are now being investigated. Whatever the motives of the divers, it seems likely that our knowledge of early ships and of the men who sailed them will gradually be greatly enlarged.

Early Ships

The earliest representations of boats are from the fourth millenium B.C.—about the time of the Biblical Flood. However, evidence from eighth millenium B.C. Mesolithic campsites on some Aegean islands proves that seafaring itself is even older. The fourth millenium representations were found in Mesopotamia and Egypt and some of them already show sails. Some depict skin-covered boats very similar to the present-day *quffas* of Irak; some depict reed boats and others, wooden boats with elaborate stems and sterns. During the third millenium B.C. (early Bronze Age) the remarkable Minoan maritime civilization appeared; it flourished until it was overwhelmed by tidal waves and heavy ash falls from a cataclysmic eruption in 1470 B.C. The Minoan vessels had high prows and low sterns; they had sails and oars. They had a mast with standing rigging and a square sail spread between a yard and a lower yard along its foot or boom.

The ancient Egyptians had many types of ships and boats. Numerous models and even a few real boats have been found in tombs and the pictorial representations are innumerable. Reed boats made from papyrus reeds were quite common and the crescent shape of the wooden ships indicates that these had evolved from the reed boat design. The wooden ships or boats were built without a keel or frames and the short planks (the only ones available) were held together by pegs and by mortice-and-tenon joints. Some rigidity was achieved by beams which were tenoned through the planking, the tenons showing through the hull. Longitudinal stiffness was often achieved by one or more stout ropes, known as hogging trusses, which were stretched from the stem to the stern to prevent the ends from sagging down or hogging. The Egyptian craft had oars or sails or both; they were steered by one to six steering oars placed on the sides near the stern. The sail was a rectangular square sail spread by a yard and, usually, a boom. Fighting ships had a ram, a raised fighting platform above the oarsmen and a fighting top at the head of the mast.

The Mycenaean Greeks, seafarers in

their own right, filled the vacuum left by the Minoans. The Mycenaean boats had a single sail and oars. They had a straight stem, a protruding keel which evolved into a ram, and an inward-curving stem. The later Greeks evolved beamy merchant ships, the *holkades*. They also had slim galleys, the earlier ones being single-banked monoremes, which grew into double-banked biremes and treble-banked triremes. The number of banks represents the number of tiers of oarsmen, with one man to each oar. The Greeks and the Phoenicians, another seafaring nation of antiquity, also had quadriremes, quinqueremes and up to eleven-banked galleys. These numbers (four to eleven) cannot possibly represent the number of tiers but must indicate the number of oarsmen on each three-tiered set of sweeps.

The Phoenician merchant vessels had a loose-footed square sail, a straight stem and they were decked. The Phoenicians traded throughout the Mediterranean, down the Atlantic coast of Morocco and up to Cornwall (for tin) and they even ventured into the Baltic.

From the days of expansion, the Romans fought their Carthaginian (Phoenician) opponents with galleys of Greek design (mainly quinqueremes), where the only modifications were of a military rather than of a naval nature: the Romans installed a wood tower with battlements, an upper deck to protect the oarsmen and to carry troops, a boarding 'draw' bridge and an artillery consisting of a heavy catapult and of carroballistas, a sort of mounted crossbow.

The Roman ships could be quite large. The ordinary large ships had a capacity

Of the many types of boats used by the ancient Egyptians, reed boats made from papyrus were the most common. This modern version, from East Africa, follows the same basic design as boats from thousands of years ago.

A Mesopotamian seal from the third millenium B.C. shows a wooden boat with elaborate high stem and stern. The crescent shape seems to have evolved from the design of the reed boat.

Musicians playing in an early Egyptian boat, from a tomb fresco at Deir-El-Medina-Pashedu. Egyptian ships were steered by large oars, here clearly shown on the side near the stern.

A wooden tomb model from the XIIth Dynasty, 1800 B.C. The hull, which is spoon-shaped, was constructed without stem, stern posts, ribs or keel. This type of craft had oars or sails and sometimes both.

A Phoenician tomb of the second/first century B.C. shows a trading vessel. The Phoenicians created trading stations across the Mediterranean, including Malta, Sardinia and Spain. They also traded with India, a voyage which took one hundred days.

Roman coins covering the period from the second century B.C. to the third century A.D. They show the development and variety of vessels of the time when Roman cargo vessels dominated Mediterranean trade, carrying produce from the Empire.

A Gallo-Roman glass painting of Jonah and the whale shows a single masted vessel with stern steering oar. The smaller boat in the Roman relief (below) also has a single stern oar but has no mast.

of about 340 tonnes but the grain ships used for transporting Egyptian grain to Rome could exceed 1,200 tonnes. The hulls of the Roman ships were built by laying down the keel, the stem and the stern posts, and by placing the thick planks known as wales. The ordinary strakes were then fitted between the wales, placed edge-to-edge and tenoned into one another. The frames were fitted in the hull once the skin was finished. Towards the end of Roman times the frames were put in as soon as the careen (the underwater body) had been planked and the topside strakes were nailed against the frames as well as being tenoned. This led eventually to the 'skeleton-first' building of the carvel ships, which appeared between the seventh and the eleventh centuries. Through-beams were tenoned through the planking, resting on the topside of the wales. The careen was often lead-sheathed, a method previously known in the Mediterranean.

Depending on their size, the Roman ships had one or two masts and there is one picture showing a three-master. The two-masters had a main mast with a loose-footed square sail and two small triangular topsails, one on each side, filling the space between the yard and the top of the mast. The fore mast or artemon was very similar to a bowsprit as it was very inclined and placed on the bows and the square artemon sail was similar to the eighteenth century sprit-sail. A second-century A.D. stele shows a Roman ship with what could be interpreted as a lateen sail with a short luff, as on modern dhows; the triangular lateen sail appears on a fourth century mosaic.

Byzantium became dominant in the Mediterranean after the collapse of Rome but its shipping never regained the volume or the individual ship tonnage achieved during the *Pax Romana*. The remains of a Byzantine ship were found at Pantano Longarini in Sicily and they are dated to A.D. 500 ± 150 years. They are those of a merchant ship 40 m long, with a square transom. The warship of Byzantium was the dromon, originally a single-banked galley with a lateen sail and a powerful ram; it evolved into a bireme. It was also armed with stinkpots and flame-throwers (Greek fire). The principal enemies of the Byzantines were the Arabs who, from the seventh century onwards, became a major power in the Mediterranean. By the seventh century the Roman square sail had almost completely been supplanted by the lateen rig and the square rig only reappeared in the Mediterranean during the fourteenth century.

The Vikings: The Oseberg Ship

From the late eighth century until the eleventh, the christianized coastal and river people of Western Europe often lived in fear of the Vikings who came from the north in their longships, plundering and destroying wherever they went. These fierce warriors also settled in some of the lands they had conquered, such as the Isle of Man, the French province of Normandy and parts of Scotland, Ireland and England. Courageous sailors, they sailed west into the Atlantic and settled the Shetlands, the Faroes, Iceland and Greenland and they even attempted the colonization of North America. To the east they crossed the Baltic and sailed down the Volga and Dnieper rivers, establishing trading posts in Russia and along the shores of the Black and Caspian Seas. They entered the Mediterranean both from the east by the Bosporus and from the west by Gibraltar.

Compared to the western Europeans and particularly to the Byzantines and Arabs with whom they fought or traded, the Vikings were barbarians, but in one field, that of seafaring, they had achieved greater technical skills than their contemporaries. In fact, the quality of their ships and the scope of their navigation were unmatched until the Age of Discovery, some four hundred years later.

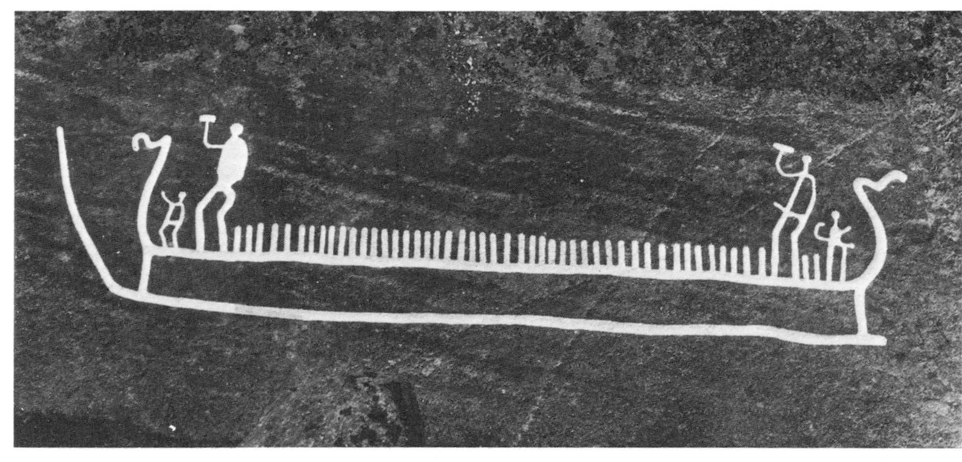

A primitive Bronze Age rock carving shows the basic structure of a longship with a high stem and stern. The figures have a warrior-like appearance, and although the drawings are ritualistic in origin, their design is realistic.

The famous and once dreaded Viking ships are well known not only from literary and pictorial sources and through folk tales, but also from several archaeological finds, of which the ship found at Oseberg, in Norway, is one of the best preserved.

The Viking ships did not appear as a sudden innovation: they were the result of centuries of nautical evolution. Bronze Age rock-carvings in southern Norway, Sweden and Denmark depict boats paddled by warriors. The oldest northern boat actually found is the 16 m paddled canoe found at Hjortspring in southern Denmark: it is dated to *c.* 350–300 B.C. It already shows the typical northern method of clinker-building, where the planks overlap one another and where the ribs are lashed into position after the hull's skin of planks has been assembled.

The use of oars appeared a couple of centuries later and the second oldest archaeological find, discovered at Nydam in Schleswig and dated from

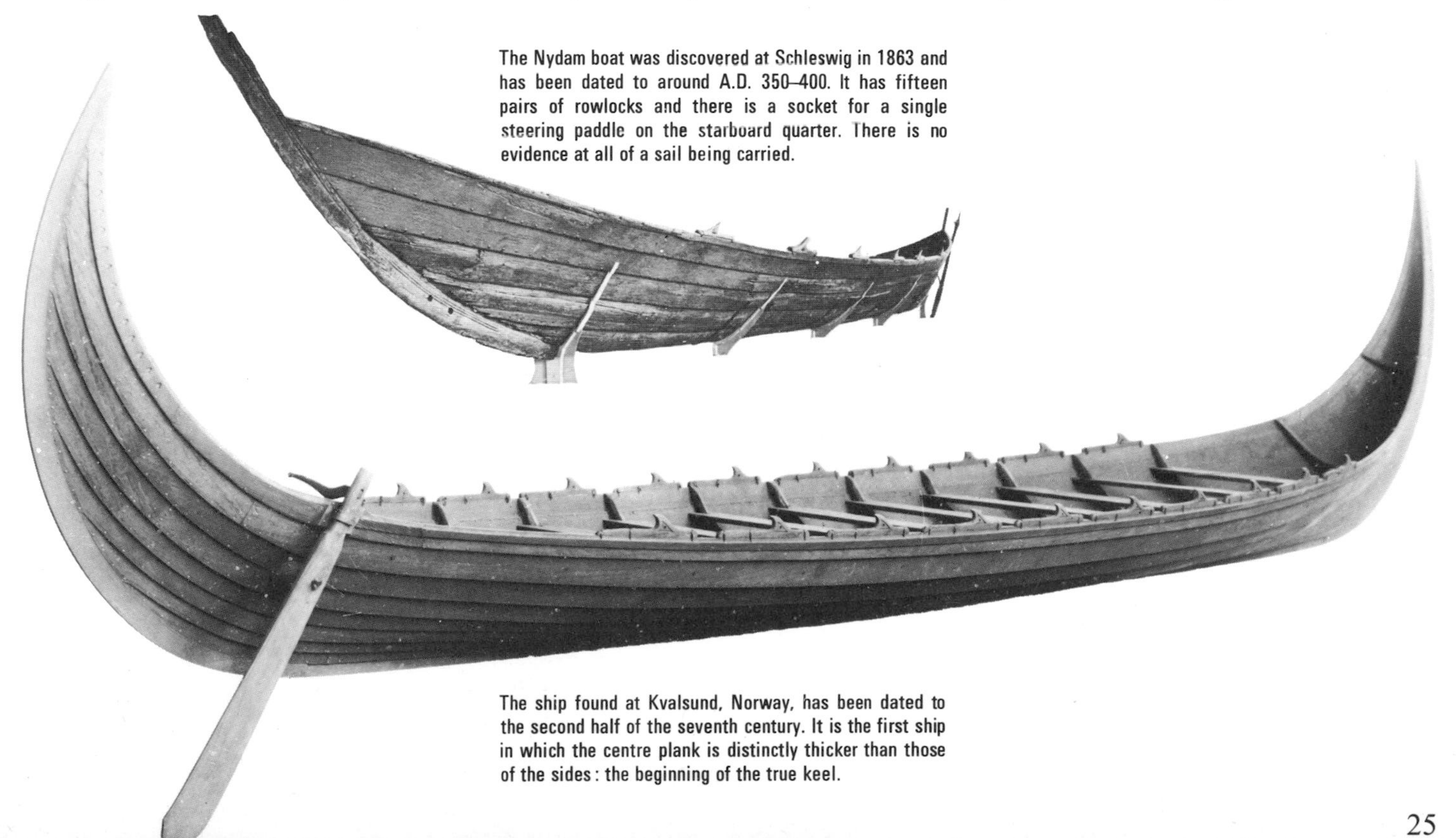

The Nydam boat was discovered at Schleswig in 1863 and has been dated to around A.D. 350–400. It has fifteen pairs of rowlocks and there is a socket for a single steering paddle on the starboard quarter. There is no evidence at all of a sail being carried.

The ship found at Kvalsund, Norway, has been dated to the second half of the seventh century. It is the first ship in which the centre plank is distinctly thicker than those of the sides: the beginning of the true keel.

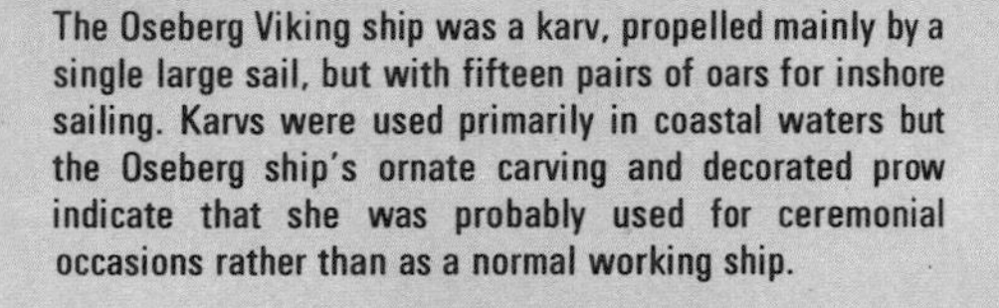

The Oseberg Viking ship was a karv, propelled mainly by a single large sail, but with fifteen pairs of oars for inshore sailing. Karvs were used primarily in coastal waters but the Oseberg ship's ornate carving and decorated prow indicate that she was probably used for ceremonial occasions rather than as a normal working ship.

A.D. 350–400, has fifteen pairs of row-locks. This 25 m boat is the sort of craft that brought the Saxons to Britain and it is similar to the Saxon ship found at Sutton Hoo in Suffolk. This last ship was larger (27 m), beamier, more sea-worthy than the Nydam boat and she is dated to *c.* A.D. 600.

Next in age is the ship found at Kvalsund in Norway, dated to the second half of the seventh century. This is the first ship where the centre plank is definitely thicker than the side ones, heralding the true keel. The keel really only developed with the sail; it was not needed for strength in a clinker-built hull but it was essential to support a mast. Although the sail had been introduced to north-western Europe by the Romans (it was known in Holland by the first century A.D.), its northward progression and adoption were astonishingly slow. None of the craft mentioned so far carried one although the continental Saxons are known to have used sails by the fifth century and the Scandinavians by the sixth or seventh.

The Oseberg ship is the next archaeological find in terms of antiquity: she is dated to A.D. 800, the early Viking Period. She was discovered in 1903 on the western side of the Oslo fjord. In common with all the boats and ships mentioned above and with two later major Viking ships, found at Gokstad and Tune, the Oseberg ship had been intentionally buried. The ceremonial use of ships as tombs, cenotaphs or votive offerings, which is also well documented in contemporary or near-contemporary literature, attests the importance of ships in the pagan cultures of the northern people.

The Oseberg ship was found in a 6 m high, 44 m diameter burial mound, partly buried in blue clay and covered in turf sods which had prevented decay. The weight of earth and stones had crushed the ship but the wood itself was in good condition and an accurate reconstruction was possible once the parts had been lifted out. The main dimensions are: length, 21·4 m; beam, 5·1 m; depth amidships from keel to gunwale, 1·5 m; height of stem and stern above the keel, 4·9 m; draught 75 cm. The ship is made entirely of oak except for the gunwales which are of beech.

A grave chamber had been built on the stern and contained two skeletons. One of them, that of a young woman aged from twenty-five to thirty years, had been half dragged out of the chamber by the Viking Age grave robbers. It is thought that this skeleton is that of Queen Asa of the Ynglinge family, the mother of King Halfdan the Black and the grandmother of Harald Fairhair. The luxury of the ship and of the artefacts she contained clearly indicate a royal burial and the date of the artefacts—between 850 and 900, when the ship was already old—fits this hypothesis. The second skeleton was that of a woman aged from sixty to seventy years, probably a servant who had been immolated (not necessarily against her will) to accompany her mistress in after life.

The Oseberg ship has both a mast and oars, though there are no rowing benches and the rowers probably sat on removable benches (not found) or on sea chests. The uppermost strake on each side is pierced by fifteen oar-holes. Fifteen pairs of elegant and decorated pine oars, 3·7 to 4 m long, were excavated but they were newly made for the funeral and clearly were not intended for use. The pine mast was also probably made specifically for the burial: it is only a stump.

As on all northern ships, the steering oar was positioned on the starboard quarter a tradition which survives in the word 'starboard', which means 'steering side'. Like the mast and oars, the Oseberg ship's steering oar was unused.

The stem and stern pieces, fitted into the extremities of the keel, are intricately carved into scroll-like, intertwined 'gripping beasts', and terminate in elegant spirals. At the prow, the spirals end in a serpent's head some 5 m above the water line.

The yard and the sail were not included in the burial but it is surmised that sails of Viking ships were made of homespun. Some pictorial references show plain red sails, others sails where the vertical cloths are of alternating colours (often red and blue or red and yellow) and others show a diagonal lattice of reinforcing tapes which were perhaps made of leather.

The Oseberg ship was loaded with artefacts but only three are of direct nautical significance: an anchor stock, a bailer and a brow (gangplank). The others represent an archaeological treasure of Viking objects: three folding beds, pillows, blankets, eiderdowns, chests and barrels, four carved head-posts and iron rattles (all presumably to ward off evil spirits), a tapestry, three looms, a four-wheeled carved cart and four sledges (three of them carved), two tents, a chair, a stave inscribed with runes, an iron knife, tubs, axes, wood platters and jugs, two iron cauldrons with folding hanging tripods, a hand mill, an ox, apples and other fruits, grains, seeds, nuts. There was probably some jewelry too, but if so, the grave robbers found it long ago.

The tents, folding beds and iron cauldrons represent 'camping' equip-

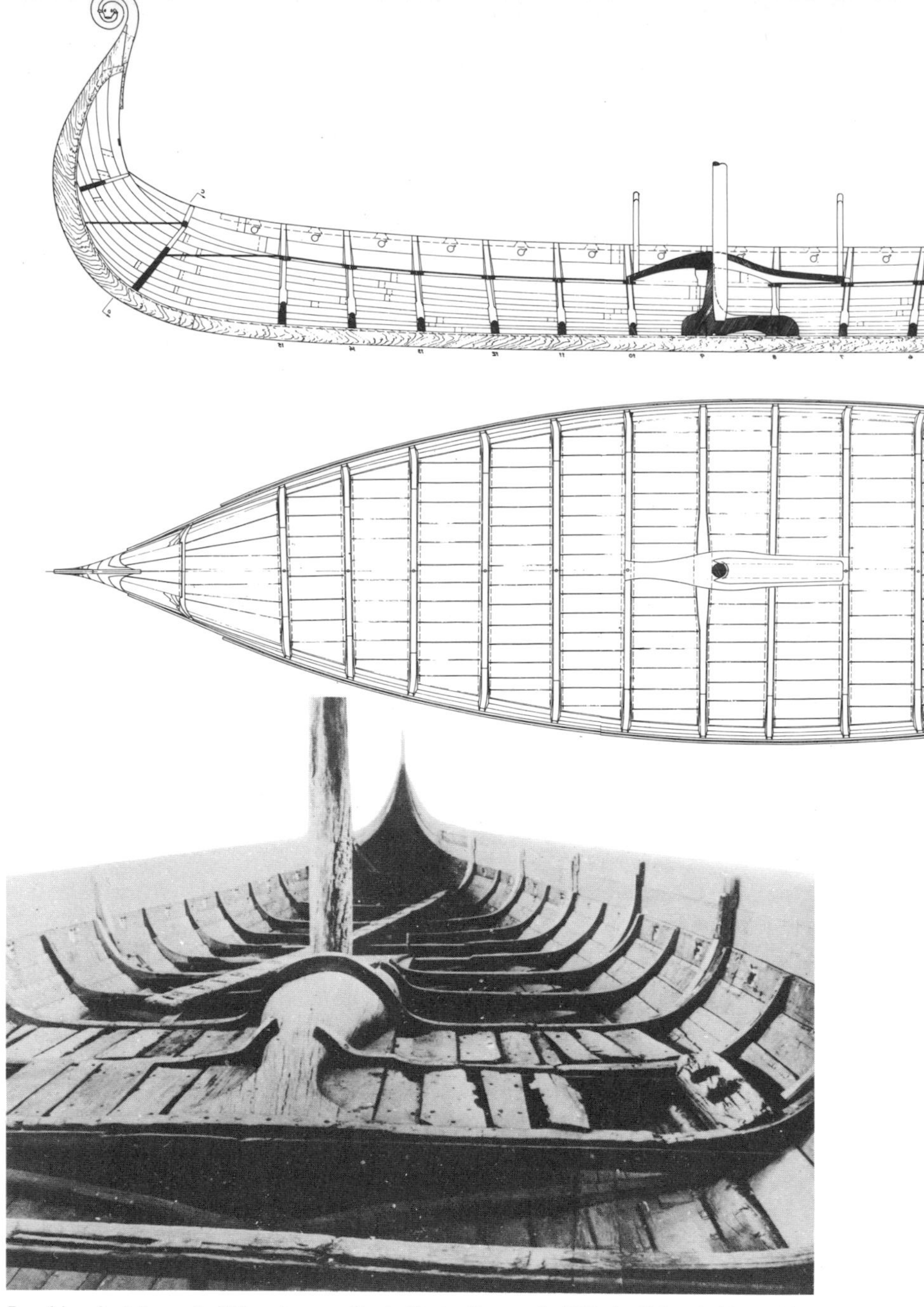

Found in a burial mound of blue clay near Sande Fjorde, Norway, in 1880, the Gokstad ship provides reliable information on the form and structure of the larger Viking ships. Looking along the interior, the substantial pine mast, measuring just over 12m, and stepped amidships, is very prominent. On either side, below the two upper strakes, are the oar-holes, which could be closed with shutters when the oars were not in use.

The Oseberg ship's prow is decorated with intricate carvings of legendary beasts, serpents and dragons. The ship itself, with its curved prow, seems intended to look like a great sea-serpent swimming through the water; the prow forms the head, the stern the tail.

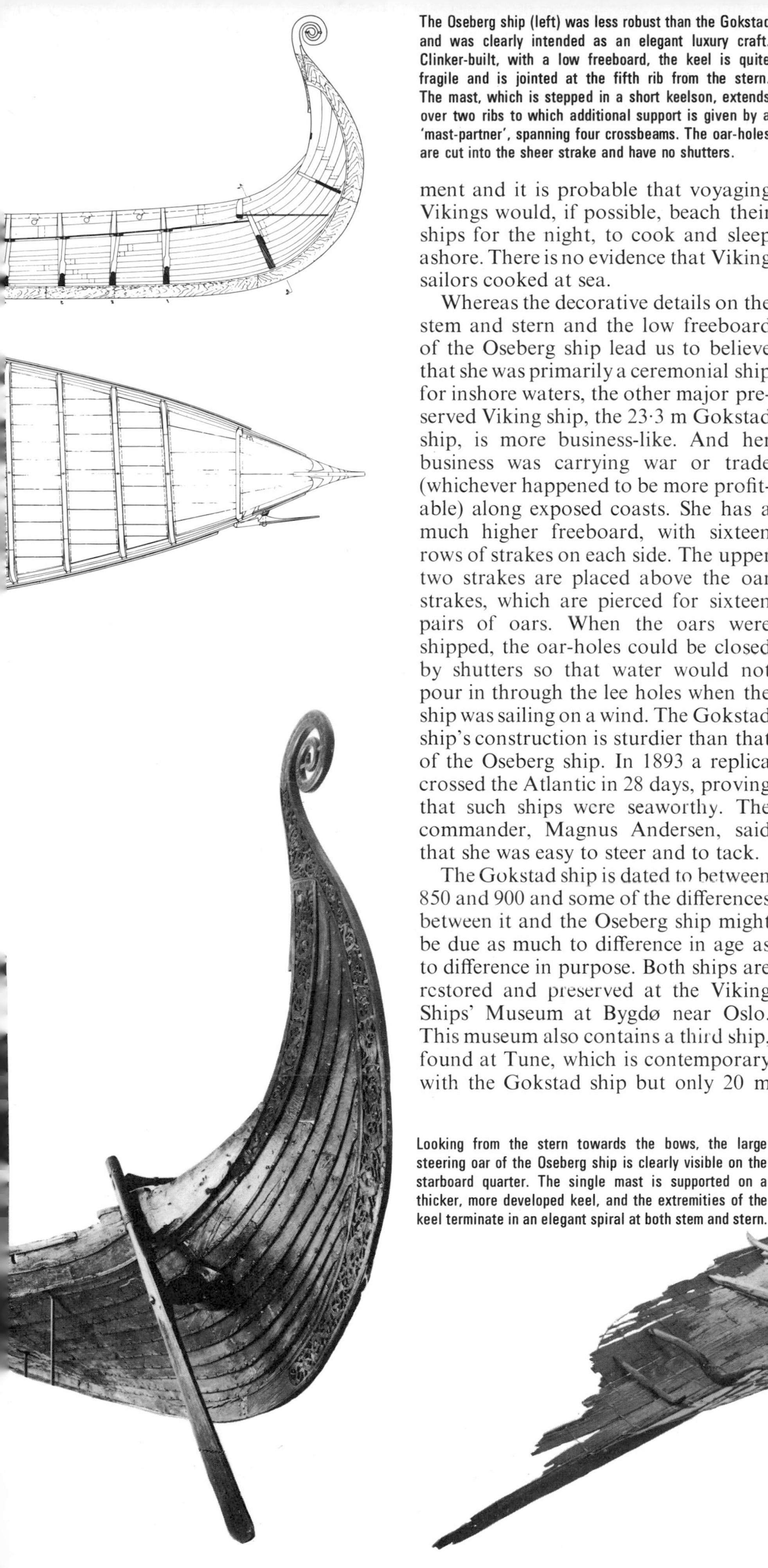

The Oseberg ship (left) was less robust than the Gokstad and was clearly intended as an elegant luxury craft. Clinker-built, with a low freeboard, the keel is quite fragile and is jointed at the fifth rib from the stern. The mast, which is stepped in a short keelson, extends over two ribs to which additional support is given by a 'mast-partner', spanning four crossbeams. The oar-holes are cut into the sheer strake and have no shutters.

ment and it is probable that voyaging Vikings would, if possible, beach their ships for the night, to cook and sleep ashore. There is no evidence that Viking sailors cooked at sea.

Whereas the decorative details on the stem and stern and the low freeboard of the Oseberg ship lead us to believe that she was primarily a ceremonial ship for inshore waters, the other major preserved Viking ship, the 23·3 m Gokstad ship, is more business-like. And her business was carrying war or trade (whichever happened to be more profitable) along exposed coasts. She has a much higher freeboard, with sixteen rows of strakes on each side. The upper two strakes are placed above the oar strakes, which are pierced for sixteen pairs of oars. When the oars were shipped, the oar-holes could be closed by shutters so that water would not pour in through the lee holes when the ship was sailing on a wind. The Gokstad ship's construction is sturdier than that of the Oseberg ship. In 1893 a replica crossed the Atlantic in 28 days, proving that such ships were seaworthy. The commander, Magnus Andersen, said that she was easy to steer and to tack.

The Gokstad ship is dated to between 850 and 900 and some of the differences between it and the Oseberg ship might be due as much to difference in age as to difference in purpose. Both ships are restored and preserved at the Viking Ships' Museum at Bygdø near Oslo. This museum also contains a third ship, found at Tune, which is contemporary with the Gokstad ship but only 20 m long. It is not completely restored.

The Oseberg, Gokstad and Tune ships are *karvs*—coasting vessels of fine lines—not to be confused with the larger *drakkars* which had from twenty to sixty pairs of oars. King Canute's *Great Dragon,* 120 oars, is said to have been 90 m long and to have carried a thousand men. On the smaller side, the sagas mention the relatively beamier and deeper *knarrs,* designed for cargo-carrying. The tenth century merchant vessels discovered in Roskilde fjord in Denmark are probably *knarrs*; the largest measures 16·5 m. It was in *knarrs* and not in longships that Erik the Red discovered Greenland and that his son Leif discovered Vinland (America).

These extensive voyages lead us to the question of the navigational knowledge of the Vikings. There is no evidence that they had instruments for measuring altitudes of the sun and stars and their knowledge was mainly one of pilotage —sailing directions transmitted by word of mouth from father to son or from pilot to apprentice. The Vikings were fine seamen who could detect land beyond the horizon by watching birds and feeling the 'mother wave'—the reflection of the swell by a coastline. Despite the dangers of the *Maelström* (tidal vortex) and their belief in the *Kraken* (a sea monster) they were far more confident at sea than their contemporaries and they did not have the fear of the open sea and of the unknown which gripped the superstitious mediaeval and Renaissance seamen of Europe until well into the Age of Discovery.

Looking from the stern towards the bows, the large steering oar of the Oseberg ship is clearly visible on the starboard quarter. The single mast is supported on a thicker, more developed keel, and the extremities of the keel terminate in an elegant spiral at both stem and stern.

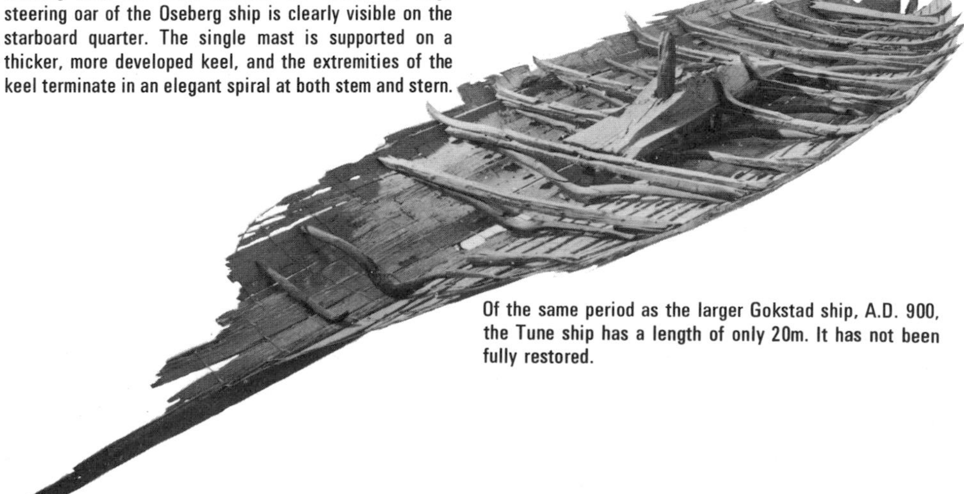

Of the same period as the larger Gokstad ship, A.D. 900, the Tune ship has a length of only 20m. It has not been fully restored.

Ships in the Dark Ages

Apart from the Viking ships that have been excavated, very little is known about the ships of the mediaeval period. During these years momentous innovations were made in the nautical field but we know little about how, when and where they first appeared. The major innovations were the fore-and-aft rig, the frame-first method of shipbuilding, the sternpost rudder and the compass.

Ever since they had appeared, ships had been steered by oars. The Egyptians used up to six steering oars, Roman ships usually carried one on each quarter and the north Europeans slung a single oar on the steering board (starboard) quarter. The steering oar gives a very high degree of control at slow speed—the nineteenth-century American whalermen used to unship the rudder from their whaleboats to replace it by a steering oar for the attack and kill—but with heavy ships or in heavy seas, steering oars are vulnerable and are also extremely tiring to use. The use of the more robust and more dependable sternpost rudder was one of the factors that allowed the European seaborne expansion that started in the fifteenth century. The first evidences of the sternpost rudder in Europe date to the twelfth century and come from northern Europe but the principle of the axial rudder had been known in China since at least the first century A.D. It is generally supposed that the idea was somehow transmitted from China.

The magnetic compass is another Chinese invention which also goes back at least to the first century A.D. It, too, reached the West in the twelfth century. The first known occurrence in the West comes from the Mediterranean and it probably arrived via the Indian Ocean/Arab trade route.

While the Vikings were still perfecting their longships, just prior to 800 A.D., the Frisian coast was the site of a thriving sea trade carried by small ships known as cogs. These cogs were probably similar to the later Hanseatic cogs described below but we have no pictorial or archaeological reference for them. This is unfortunate as, with their presumed straight sternposts, they may have been closely associated with the development or adoption of the stern rudder.

Hulks were boats from the same period which were used in the non-Scandinavian North Sea area. They had no keel or posts and their hull was shaped like a banana, with lapped strakes converging at the ends where they were lashed together with rope. The remains of such a boat, which was twenty metres long, have been found at Utrecht in the Netherlands and they have been dated to *c* 800. This was obviously a towed boat for inland waters but similar boats were also used with sails for coastal trade. The font in Winchester Cathedral, dated to 1180, shows a hulk fitted with an axial rudder; it is the oldest known representation of a rudder in Europe.

Coastal trade in northern Europe declined during the height of the Viking expansion but it flourished anew during the twelfth century and from the Dutch coast to the Baltic a series of towns prospered from dealings in Baltic herring, Swedish copper and iron, German silver and salt and Norwegian cod. These towns were to form a powerful monopolistic association in the following century, the Hanseatic League which dominated mediaeval North European economic life. Ships, again called cogs, were used to carry the valuable cargoes and these twelfth to fourteenth century vessels are well known from numerous town seals, paintings and even an archaeological find near Bremen, one of the Hanseatic towns.

Norman ships of around 1066, from the Bayeux tapestry. At the time of the Norman invasion of England ships were little different from the Viking longships, except for an increase in beam and greater depth to carry a larger sail.

Portuguese carracks of the first half of the sixteenth century, a period of amazing nautical activity. Pictures of ships from this time are very rare, and not always accurate. This, by Cornelius Anthoniszoon, shows typical multi-decked carracks with tall poops and overhanging forecastles. A galley is in the foreground.

Right: A reconstruction of the *Santa Maria,* the flagship of Christopher Columbus on his first voyage across the Atlantic in 1492. She was a carvel (a name derived from caravel). Special mention of her spritsail, foresail, main topsail, mainsail and mizzen, is made in Columbus' diary of the voyage.

Double-ended cogs with a single mast and single square sail were used to carry valuable cargoes in Europe during the twelfth to the fourteenth centuries.

The cog was developed for coastal trade, which had once more begun to flourish in the twelfth century. Single-masted vessels with a square sail, they became the most commonly used ships of the HANSÁ, Union of European Harbour Towns, founded in 1241. The name 'cog' is derived from the wine barrels which were at one time the main cargo. In the fifteenth century they were modified by the addition of a smaller fore mast to the main mast; a smaller mast was placed aft, set with a lateen sail.

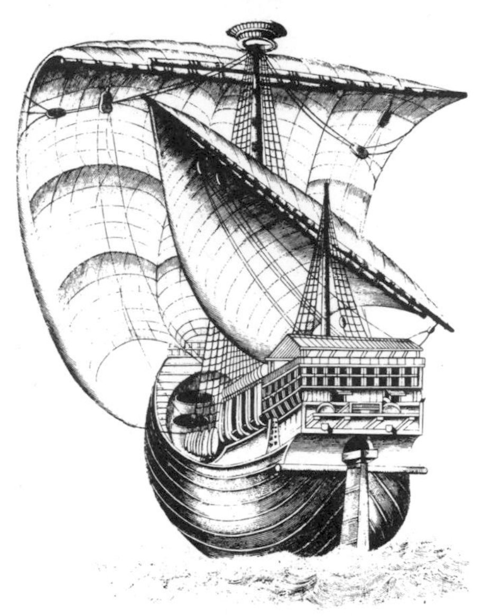

Sixteen types of ship, from an engraving c. 1560. The development of various types of ship from the northern European cog to the carracks and caravels of the Mediterranean was influenced by the growth of trade between the regions. The shape of the hull and type of sails was influenced by the ship's area of operation.

These cogs were double ended, single masted and single square-sailed vessels twenty-one to twenty-nine metres in length with an eight to nine metre beam. They had a flat bottom made by planks placed edge to edge (not overlapping) and tall lapstrake sides. The stem and stern posts were straight, making angles of about 60° with the horizontal, and the stern-post carried a rudder. Compared to the Viking longships these cogs were slow and cumbrous but they were ideally suited for trade. They could not run away from Scandinavian pirates in fast longships but their tall sides protected them from boarding. In an attempt to overcome the disadvantage of a low free-board, the longships were fitted with platforms fore and aft—castles—but the advantage thus gained was nullified when the cogs were similarly fitted, regaining the superiority of height. The longships were helpless and in 1304 the Danish naval defence organization, the *Leding*, officially switched from longships to cogs.

The castles were small, triangular platforms perched right atop the posts and they were light, flimsy and removable: they were only fitted on the cogs for voyages where trouble was anticipated.

Meanwhile, in the Mediterranean, sleek galleys with oars and lateen sails waged war and carried luxury or perishable goods. Heavy cargoes were carried in 'round ships', the largest of which had two lateen-rigged masts, three continuous decks, a protruding and covered forecastle and a two-tiered after castle or poop. The hulls were built frame-first and were carvel-planked. They were steered by two huge steering oars, one on each quarter.

The northern cogs had been adopted all the way south to the Gulf of Biscay and they were commonly trading to the Mediterranean in the thirteenth century when the Hanseatic merchants would meet their Venetian, Genoan, Pisan and Amalfian counterparts. By 1304 the cog had been copied by Venice, Genoa and Catalonia and had displaced the heavy round ships. The general lines of the cog and the stern rudder were retained but the hull was carvel-built. The rig was optional, square or lateen.

Northern European literature and archives show that the cog was superseded by the hulk around 1400 but it is not certain how different the last cogs looked from the new style hulks: the expression 'hulk' is not found with a picture during that period. However, seals and other representations show ships that look broadly similar to large cogs but with a curved stem and what appears to be a round bottom. These may be the hulks, perhaps the descendants of the curved banana-shaped hulks of the eighth century.

The predominance of the hulk did not last very long. By the mid 1400s it was being replaced by a larger ship with a more substantial forecastle and a Mediterranean-style high poop deck and it had acquired a second mast, a mizzen, that carried a lateen sail. The square sail on the main mast had discarded the reef points found on the sails of cogs and hulks in favour of a bonnet, a removable strip of canvas laced to the foot of the sail. This new ship type was the carrack. It was used both in the Atlantic and in the Mediterranean but there were some significant regional differences: in the north the carracks were lapstrake or clinker-built and they had ratlines in the shrouds; in the Mediterranean they were carvel-built and had no ratlines.

The carrack type evolved very fast and during the hundred years that it dominated the seas it literally 'sprouted' in all directions, increasing in size, 'growing' up to four masts, budding topsails and topgallant sails, throwing up huge multi-decked and overhanging forecastles and tall poops and bristling with weapons entirely new at sea: guns. Somewhere along the line it shed the double-ended stern of its northern and Mediterranean forebears and developed instead the space-giving transom stern. The period was one of amazing nautical activity and was concluded, about 1550 by the appearance of the galleon.

Although the carracks grew in size and bulk, there was still a demand for smaller ships. Some of these, such as the Spanish naos, were built along similar lines and with a similar rig; others, such as the caravels, were essentially lateen-rigged and slimmer hulled. Both the naos and caravels were suitable for oceanic travel: the combination of the northern and Mediterranean shipbuilding traditions, the stern rudder and the compass from China were about to change the face of the world.

The Age of Exploration: The Victoria

In the year 1519 a fleet of five vessels under the command of Ferdinand Magellan, a Portuguese navigator in the service of Spain, sailed with 270 men from San Lucar at the mouth of the Guadalquivir. It was bound on a voyage of trade and exploration, the purpose of which was to seek a westerly route to the spice islands of the Moluccas. Three years later a single ship, the *Victoria,* returned with eighteen survivors under the command of Juan Sebastian de Elcano, having completed the first circumnavigation of the world.

In the sixteenth century, voyages of exploration were not undertaken for purely scientific reasons. Magellan's most important task was not to prove that the world was round, or even to find new lands to conquer, but to find a new trade route, avoiding Portuguese-controlled southern Africa.

There are no contemporary plans or trustworthy pictures of any of the ships employed for the great voyages of discovery and contemporary writings and reports only give the scantiest of clues. Thus the description given here of the *Victoria* is largely one of interpretation and it is more a general description of her type than of her self.

During the late fifteenth century and the first half of the sixteenth there were three types of ocean-going vessels: caravels, carracks and naos. Caravels were small vessels with two to four masts which usually carried lateen sails. They were handy and were used for voyages of discovery (Columbus's *Pinta* and *Niña* were caravels) but their size was limited by the nature of the lateen rig which does not lend itself to more than one sail per mast. Because they were small—not exceeding 70 tonnes and 25 m overall—they could not carry much in the way of provisions and larger ships were preferred. The large square-rigged carracks, the 'great ships' of the time, had a big carrying capacity, but their towering superstructures and deep draught made them too awkward for exploration purposes. Naos were similar

In 1519 the Portuguese explorer, Ferdinand Magellan, set sail on his voyage to circumnavigate the world. Almost a hundred years later the Dutch explorer Willem Cornelison Schouten in his ship *Unity* undertook a similar voyage. The map, below, shows both the Magellan Strait and Le Maire's Strait, named after a merchant who accompanied Schouten.

Ship's guns from the time of Magellan
1. Wrought-iron gun, 1350–1525, made of wrought-iron bars running the length of the gun with iron rings shrunk around them. The guns were lashed to 'stocks' which were fastened to the deck and could not be run in and out. They were therefore breech loaded. (About 4m long.)
2. Sixteenth century 'brass' breech loaded Falconet. (About 2m long.)
3. 'Brass' Culvering 1500–1800. Although called 'brass' guns, they were actually made of bronze. At the beginning of the sixteenth century two small wheels were attached to the front of the stocks, changing them to 'trucks' which could be run in and out, allowing the gun to be muzzle loaded. (About 4m long.)

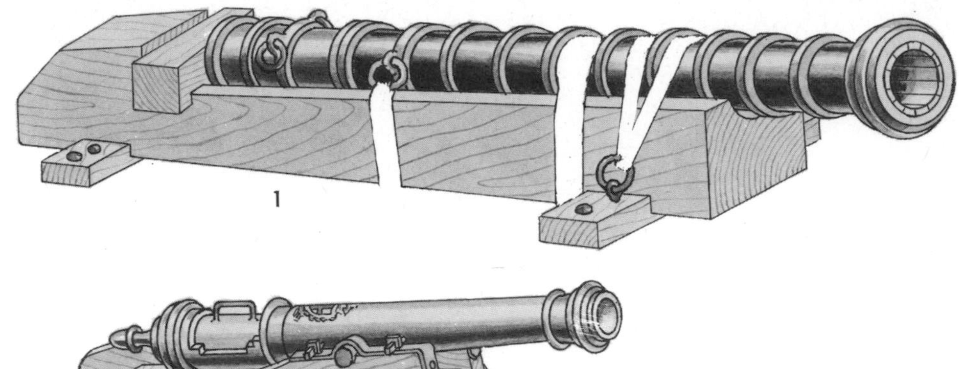

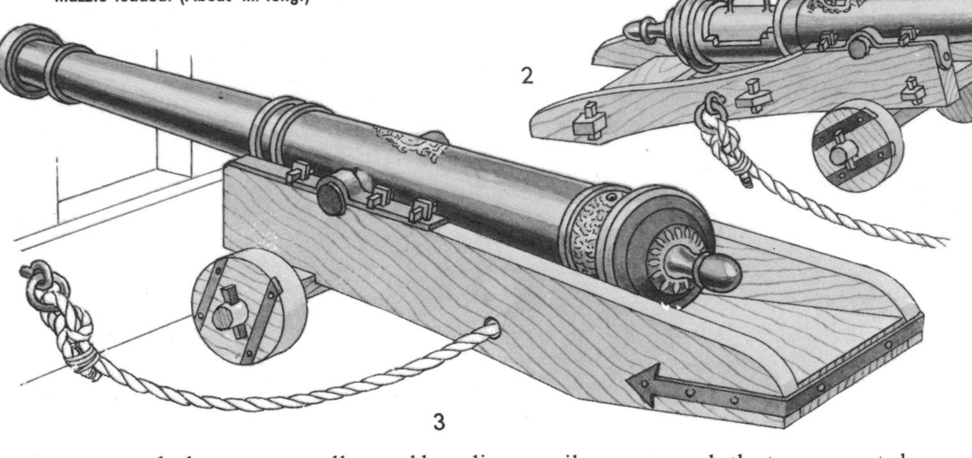

The *Victoria* was the sole survivor of the five ships which set out on Magellan's voyage round the world in 1519. She was of the naos type, with three masts. Her sails and rig followed a basic pattern which is still largely retained by square riggers of today.

to carracks but were smaller and handier to sail. They had sufficient hold space for provisions and were the navigators' favourites. They were ordinary trading vessels but few explorers had the luxury of purpose-built or even new ships. The *Victoria* and the other ships in Magellan's fleet were naos. They were second-hand and the low price paid for them shows that they had known better days.

Tonnage measurements in those days were represented by the deadweight capacity of the ships when loaded with a standard commodity which varied from port to port: at Seville and on the Atlantic coast of Spain and Portugal the unit was the *tonelada* of wine—about 900 kg or 0·9 cubic metres of liquid. The *Victoria*'s tonnage is reasonably well known as her capacity in Sevillan *toneladas* was recorded: in modern units she would measure 90 tonnes. A tubby and heavy displacement hull of that tonnage would probably be about 26 m.

Whereas the big carracks had up to four masts, the *Victoria* was an ordinary three-masted vessel. The bowsprit carried a single sail, the spritsail, which did not impart much extra speed to the ship but which helped, by correct setting, to keep the ship on the desired course. The main and fore masts were in two parts each: a thick, tall lower mast stepped on the keel of the ship and a shorter, lighter topmast above it. As trees of sufficient size could not be easily obtained for the lower masts, these were made of several baulks assembled together by rope bands or wooldings.

The lower masts carried a large square sail on a yard that was not lowered except for repairs. The sail was therefore furled *up* to the yard and to secure it, the men had to 'lay out' on the yard arms to tie short lengths of rope known as gaskets. This is still the practice in modern square riggers but it must have been particularly perilous in those days as footropes were not yet invented.

The lower sails were very baggy and some contemporary paintings show a rope, the bowgee, leading from the middle of the foot of the sail down to the deck, to prevent the sail from lifting and spilling its wind. In light winds the surface of these sails could be increased by lacing a strip of canvas, the bonnet, to their foot. The topsails (on the topmasts) were considerably smaller than the lower sails and their yards were lowered to the top when the sails had to be taken in.

The mizzen mast was more slender than the lower fore and main masts and it was stepped on deck. It carried a lateen sail called the mizzen; such a fore-and-aft sail improved the windward performance and the general balance of the ship under sail. The mizzen was handed by lowering the lateen yard to the deck.

The rig of naos and carracks was the result of the blending and cross-fertilization of mediaeval North European and Mediterranean rigs. The square sails and their running rigging, the standing lower yards and the ratlines were of northern origin; the lateen sails and the bonnets came from the south. This three-masted rig, with square sails on the fore and main masts and a fore-and-aft sail on the mizzen mast is the basic pattern retained by square riggers up to the present day.

The hull, too, was of mixed northern and southern ancestry. Its broad, tubby and buoyant lines had been developed for riding the rough seas of the Atlantic. The Mediterranean carvel method of planking was adopted but the thicker reinforcing strakes, known as wales, and the vertical external ribs, known as skids, had evolved in connection with the clinker-built hulls of the north. The stern rudder had reached northern Europe from China some time during the twelfth century and it had quickly spread around the coasts of Europe. The *Victoria* was steered by a plain tiller, as the steering level or whipstaff (let alone the wheel) was a later invention. However, in heavy weather, relieving tackles may have been clapped on the tiller to reduce strain on the helmsman.

The castles were superstructures built over the hull proper. In carracks they reached ridiculous proportions, with three decks or more: their original purpose was defensive, like towers on land. Naos, being smaller, had lower castles. The poop structure contained the captain's cabin, his day cabin and bunks for the master, pilots and gentlemen. The hands slept where they could, on deck or on the cargo; hammocks were not yet used at sea.

The *Victoria*'s original complement was about fifty strong and the ship must have been very crowded at the start of the voyage. A large crew was necessary

Magellan's voyage—and his ship—embodied the spirit of the Age of Exploration. This early German engraving is more an 'artist's impression' than an accurate representation of the *Victoria*.

Below:
An allegorical picture of Magellan the Navigator. He is surrounded by the simple navigational instruments with which he sailed round the world. The *Victoria* is shown in the midst of the perils faced on a voyage at that time: strong winds, sea monsters, and fearsome natives—at whose hands Magellan was to meet his death.

both for sailing the ship and because allowance had to be made for an expected mortality rate of about fifty per cent. No wonder there were few volunteers and that the manning of deep-sea vessels was a major problem! Magellan's expedition had one of the worst fatality records, with deaths from starvation, scurvy, accidents, skirmishes and mutiny. Despite the dangers, there was a tourist who joined simply for the adventure. He was Antonio Pigafetta, a native of Vicenza in Italy and his narrative of the circumnavigation is the only original one we have, Magellan's papers having been destroyed during the voyage.

The expedition's victuals were like those carried in ocean-going sailing ships until this century: sea biscuits, salt beef, salt pork, cheese, dried beans and chick peas, wines, onions, raisin, dried figs, honey, rice, flour, lentils and olive oil. The cooking was done, as it still is today in Indian Ocean dhows, on an open wood fire placed in a sand box. On the way, Magellan's crews salted down penguins, sea-lions and guanacos but later, in the Pacific, they were reduced to eating rats and the leather from the chafing gear.

The fleet carried seventy-one guns of various types, including fifty-eight culverins (heavy guns weighing 2 tonnes and firing a 7·8 kg shot with a range of 2,500 paces) and seven falconets (light guns weighing 230 kg, firing a 0·57 kg shot with a range of 1,400 paces). Small arms included fifty arquebuses and sixty crossbows; there were also one hundred sets of corselets, breast plates and helmets and two hundred shields.

This was not, however, a military expedition but an exploring and a commercial one. The naos carried enough trade goods to barter against a full return cargo of pepper: copper bars, quicksilver, bracelets and other trinkets, knives, fishhooks and coloured cloths.

The navigational equipment included twenty-one wooden quadrants and seven astrolabes, thirty-five compass needles and forty-eight parchment charts (which were useless). The longitude could only be estimated by dead reckoning and the speed of the ships was assessed by pure experience.

Apart from the *Victoria,* the ships in Magellan's fleet were the *San Antonio* (121 tonnes), the *Trinidad* (111 tonnes) the *Concepción* (91 tonnes) and the *Santiago* (76 tonnes). The *San Antonio* deserted as the fleet struggled to round Cape Horn and returned to Spain. It took the rest of the ships five weeks to sail the 480 kilometres now known as the Strait of Magellan, and notorious for its stormy seas. Perhaps because of its contrasting calm, Magellan named the ocean he entered the Pacific—or peaceful—Ocean.

The *Trinidad,* Magellan's flagship, foundered in the Moluccas after Magellan himself had been killed in the Philippines. It was in these islands that the *Concepción* was declared unseaworthy and burned. The *Santiago* had been wrecked earlier on the coast of Patagonia. The only ship to complete the voyage, the *Victoria,* was hauled ashore at San Lucar when she returned, as a memorial to her great circumnavigation. Unfortunately this attempt at preservation failed, but though the ship itself has perished, her achievement is remembered to this day.

An Elizabethan Galleon: The Mayflower

Just over three and a half centuries ago, in 1620, the *Mayflower* landed 102 emigrants, who called themselves 'Pilgrims' on the bleak, wild shores of New England. They were not the first European settlers, nor even the first English ones in what is today the United States of America. What gave them a special status in history was their attitude: they had arrived in the New World not for a colonial venture controlled and administered from England, to provide colonial products for the parent country, but to found there a new society to their own taste. They were the first Americans.

The *Mayflower's* name has gone down in history and, with Noah's Ark and Columbus' *Santa Maria*, she is one of the most widely known ships. Like those two vessels, she appears in no contemporary plans or pictures and her appearance can only be reconstructed by detective work, circumstantial evidence and comparisons with what is known about the ships of her time.

The *Mayflower* was a galleon, a type of ship that appeared in the 1540s and which superseded the carracks and naos. The main differences between the *Mayflower* and the slightly earlier *Victoria* are not immediately apparent as they are connected mainly with finer underwater lines and a slimmer hull. On galleons the forecastle was brought well inboard of the stem and the sides were flush with the hull, whereas on carracks the forecastle usually jutted forwards. The beakhead, evolved from the galley's ram, is also characteristic of galleons. On galleons of the *Mayflower's* period, the high ratio of superstructure height to the length of the hull was still, however, reminiscent of the carracks.

It is from the official papers of the New England Colony and from British shipping registers that some information can be gleaned on the *Mayflower* and her master. She appears to have had a tonnage of nine score (180). Using the contemporary tonnage rules and assuming the ship was built along certain proportions, the main dimensions can be calculated. William Borough, comptroller of the Navy in 1589–98 wrote that 'the mean and best proportions' for a merchant ship would be a keel length two-and-a-quarter times the beam and a depth eleven-twenty-fourths of the beam; it is quite possible but not certain that the *Mayflower* was built to these common proportions. If so, her main dimensions were: 180 tons (contemporary measurement); keel length 21 m; length from the stem to the taffrail, 35 m; rake (inclination from the vertical) of the stern post, 20°.

An infinite variety of hulls could be designed with these dimensions and here again assumptions have to be made. The best information we have about naval architecture of the *Mayflower's* times are contained in a 1620 manuscript in the Admiralty Library recently published as *A Treatise on Shipbuilding* and in a manuscript in the Pepysian Library known as *Fragments of Ancient English Shipwrightry*, written about 1586 by Matthew Baker, a master shipwright. The midship hull sections were flat-floored and the sides were drawn by compass, with three intersecting arcs or 'sweeps': the floor, futtock and upper sweeps. The hull lines produced accord-

The small Elizabethan galleon *Golden Hind* had a long, projecting beak and a forecastle set well back from the stem. The deck, incorporating gratings, extended forward to the beakhead. The stern gallery formed a walkway. Below deck, maximum use of space was essential because of the length of the voyages undertaken. Only a light armament was carried.

The *Mayflower* is perhaps one of the most widely known ships of the galleon type. She was a merchant ship with a rig similar to that of the naos and carracks of the early sixteenth century. In 1620 she set sail on a voyage that was to make her famous: carrying the Pilgrim Fathers to found a new society in America.

ing to the Treatise are those of a fast and handy ship with a good hold capacity. A 'replica' built in 1957, which re-enacted the historical voyage, proved to be quite a good sailer (reaching seven knots) but there is no proof that she is closely similar to the original ship.

The *Mayflower* had a curved stem with a straight projecting beakhead about six metres long. The main deck, which ran the length of the hull, had a forecastle or foc'sle structure built above it, on its fore part, around the fore mast. This foc'sle formed a cabin, probably for the crew and the galley and its 'roof' was a working deck surrounded by railings. The after quarter of the main deck was covered by a quarter deck. The space at main deck level and below the quarter deck was made into cabins for the officers, to port and starboard of the helmsman's position, and with the captain's great cabin occupying the whole rear section. The headroom was very low—much less than two metres—except in the great cabin where the main deck was dropped a little. The quarter deck above the great cabin was surmounted in turn by a poop deck, which sheltered the captain's private cabin. The stern was square, of the transom type and the sides leaned inboard so that the captain's cabin and the poop deck were very narrow.

Below the main deck, within the basic hull, was the 'tween deck. The headroom there was even lower, obliging the crew and passengers to crawl. The tiller entered inboard at this level and it was controlled from the main deck above by a steering lever, the whipstaff. The helmsman stood in front of the great cabin with its head peering through a hatch in the quarter deck. The hold was below the 'tween deck and it was probably loaded through a single hatch in front of the main mast.

Being a merchant ship, the *Mayflower* probably only had a light armament, perhaps a couple of falcons (firing three-pound shots) a-side, on the main deck, and a few railing pieces.

The rig of the *Mayflower* was similar to that of the naos and carracks of the early sixteenth century such as the *Victoria*. Bonnets were still used on the lower sails but bowgees had gone out of fashion. Topgallants were not usually carried by medium-sized merchantmen such as the *Mayflower*.

The *Mayflower* was not a new ship when she sailed for America. It is not known for certain where or when she was built but she was definitely in existence in 1606 and she may be far older. There had been two *Mayflowers* in the English fleet fighting the Armada in 1588 and one of these, from London and owned by John Vassal, was measured at 200 tons (contemporary measure). This was certainly the same ship as the 250-ton *Mayflower* from London, also owned by Vassal, which was entered in several archives of the early 1590s. Tonnage measurements at the time are known to have been inconsistent and it is quite possible that the Vassal *Mayflower* of around 200–250 tons and the Pilgrims' *Mayflower* of around 180 tons were the same ship. Further clues that the Pilgrims' *Mayflower* was the same ship that had fought the Spanish Armada comes from records dated 1606 which refer to a *Mayflower* from Lee with a Lee captain, Robert Bonner. Vassal had moved from London to a place near Lee in 1602 and it seems reasonable to suppose that he had taken the ship with him.

The Lee *Mayflower* reappears in records from 1607, again with Bonner in command, but this time with London as her port of origin. The variation of the port of origin is not critical as there were no ports of registry in the modern sense. A ship was sometimes listed as being from the port where her owner lived, sometimes as being from the port she usually sailed from.

The final clue to the identity of the Pilgrims' *Mayflower* lies in records of her masters. In 1608 Bonner, who had

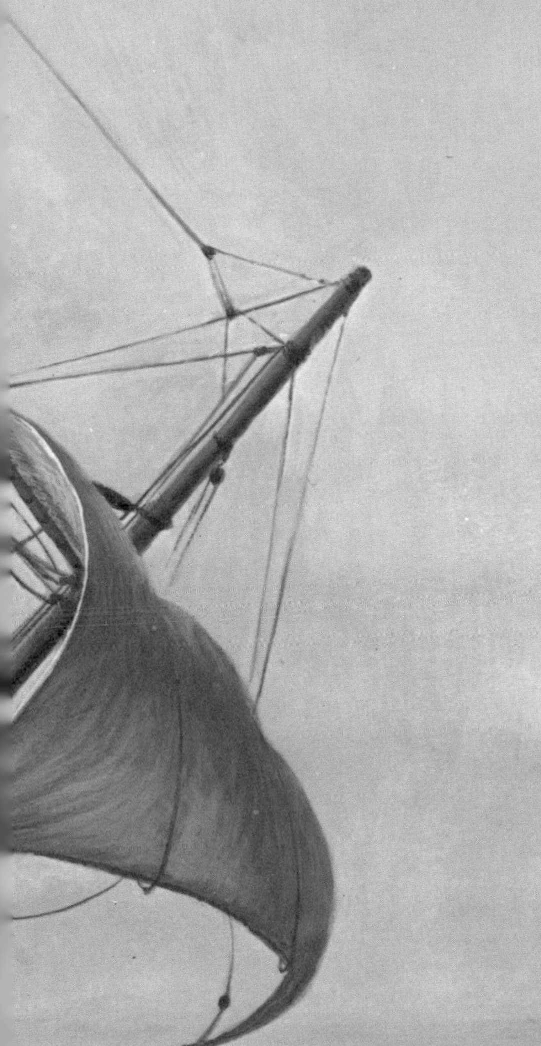

The defeat of the Spanish Armada by the English fleet under the command of Lord Howard of Effingham, Lord High Admiral of England, marked the beginning of tactical naval warfare. The English fleet fought using the full force of its superior gunnery, making it impossible for the Spanish, who had far more men and ships, to close and board. It is possible that the *Mayflower* may have taken part in the battle.

previously been listed as the Lee *Mayflower*'s master, became master of a ship called the *Josan*. The *Josan*'s previous master, Christopher Jones, appears in records of 1609 as the *Mayflower*'s master and it was the same Christopher Jones who, in 1620, commanded the historic voyage to America. It is possible that Bonner, who took over Jones' command on the unusually named *Jonas* handed the Lee *Mayflower* to another master and that Jones' *Mayflower* was a completely different ship. But it is surely far more likely that he and Jones simply swapped ships. Whatever her previous history, the *Mayflower* of 1609, now registered at Harwich, certainly became the Pilgrims' ship.

From 1609 until 1620 the *Mayflower* sailed with Jones to such ports as Trondheim in Norway, Bordeaux, La Rochelle, Hamburg and Malaga. She may also have engaged in seasonal Greenland whaling.

In the early years of the seventeenth century Brownists (Puritan separatists from the Church of England) had gone into voluntary exile in Holland to avoid religious persecution. They desired, however, to retain an English identity for their children and feared that they would be assimilated by the friendly but foreign Dutch. With the permission of King James I of England and of the Virginia Company, they arranged to form a new colony to be situated in Virginia, to the North of Jamestown. They bought the *Speedwell*, a sixty-one-tonne vessel and chartered the *Mayflower* for a year. On 5 August 1620 the two ships sailed from Southampton with 120 Pilgrims. The *Speedwell* soon proved to be unseaworthy and they had to return twice to England.

Finally the *Mayflower* alone sailed from Plymouth with 102 Pilgrims: eighteen could not find place on the ship but by that time about that number had seen enough of the sea and had changed their minds anyway. The emigrants consisted of fifty men, twenty women and thirty-two children. There was also the ship's company, forty strong. We can imagine the conditions in the thirty-five metre hull, particularly for the passengers who were battened down in the 'tween deck as soon as bad weather threatened. They were not allowed to use the galley and they had to bring their own provisions; they ate cold meals throughout the passage which lasted more than two months. The voyage was plagued by storms and the *Mayflower* was nearly lost on several occasions. She was blown well to the north of her intended destination making her landfall at Cape Cod on 9 November. The winds prevented the ship from sailing south and finally the Pilgrims landed on Cape Cod where Provincetown is now built. This was not a suitable site and after a reconnaissance of the area, the Pilgrims decided to settle on the opposite side of Cape Cod bay at a spot that had been named Plymouth by Captain John Smith who had explored the New England coast in 1614. The Pilgrims' hardships had barely begun and half the colonists were to die within a year of arrival.

The *Mayflower* had been used during the winter as a support vessel but she

Above: One hundred and two Pilgrims sailed from Plymouth in August 1620. Some 350 years later a replica (below) repeated the historic voyage to America.

A model of the *Mayflower*, showing her typical galleon features. The main deck, running the length of the hull, had a foc'sle structure around the fore mast and a quarter deck over its after quarter. The poop deck, sheltering the captain's cabin, rose above the quarter deck. Her stem was square, of the transom type, and her sides leaned inboard.

Right: The Pilgrims first landed at Cape Cod, but built their settlement on the opposite side of the bay, at a place appropriately named Plymouth.

left the struggling colony in April 1621 and reached England in only thirty-one days. She resumed her trade to La Rochelle—but not for long. Captain Jones died at Rotherhithe in 1622 and his ship may have been laid up after his death and allowed to get out of repair for in 1624 she was reported to be *in ruinis* at Rotherhithe. According to unproven and doubtful traditions, some of the *Mayflower*'s timbers are part of a barn in Buckinghamshire and two of her masts are used as pillars in a chapel at Abingdon, by the Thames.

A Seventeenth Century Warship: The Wasa

In 1961, three hundred and thirty-three years after they had been drowned, two knights rose slowly from the murky waters of Stockholm's harbour, hardly the worse for their long immersion. In fact, if they had not been submerged, they would probably never have been preserved at all, for the knights were carved wooden bitts by the fore mast emplacement on the upper deck of the seventeenth-century warship *Wasa*. As the water was pumped out of the wreck, more and more of the hull appeared until, before long, the salvage was completed and marine archaeologists could start working in earnest on a unique and invaluable find: an almost undisturbed man-of-war complete with stores and crew's belongings.

The *Wasa* did not survive long enough as a warship to become famous or even to be painted on canvas. Until her recent salvage very little was known about her apart from the fact that she had capsized and sunk on her maiden journey in 1628.

Although she was the largest ship in the Swedish fleet, there was nothing particularly exceptional about the *Wasa*: despite her tragic and untimely end she was not the result of some freakish experiment in ship design. In other words she was not salvaged because of her design or her history but because she happened to be a remarkably well-preserved example of a large warship of her time.

It is astonishing how little we know about ships of the sixteenth and of the first half of the seventeenth century. Contemporary paintings and other pictures must be used with caution. Most of them are technically incorrect and they do not give much information about the underwater shape of the hull and the internal layout. The *Wasa* is therefore of particular interest, as much of the missing information on shipbuilding of the period can be obtained by direct study. She is also the oldest salvaged ship in existence for which we know the name, the exact dates and other similar details.

The *Wasa*'s history goes back to 1626 when King Gustav II Adolf of Sweden decided to have four new warships built. The largest, which was to be larger than any other ship he had previously owned, was to be called *Wasa,* from the name of his dynasty. This name was spelled variously *Wasa, Wasen* or *Wasan* and is often written *Vasa* today.

The Swedes, with their Viking background, were competent producers of small ships but the task of designing and building such a large ship as the *Wasa* was entrusted to a Dutchman, Henryk Hybertson. The Dutch were then the uncontested leaders in such matters—the contemporary French ship *Saint-Louis,* was Dutch-built for the same reason. English design at this period had, if anything, regressed to pre-Armada extremes of very tall hulls with poor sailing performances. The building of the *Wasa* took place at the Royal Dockyard on Blasieholmen

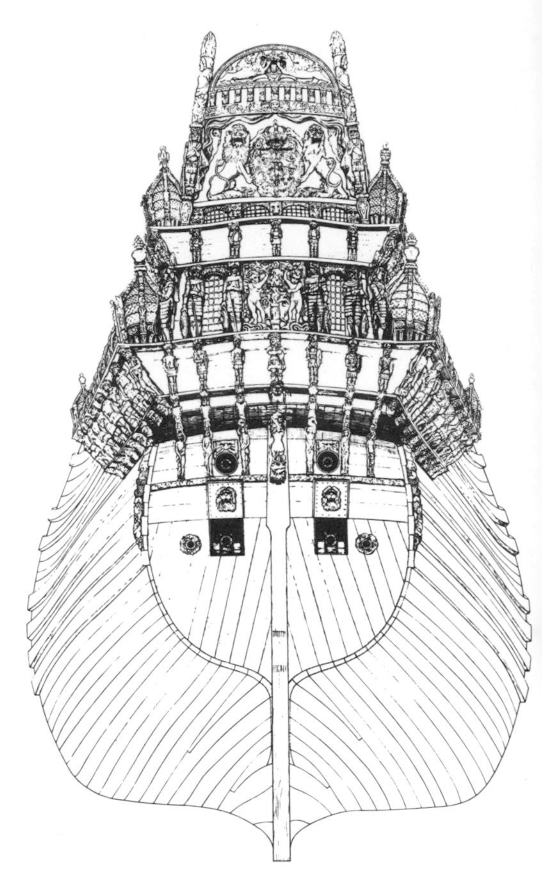

Left: The stern of the *Wasa* towered some 16m above the water. At its uppermost part, a large crossbeam bears the initials GARS—Gustavus Adolphus Rex Sueciae. Underneath, supported by two crowned lions, is the national coat of arms of Sweden. Lower still, between the two large window openings, and held by two cherubs, is the Wasa or cornsheaf, the symbol of the Wasa family.
Below: In spite of her decorations, the *Wasa* was built as a warship and was intended to be the largest in the Swedish navy. Instead, she sank in Stockholm harbour on her maiden voyage.

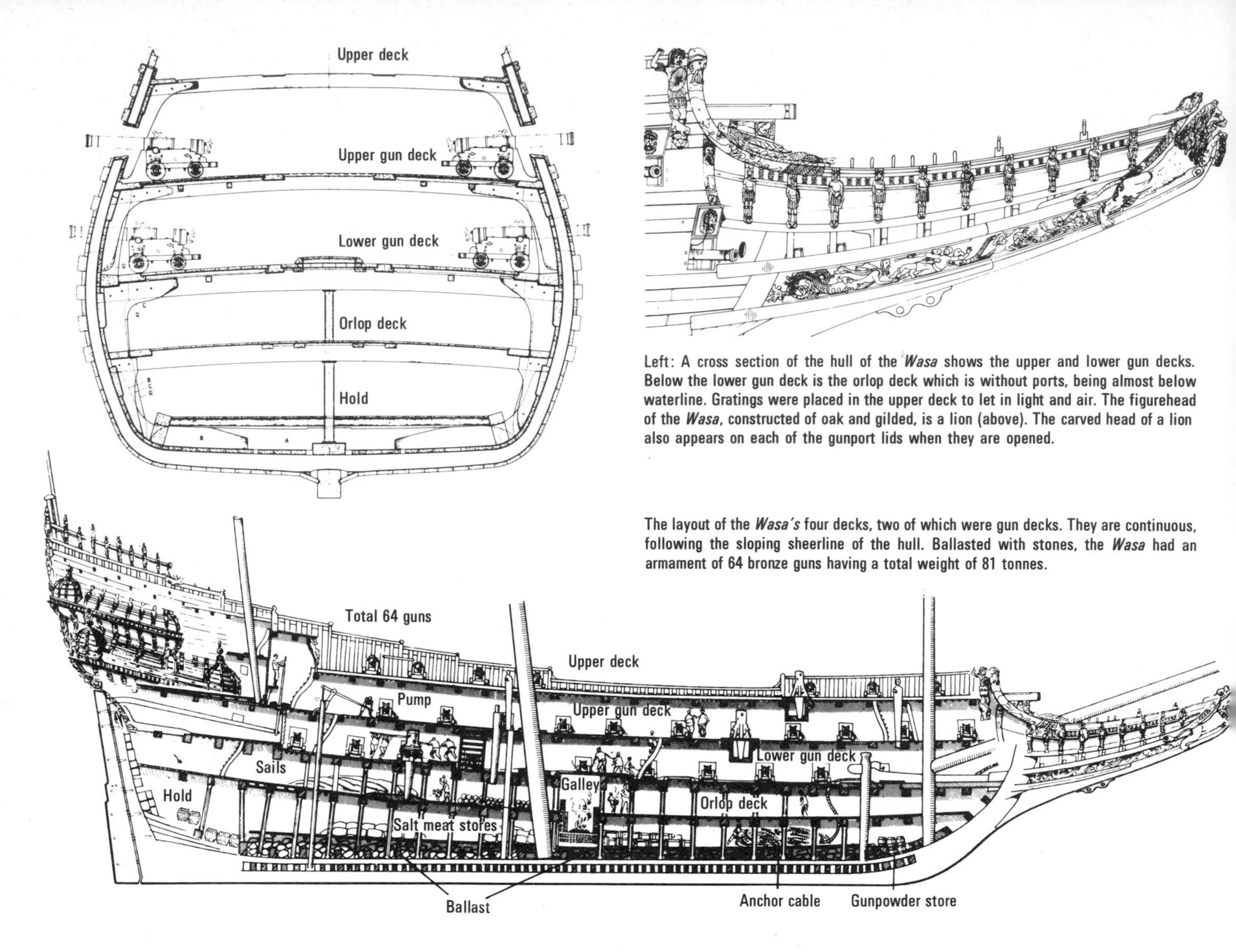

Left: A cross section of the hull of the *Wasa* shows the upper and lower gun decks. Below the lower gun deck is the orlop deck which is without ports, being almost below waterline. Gratings were placed in the upper deck to let in light and air. The figurehead of the *Wasa*, constructed of oak and gilded, is a lion (above). The carved head of a lion also appears on each of the gunport lids when they are opened.

The layout of the *Wasa's* four decks, two of which were gun decks. They are continuous, following the sloping sheerline of the hull. Ballasted with stones, the *Wasa* had an armament of 64 bronze guns having a total weight of 81 tonnes.

island but was contracted to a private shipbuilding firm.

The *Wasa* was launched in 1627 and the following year she was moved a short distance to Stockholm Castle to be ballasted (with stones) and to take on her armament of sixty-four bronze guns. These consisted of forty-eight 24-pounders, eight 3-pounders, two 1-pounders and six mortars. This artillery weighed eighty-one tonnes, all above the waterline, posing a stability problem that was common to all men-of-war. Stability trials were held by the simple expedient of having thirty men running from one side of the ship to the other. The rolling motion thus created was so alarming that the trials were stopped.

Finally, on 10 August 1628, the *Wasa* was ready for her inaugural cruise—a short sail to Alvsnabben island in the Outer Stockholm Archipelago, with many guests and personalities aboard. She was certainly a beautiful ship. Her displacement was 1,422 tonnes and her hull was 54 m long (75·5 m with the bowsprit) by 12·5 m beam. Her draught was 5·25 m and her stern towered some 16·4 m above water. She had two gun decks pierced by fifty-two gun ports, and a continuous upper deck which consisted partly of gratings to allow light and air below. Above the forward upper deck stood the forecastle, around the fore mast; and abaft the main mast a half deck extended to the poop where it was in turn surmounted by a raised quarter deck.

The bows and stern were profusely decorated with painted and gilded carvings. The figurehead was a 508 cm gilded lion. The head bulkhead, standing like a wall above the bow, was decorated with sculptures of Roman emperors. The stern, with galleries, was an intricate mass of carvings which included the national coat of arms held by two grinning lions, a *wasen* or sheaf (the symbol of the Wasa family) held by two cherubs, and a collection of knights and Greek mythological heroes. The sides were unadorned except that the open gun port lids, each showed a carved lion head.

In contemporary paintings rows of gun ports like these follow the marked curve or sheer of the thick strengthening wales which run the length of the ship. Until the salvage of the *Wasa*, it was not known whether the guns were placed on sloping decks, on special horizontal platforms or even if the decks themselves were staggered. The *Wasa* shows that the decks were continuous, following the sloping sheer line of the ship; the gun carriages, rolling directly on them, must have been very difficult to handle. Half a century later, by the time of the *Zeven Provincien*, the gun decks had become horizontal so that the gun ports intersected the wales. This weakened the hull and from about 1750 until their disappearance, most sailing men-of-war had uncambered sides so that both the wales and the gun decks were horizontal.

The tiller, in the after part of the lower gun deck, was connected to a whipstaff, which swivelled through a harwood hub in the upper gun deck floor and was used as a lever for steering. The whipstaff was replaced on ships by the

The *Wasa*'s sails and rig have not yet been restored. It is known, however, that she was a three-master, rigged with topsail and topgallant on her fore and main masts and two sails only on her mizzen. The masts were of pine and she could set some 1,150 sq.m. of canvas in all.

On 24 April 1961, after 333 years on the bottom, the *Wasa* was brought to the surface again. Made fast between the salvage pontoons *Odin* and *Frigg* she was towed to shallow waters and was later mounted on her own permanent concrete pontoon. Continuous spraying with a preservative solution to replace the water in the wood fibres was necessary to prevent the wood splitting.

Raising the pontoon.

On the permanent concrete pontoon.

Restoration work inside the ship.

The *Wasa* today.

modern wheel at the beginning of the eighteenth century.

The orlop deck, below the lower gun deck, has no ports as it is almost all below the waterline. Most of the crew slept in hammocks on these two decks. Another interesting feature of the *Wasa* is the galley, built in the hold just forward of the main mast. It is a simple brick-floored structure with an open fire on its floor. Two brick walls support an iron rod on which was slung a 200-litre iron cauldron—a primitive method of gimballing to prevent the soup from spilling on the fire in rough seas. By the end of the century galleys on ships had become a proper brick and iron stove and had migrated to just abaft the fore mast on the upper gun deck.

As we now know, this is how the *Wasa* appeared to her passengers on that fateful August day in 1628. Contemporaries would also have noticed her rig, but little of this has been preserved although enough is known about the rigs of the time to reconstruct it. Under her bowsprit she carried a square sail, the spritsail. A small, precarious mast was perched at the far end of the bowsprit, carrying a spritsail-topsail. The fore mast carried three sails (fore sail, fore topsail and fore topgallant), as did the main mast (main sail, main topsail and main topgallant). Her mizzen mast was much smaller, stepped on the upper gun deck instead of resting on the keel like the fore and main masts. It carried a triangular lateen sail, the mizzen, and perhaps a small square topsail. In all, the *Wasa* could set some 1,150 square metres of canvas.

The ship's normal complement would have been 433 men: 133 seamen and naval officers and 300 soldiers. The preponderance of soldiers was traditional and only disappeared later in the century when seamanship and gunnery became more effective than boarding tactics. When the *Wasa* sailed, the soldiers had not been embarked but there were many guests, including the Dutch architect, and all together between 200 and 250 people were aboard.

The *Wasa* had only sailed a few

The bows and stern of the *Wasa* were covered with brightly painted and gilded carvings. The figures around the bow are sculptures of Roman Emperors, while those beneath the stern galleries are of heroes of Greek mythology and knights. After careful restoration work, traces of the original gilding can still be seen.

Resting upon its own keel, the hull of the *Wasa* is now supported on a vast floating pontoon over which has been constructed a large hall which protects her from the weather. The hull timbers are still frequently treated with a polyethylene glycol preservative with a fungicide to prevent wood rot.

hundred metres when she suddenly heeled to port in a gust of wind. The water rushed in through the open gun ports and she sank very quickly in 30 m of water, drowning fifty people, including the architect. The Court of Enquiry did not reach a conclusion and no-one was punished but it is probable that the weights were badly distributed inside a hull of basically sound design. Gun ports had always been a danger and the English *Mary Rose,* perhaps the first ship to have them, had sunk in 1545 with 700 people, in similar circumstances. Her wreck has recently been found in Portsmouth harbour and there are plans to salvage her too, although she is in a far worse state than the *Wasa.* The main reason for the *Wasa*'s remarkable preservation lies in the nature of the water of Stockholm's harbour. It is brackish and unsuitable for teredos and because it also lacks oxygen, organic matter does not easily decay. Even clothes, leatherware and ropes were in good condition although the twelve bodies found were skeletons.

Because the *Wasa* had sunk in relatively shallow water, attempts were soon made to salvage her. Ian Bulmer, an Englishman, started the work on a 'no cure, no pay' basis. He managed to get the hull on an even keel but that was all. In 1664 Hans Albrekt von Treileben, a Swede, and his German associate, Andreas Peckell, started a series of salvage operations. They did not refloat the ship but they salvaged fifty of the guns. Made of bronze and weighing between one and two tonnes each, these were worth a small fortune. The divers used a diving bell and fresh air was brought down to them in weighted casks. When these operations ceased in 1683, the *Wasa* sank further into the mud and into oblivion until even her exact location was forgotten.

In 1920 the wreck of another Swedish man-of-war, the *Kiksnickeln,* which had sunk the same year as the *Wasa,* was accidentally located and this spurred the interest of the Swedish marine archaeologist Anders Franzen. He compiled a list of a dozen sixteenth and seventeenth century wrecks in the Stockholm area and concluded from circumstantial evidence that the *Wasa* would be the best preserved. Direct exploration by divers was ruled out because of the murkiness of the water and in 1953 Franzen started the search by towing grapnels and a wire sweep along the harbour bottom. Obstructions were sampled by means of a specially designed gravity corer which, in 1956, finally brought up a plug of very old oak. Divers confirmed that the *Wasa* had been found and that she was on an even keel, buried to the water line in blue clay and organic mud.

Salvage operations began the following year. Hard-hat navy divers tunnelled six shafts right under the hull, using a

During the seventeenth century guns weighing some 70 tonnes were removed from the *Wasa*'s hull. This is why very few of the gun carriages now bear their guns. It is believed that these early divers, by removing this great weight of armament from the decks, may in fact have prevented the *Wasa* from collapsing.

high-pressure recoil-less Zetterström water-jet and an air lift to carry away the mud debris. This tunnelling, in zero visibility under 6 m of soft mud and 30 m of water was an extremely perilous enterprise. The top of the tunnels was the hull itself—old rotten planks supporting tonnes of stone ballast.

Many loose carvings were found lying around the hulk and were brought back to the surface. Accurate plans were made to show exactly where each object lay, to help the marine archaeologists with reconstruction later on. Waterlogged wood will shrink and split if it is allowed to dry, so a special method of preservation was devised. The objects were continuously sprayed with a polyethylene glycol solution, the dripping being recycled. Polyethylene glycol gradually seeps into the wood fibres and replaces the water. It eventually dries as a waxy substance that hardens and protects the wood; further protection is provided by adding a fungicide.

The tunnels were successfully completed in 1959 and 1,450 m of 4·85 cm diameter steel wire were drawn through. The ends were made fast to a pair of salvage pontoons called *Odin* and *Frigg* which were then flooded until they were barely afloat. The wires were tightened and as the pontoons were pumped out they began to rise, lifting the *Wasa* out of the mud. The whole assembly was then towed to shallower waters until the *Wasa* touched the bottom again. The pontoons were flooded once more, the slack was taken up on the lifting wires and the pontoons and the *Wasa* were raised a further few metres. This operation was repeated eighteen times until the ship rested on the bottom at 15 m.

The *Wasa* stayed there for a further nineteen months while plans were made for bringing her to the surface—a very difficult technical problem. Divers sealed all the holes in the hull and the 4·85 cm wires were replaced by larger, 7·3 cm diameter ones. The *Odin* and the *Frigg* had been modified for the final lifting operation and were back above the *Wasa* on 4 April 1961. Everything was set by the 24th and at last the carved fore mast bitts broke the water. When the upper deck came to the surface, powerful pumps started pumping the water from the sealed hull.

Partly supported by the salvage pontoons and by inflatables placed under her stern, the *Wasa* floated on her own keel into a dry dock and over a large concrete pontoon specially designed to support her. This pontoon is now afloat, with the *Wasa* on its deck and a hall has been built on it to protect her. This is a semi-provisional structure to allow restoration work to be carried out and also to make public viewing possible. It is hoped that one day the *Wasa* will be in a larger, permanent museum, perhaps even with new masts and rigging.

The Dutch Fleet: The Zeven Provincien

The seventeenth century was the golden age of the Netherlands, the period during which the United Provinces (as the Netherlands were then called) were the major sea-trading power in the world, during which they founded the wealthiest colonial charter companies, gained independence from the Spanish Crown and promoted the arts and sciences. Such supremacy was not acquired without a few setbacks, nor was it maintained by unchallenged peace. As a nation whose economy mainly rested on seaborne trade, their security had to be acquired and defended at sea. Amongst the many brilliant Dutchmen of the time, Admiral Michiel Andriaszoon de Ruyter (1607–76) is one of the most outstanding, having repeatedly saved his country from defeat or foreign invasion and having maintained its overseas possessions and trade in the face of European competition and hostility. He is to the Dutch what Nelson is to the English and his ship, the *Zeven Provincien*, is their *Victory*.

De Ruyter's *Zeven Provincien* was the second Dutch Navy ship of a long line to bear that name. The first *Zeven Provincien* was launched in 1653 and fought during the First Dutch War (1652–54). She was named for the seven Dutch provinces—Holland, Zeeland, Utrecht, Guelderland, Overijssel, Groningen and Friesland—which had declared their union and their independence from Spain in 1579.

De Ruyter's *Zeven Provincien* was launched at Delfshaven in 1665, the year the Second Dutch War started, and was named after her predecessor. She was an 80-gun two-decker man-o'-war. She was larger in size than the *Wasa* and her gun decks were horizontal instead of following the sheerline and wales. This was certainly preferable from a gun-handling point of view, although it meant that some of the gunports would have to be cut through the wales, a practice that did not improve the solidity of the hull. It was only about a century later that the obvious best solution was found: ships with a straight sheer.

The *Zeven Provincien* was large for an 80-gun ship. This enabled her to have the sills of her lower gunports further up than on her English counterparts. The gunports could therefore be opened and the guns used in sea conditions where other 'eighties' would have had to keep them closed and fight only with their upper batteries.

The great cabin was in the after part of the upper gun deck; it was lighted by four square stern windows. As in the *Mayflower*, the helmsman was stationed just forward of this cabin, with his back to the bulkhead and with the whipstaff in his hands. Whereas on the *Mayflower* the helmsman could at

Admiral Michiel Andriaszoon de Ruyter (1607–1676) the most famous of the Dutch admirals, and a peerless seaman. De Ruyter began his naval career as a cabin boy and rose to the rank of Lieutenant-Admiral-General.

The *Zeven Provincien* was an 80-gun, two-decker man-of-war. A ship of the line, she fought in both the Second and Third Dutch wars against the English. As it was necessary for their vessels to have a shallow draught, the Dutch did not build three-deckers, but the *Zeven Provincien's* armament was almost equivalent to that of an English three-decker or first rate.

The Dutch East Indiamen, although essentially merchant vessels, were heavily armed for protection against pirates. In times of war they were used as naval vessels and up to the middle of the eighteenth century they formed a major part of the Dutch fleet.

least peer at the sails through the hatch in the low deckhead, on such large ships as the *Zeven Provincien* the helmsman could not see anything at all and had to steer by orders given from above. The tiller on such ships was very long and therefore the angle imparted to the rudder by the maximum inclination of the whipstaff was very small. Much of the steering must have been assisted by bracing the yards, trimming the sails and balancing the ship under sail. The whipstaff could probably be quickly disconnected and relieving tackles put to the tiller to be manned by sailors on the lower gun deck.

The midship part of the upper gun deck, the waist, was open to the sky and the forward part of this deck was covered by the fo'csle where the galley was located. The deck which covered the great cabin and which extended forward of it, almost to the main mast, was known as the half deck; it carried some sixteen guns and its after part was in turn decked over by a small quarter deck so as to form a cabin called the roundhouse or cuddy. This may have been used by the captain as a state cabin when the Admiral was occupying the great cabin. In the eighteenth century, the half deck became known as the quarter deck and what we have called here the quarter deck would have been referred to as a poop deck—except that such poop decks were by then no longer built on two-deckers.

The seventeenth century was a century of rococco and profuse hull decorations and the *Zeven Provincien* had her fair share. The stern was overloaded with carvings and what was not gilded was painted in bright colours. Above the great cabin windows there was a huge carved coat of arms consisting of two lions rampant holding the coats of arms of the seven Provinces, arranged on the sides and underside of a larger coat of arms, that of the United Provinces. The taffrail crowning the stern supported five great lanterns big enough for men to stand in. These heavy highly unseaworthy lanterns were usually taken down upon leaving harbour.

The sterns of men-o'-war of the period had definite architectural styles which varied from country to country and which were fairly typical of each country. The *Zeven Provincien's* stern is typically Dutch: fairly beamy and wide at the water-line, with a pronounced tumblehome. The latter is partly hidden by the quarter galleries which were external to the structural hull. These galleries, despite their fancy decorations, had a very mundane function: they were the officers' toilets. As with English ships, the stern itself did not have any galleries, although these existed on French and Spanish ships of the period. The lower part of the Dutch and French sterns had a square tuck (as on the transom sterns of modern motor-cruisers), as if the after part of the hull had been sawn off. On English ships there was a round tuck, where the side and bottom planking curved round to meet a transom above the waterline, thus creating less drag.

The sides were relatively unadorned apart for the quarter galleries but the bows were another area left to the exuberant attentions of the sculptors and gilders. The figurehead was the traditional red lion. This luxurious part of the ship was used by the crew for the same purposes as the quarter galleries were used by the officers: to the present day a ship's toilet is referred to as the 'head'.

De Ruyter, who was a thorough seaman and who was renowned for his sober and unassuming tastes and habits would probably have dispensed with the whole paraphernalia of carving and sculptures, if he had had the final word on such matters. The cost of decorations on seventeenth century ships could reach a very appreciable proportion of that of the whole ship and a single enemy broadside could cost a fortune in smashed sculptures.

The *Zeven Provincien*'s underwater body was beamy and had a shoal draught, in the Dutch fashion. This was a desirable feature owing to the shallowness of the waters off the Dutch coast and more than once Dutch ships escaped English ships of superior force by sailing into shoal waters where the latter could not venture without the risk of running aground.

The rig of the *Zeven Provincien* was basically the same as that of the *Wasa* but with two significant innovations. Firstly, the lateen mizzen yard only carried canvas on its part abaft the mizzen mast: the original triangular sail had been in effect cut in two and the remaining part assumed the shape of a gaff sail. The lateen yard was kept in men-o'-war until about the middle of the following century as it was considered a useful spare topsail yard for emergencies; it eventually, however, gave way to a standing gaff. On the *Zeven Provincien* the half mizzen was already brailed up to the yard and mast in standing gaff fashion, showing that the old practice of lowering the yard for furling had been abandoned by then. The second significant change was an addition: that of staysails. The stays, however, were still encumbered with brace blocks, bowline fairleads and crow's feet and the jib had to contend with the spritsail topmast. In time all this gear was either to be re-led (braces, bowlines) or dispensed with (crow's feet, spritsail topmast) as they interfered with the new, extremely useful fore-and-aft

The *Zeven Provincien* was launched in 1665, when the Netherlands were the most important sea-trading power in the world. She had a characteristically Dutch stern, fairly beamy and wide at the water-line, with a pronounced tumblehome. Both bows and stern were covered in brightly painted and gilded carvings.

It was under the direction of Richelieu that in 1624 the French recognized the need for power at sea. To meet this need Richelieu turned to the Dutch, the finest and most experienced shipbuilders, ordering from them five large, 60-gun ships. These proved successful and the French were soon building their own fine ships. By the mid-seventeenth century it was the French ship which, when captured, was copied by its captors.

sails. Another, minor change was the suppression of the small round 'top' at the foot of the topgallant mast; it was replaced by spreaders or cross-trees.

The *Zeven Provincien* was a ship-of-the-line. The fleet battle-order in line ahead was a strategy first applied during the First Dutch War and the expression 'ship-of-the-line' appeared at the time to denote the ships powerful enough (two- and three-deckers) to take place in the line of battle where they would be facing enemy ships of the same class. The line of battle presented a formidable wall of batteries and the ships in line would mutually protect their weak and under-gunned bows and sterns. A line would attempt to pierce an enemy line through any gap left open by the disablement of ship; as the ships sailed through the gap they would pour raking broadsides into the enemy ships on either side and the van of the piercing line could double up so as to attack the isolated enemy line from both sides. There was a lot of theory and much jockeying to get the wind gauge and all the ships in their correct stations, but once a battle was started it often wound up in a general melée with ships of the same side often firing at one another through the dense gunsmoke.

A few years before the First Dutch War, during the reign of Charles I, the English had introduced the concept of rates. The ships were divided into six classes, from first rate to sixth rate according to the number of men they carried (and therefore to the rate of pay of their captains). Soon the rating was defined by the number of guns carried, which was usually more or less the same thing. During the Dutch Wars first rate ships (with up to 100 guns) down to fourth rate ships (with as few as 30 guns) formed the line-of-battle. When the Second Dutch War started, the English had three three-deckers, which were first rates, of 100, 80 and 70 guns respectively; the second rates only had two decks and from 66 to 52 guns. The Dutch never had any three-deckers during those wars but their largest two-deckers, such as the *Zeven Provincien*, had a number of guns similar to the English three-deckers or first rates.

One of the reasons the Dutch did not have three deckers was because they needed shallow draught vessels. The Dutch naval vessels, being beamy, provided a more stable gun platform. The extra beam also created a larger stowage space: they could be used as merchant vessels in time of peace. Interestingly, the merchant Dutch East-Indiamen could be used as naval vessels and in fact a large part of the Dutch fleet until the mid-eighteenth century consisted of East-Indiamen. The *Zeven Provincien* differed from these only by her larger size.

The *Zeven Provincien* fought in the Second and Third Dutch Wars (1665–7 and 1672–8). She was severely damaged during the Battle of Barfleur against the French in 1792 and was broken up in 1794. Although they were disparagingly nicknamed 'cheese merchants' the Dutch battleships showed that they could more than hold their own against the larger English and French vessels.

A French Frigate: The Boudeuse

The second half of the eighteenth century was characterized by a revival of the spirit of discovery. For the first time the traditional mercantile and territorial motivations were overshadowed by a genuine scientific interest. The most outstanding voyages of the period were those of the Englishman James Cook (1728–79) and of the French Count Louis Antoine de Bougainville (1729–1811). Bougainville's expedition, with the frigate *Boudeuse* and the store ship *Etoile,* was the first French expedition to sail round the world. Although engaged at first in geographical work, the *Boudeuse* was an ordinary naval frigate and her career is typical of her age for she fought during the Anglo-French wars that followed both American Independence and the French Revolution.

The *Boudeuse* was a twenty-six gun frigate built at the yard of Lamothe, at Indret near Nantes, in southern Brittany. Her keel was laid in 1764 and she was launched in 1766 to be immediately commissioned for Bougainville's voyage. She was 42 m overall and had a beam of 10·9 m. Her draught was 4·8 m aft and 4·45 m forward; her gun deck was a comfortable 2·1 m above the water. The hull below the waterline was sheathed with wood for protection against teredos, 'ship worms' which bore through the hardest of woods. They might burrow into the expendable sheathing but would hopefully be stopped by the tarred and sulphured felt layer placed between the sheathing and the hull. The masts were plumb, with no rake; they and the yards were made from timber imported from Riga, in the Baltic. The ropes were made at Nantes and the sail cloth came from Angers.

Like all frigates, the *Boudeuse* had a single continuous gun deck. She had a discontinuous upper deck level above it, consisting of the quarterdeck (extending from the main mast to the stern) and the forecastle (from the head of the ship to just abaft the fore mast). These two upper decks were separated by the waist where the gun deck was open to the sky. They carried only six 6-pounder guns; more or heavier guns here would have upset the stability of the ship. The gun deck carried twenty 12-pounder guns but the frigate's beam was 65 cm, too narrow for their proper use: she could not fire from both sides at the same time. The galley was located on the gun deck under the forecastle and was fitted with a sea water distilling apparatus. The after end of the gun deck was partitioned off to form the captain's quarters.

The mess deck (at water level and with no gun ports), was situated below the gun deck. It was here that the hammocks were slung at night. Its after end had small cabins for the officers, placed on either side of the wardroom (the officers' mess). There was one more deck below the mess deck, the orlop deck, which contained the cable tyers (anchor cable stowage space), the sail locker, the powder magazines and the sick bay. The hold, with the stores, water casks and ballast, was just beneath the orlop deck.

A report has been preserved which was written on the *Boudeuse* in 1783 by her captain after a year spent in the Mediterranean some thirty years after Bougainville's voyage. He states that the steering was good, that her pitching and rolling motions were easy and that her sail-carrying ability was good. She had a satisfactory balance under sail, could tack and wear easily and she was good when running. However, she was somewhat wet forward, a poor sailer when close hauled and an indifferent performer on a beam reach.

It is interesting to read Bougainville's own opinion when he took her fresh from the stocks. Although one of the few explorers to be given a new ship, he would certainly not have chosen her himself for the Cape Horn waters he was to face. She was hogged, that is, her keel was warped for she had grounded on a sand bar just after her launch, opening some of the seams in her forward topsides. Her masts were too lofty and they were insecurely stayed as the excessive inward slope of her sides (called tumblehome) prevented the shrouds from spreading out at a sufficient angle. As loaded for the voyage, with heavy stores, twenty tonnes of pig iron and twelve of her guns in the hold, she was too stiff and threatened to roll her masts out in a seaway. James Cook had a much more suitable ship in his *Endeavour,* a capacious, seakindly and sturdy former Whitby collier.

The *Boudeuse* left on 15 November 1766; two days out she encountered a severe gale, which proved the worst of her captain's fears. Her new standing rigging, which had not had time to stretch properly, became loose as the ship rolled violently. Her mizzen topmast carried away and the main topmast had to be sacrificed in order to save the main lower mast. She took in tonnes of water through her leaky forward seams. She had to put in to Brest on 21 November for repairs. Her masts were shortened, the top sides were recaulked and her twelve-pounders were exchanged for eight-pounders, saving twenty tonnes weight.

Count Louis Antoine de Bougainville (1729–1811) was the first Frenchman to sail around the world. He commanded ships-of-the-line during the American War of Independence, but retired from the navy after the outbreak of the French Revolution.

The *Boudeuse* made her second departure on 4 December 1766 with eleven officers, three volunteers and 203 men. Her normal complement for an ordinary commission would have been 360 officers and men. When Bougainville eventually arrived in Tahiti, he was only the second European to land there, just a few months after Samuel Wallis in HMS *Dolphin.* They were soon followed by Cook and Bligh and these first calls at Tahiti started a legend, the romance of which is still so much alive today.

The *Boudeuse* returned to St Malo on 16 March 1769, having lost only ten men during the journey—a vast improvement on Magellan's voyage when 270 men sailed and only eighteen returned.

After her return, the *Boudeuse* was put 'in ordinary' (we would say 'mothballed' today). Because of the American Revolutionary war and the ensuing Anglo-French war, she was refitted in 1776. In 1778 she was part of Count d'Orvillier's squadron of thirty ships-of-the-line and sixteen frigates which engaged a squadron of equal strength commanded by Admiral Keppel off Ushant. This fleet action was a draw. The following year the *Boudeuse* helped to take the West Indian island of St Barthélemy, and she captured the sixteen-gun sloop *Weasel* off St Eustatius. Back in France, she left Toulon in 1782 to escort a merchant convoy bound for America, returning the same year with another; the following year she escorted an eight-ship convoy to the Levant. During the short peace that followed she remained in commission as part of

The *Boudeuse* which, with the store ship *Etoile*, made the first French scientific expedition round the world was in fact an ordinary naval frigate and later saw action against the Americans and the British. In 1768 her captain, Bougainville, became the second European to land on the island of Tahiti.

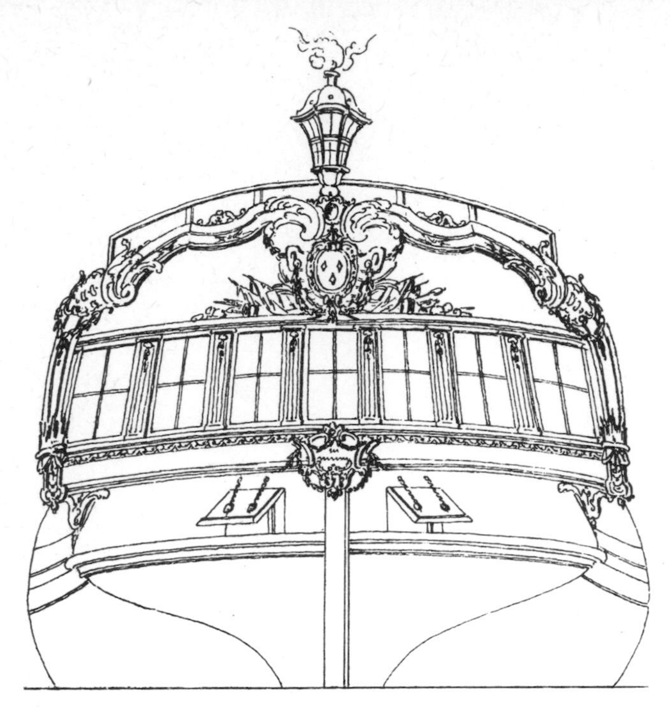

A contemporary sketch of the stern of the *Boudeuse* shows far fewer carvings than had been usual in the early part of the eighteenth century. The *Boudeuse* was launched in 1766.

Right: Bougainville visited several Polynesian Islands, though it was not always possible to land among the coral reefs. Here at Akiaki in the Tuamotu archipelago (which he called the Île des Lanciers) he thought at first that the light-skinned inhabitants were shipwrecked Europeans, and put ashore to rescue them.

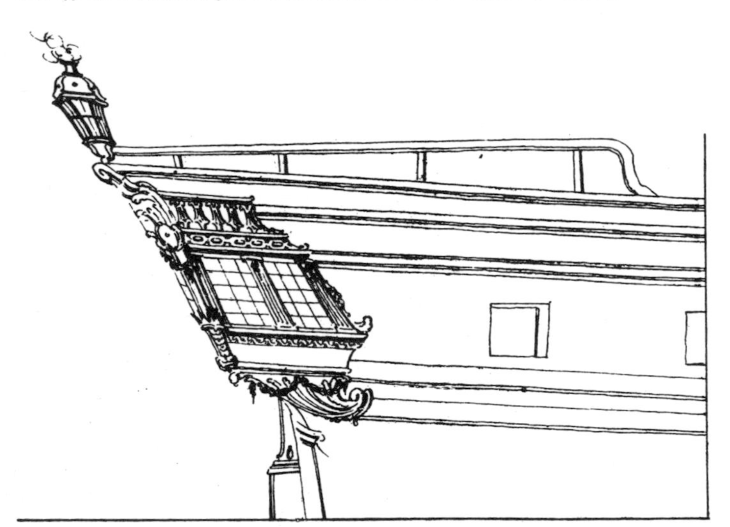

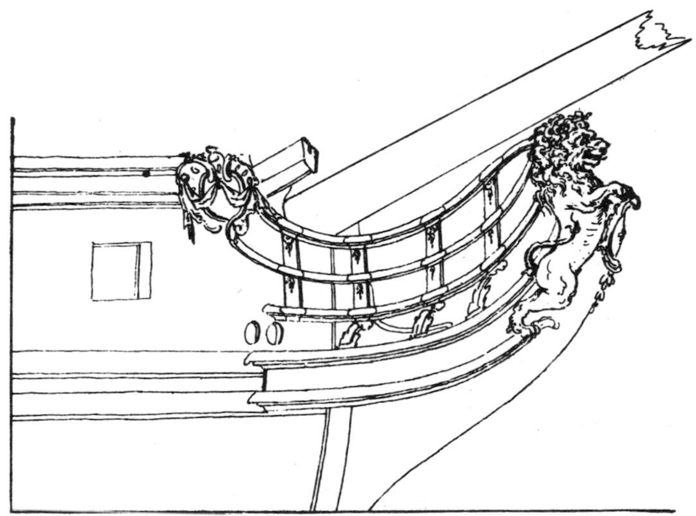

Seen from the side, the stern (left) and bows also show less decoration than was usual on those areas at the time she was built. Her structure as a whole, however, was typical of French frigates of the second half of the eighteenth century.

the Mediterranean Command.

The French Revolution brought peace to an end and the *Boudeuse* narrowly escaped being burned by the retreating British at Toulon in 1793. Now armed with thirty-two guns, she made two prizes which she took into Toulon during messidor, Year II (19 June–18 July 1794). The first, the *Alceste,* was a French-built frigate which had been captured by the English and then given to Sardinia. She struck her colours after a two-hour fight. The second was a Danish brig bound for Leghorn in Italy. The following month the *Boudeuse* sunk a Spanish brig and on 26 thermidor (14 August) she captured an English brig, the *Peggy*. Against the will of the *Boudeuse*'s captain and through the insistence of revolutionary elements amongst her crew, the prisoners from the *Peggy* were executed.

The *Boudeuse* took part in 1795 in the siege of Rosas in Spain, and in 1798 she acted as a troopship and as a convoy escort to Corsica. Finally, with a ballast cargo of cannon balls, she ran the British blockade of French-occupied Malta where she arrived on 16 pluviôse, Year VII (5 February 1799). Having reached the end of her useful life, she was broken up for firewood in Valetta, Malta in 1800.

Venetian Galleys: The Bucentaur

Every year, for more than six centuries, a special ceremony was held in Venice aboard the Doge's unique, almost fabulous State barge, the *Bucentaur*. The ceremony, called the *Sposalizio*, symbolized Venice's maritime supremacy in the mediaeval world.

When northern Italy was overrun in the sixth century A.D. by Barbarians, the Lombard refugees settled on a marshy island in a lagoon on the north shore of the Adriatic Sea. Here they founded Venice. By the end of the tenth century this small town had become a local maritime trading power and a small republic headed by an elected Duke, the Doge.

Venice was ideally located for trade for she was at the crossroads of the Byzantine, Germanic, Slav and Muslim worlds. During the eleventh and twelfth centuries the town's wealth expanded with an active trade in Slav slaves, Dalmatian timber and pitch, Alpine iron and woollen cloth, all of which were sent to the East. Her ships returned with cargoes of silks from Byzantium and spices from Alexandria, for re-export throughout the West. It was during this period that the basilica of San Marco was built, and that the great international market was opened beside the Grand Canal.

In 1177 Venice helped Pope Alexander II to obtain an advantageous settlement of his dispute with the Holy Roman Emperor Frederick Barbarossa. Thanking the Doge, the Pope remarked: 'May the sea be submitted to you as the wife is to her husband.' It was these words that the ceremony of the *Sposalizio* (marriage—of Venice and the Sea) commemorated. An earlier celebration, known as 'the Blessing of the Sea' was merged with the new one and the first *Bucentaur* was built for the occasion.

The best years of the Venetian republic were between 1204 and 1453, beginning with the success of the fourth crusade which enabled Venetians to establish new *fondouks* (trading posts) in the Middle East and along the shores of the Black Sea. Merchant galleys carried precious or perishable cargoes; sailing ships carried the heavier trade. The only serious rival to Venice was Genoa but even this town was far behind.

From the beginning of the fourteenth century regular yearly convoys of galleys sailed from Venice around Gibraltar to

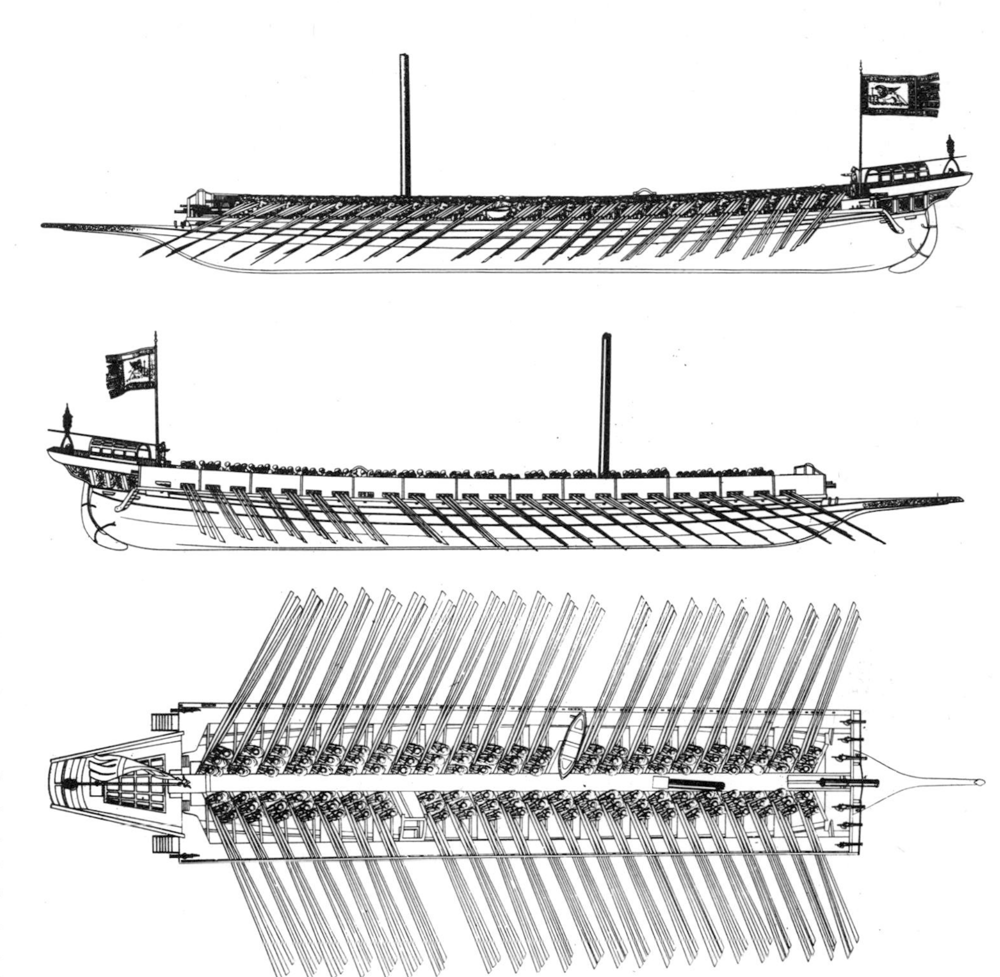

The Venetian galley in the sixteenth century had an overall length of between 30 and 40m and was propelled by oars, each oar handled by three men. The mast carried a lateen sail suspended from a yardarm. War galleys were equipped with 2 or 3 guns mounted in the bows. The stern carried a superstructure, providing quarters for the captain. The sharp protruding ram and shallow hull are characteristic features of the galley.

Below:

The first *Bucentaur* was built in the twelfth century, to be followed by a succession of similar ships. This is the 1605 *Bucentaur*.

Southampton, London and Bruges. It was the meeting of these long, slim Mediterranean galleys with their oars and lateen sails and the broad, buoyant and square-rigged carracks of the Atlantic which resulted in a new type of ship incorporating the best features of both: the galleon.

The end of Venetian supremancy is linked with the fall of Constantinople to the Turks in 1453. The muslims now held the upper hand in the eastern Mediterranean and when they were not actively at war with Venice they charged what they wanted for silks and spices and trade declined. A further blow to Venice was the discovery, in 1497, of a direct route to the spice-producing East by the Portuguese Vasco da Gama. This bypassed not only the Arab middlemen but the Venetians as well. Venice did not fall into immediate decline: many of her most beautiful houses and monuments, such as the Doges' Palace and the Piazza San Marco were built at that time. By the beginning of the eighteenth century, however, the inevitable decline had become apparent although each year the *Bucentaur* was still rowed out to the harbour entrance to renew the supremacy of Venice over the sea. When the last *Bucentaur* was built in 1727 the dominance of the sea trade by Venice was a thing of the past and the city, living on her former reputation for wealth had become a carnival town addicted to luxury and pleasure.

There are several proposed derivations for the name *Bucentaur*. One proposes that the first *Bucintro* had an ox with a human head (which could be called a 'bucentaur') as figurehead; a second proposal was that the first barge was built to carry two-hundred people and that the latin word for two-hundred (*ducentorum*) had become corrupted to *Bucintoro*. A third proposal derives the word from *buzo d'oro*, 'golden ship'.

There was, of course, a succession of *Bucentaurs*. A Spaniard, Pero Tafur,

visiting Venice in 1438 described the *Bucentaur* of his day as being draped with rich cloth of gold. The richness and luxury of the 1520 *Bucentaur* was widely publicized and the 1605 *Bucentaur* was the subject of a eulogy by a Venetian poet and of much admiration by foreigners. An Englishman, Peter Mundy, saw her in 1620 and described her as 'a vessel like a gallye but shorter, thicker and higher, whereon is shewed the uttermost of Art for carved works being overlayed with gold soe that when she is in the water she appears all of pure gold'. Twenty-five years later the same vessel was seen by another Englishman, John Evelyn, who wrote about the 'gloriously painted, carved and gilded *Bucentora*'. The next *Bucentaur* was not built until 1727.

The Bucentaurs were made to last, with good reason, for they must have been fantastically expensive to build. Their durability was also helped by the fact that they were purely ceremonial, being used mainly for the *Sposalizio*, and occasionally for entertaining important foreign viitors.

The 1727 *Bucentaur*, which was launched in 1728, was to be the last. She was about forty-two metres long, built in an archaic style which preserved much of the earlier tradition of her predecessors. Except for her shallow draught, gorgeous awning and decorations, she was very like the Mediterranean galleasses of the seventeenth and eighteenth centuries. She had two decks, the lower one for the oarsmen, and the upper for the dignitaries.

The *Sposalizio* was always a ceremony of great importance. Each Ascension day the *Bucentaur* was brought round from the Arsenal (the dockyard) in the morning, with the flag of St Mark flying on her single mast. The Doge and the Signory in their robes of office, the ambassadors from abroad and other important visitors boarded the *Bucentaur* at the Piazzetta and the barge, propelled by forty-two oars with four men at each loom, began her short journey amongst a crowd of gondolas and other vessels. The procession passed the Riva degli Schiavoni and landed at the island of Santa Elena where the Patriarch and clergy of the San Pietro cathedral came aboard. A gold ring was duly blessed by the Patriarch and the *Bucentaur* was rowed through the Lido pass. When she had travelled a short distance in the Adriatic Sea, the Doge dropped the ring in the sea, from a window by his throne in the stern, saying: *'Desponsamus te, Mare, in signum veri perpetuique dominii'* (Sea, we marry thee, in gesture of real and everlasting sovereignty). Mass followed in the church of San Nicolo in the Lido and the *Bucentaur* returned to the Palace where a large reception was organized.

The end of the *Bucentaurs* and of the *Sposalizio* ceremony came when Napoleon Bonaparte arrived in Venice in 1797. The city surrendered without a

Venetian galleys dominated trade in the Mediterranean for around 150 years, from the beginning of the fourteenth century. The *Bucentaur*, a richly decorated ceremonial two-decked galley, was used only on state occasions.

Of all the sea fights fought between galleys the greatest and most decisive took place in the Gulf of Lepanto on 7 October 1571. The Christian Fleet of some 202 galleys and 63 other vessels, under the command of Don Juan of Austria, completely overwhelmed the Turkish naval force of 208 galleys and 60 ships of other types, under the command of Captain Ali Pasha.

As late as the end of the seventeenth century, French sailing galleys remained an important type of vessel in the navy of Louis XIV. Such galleys usually had two or three masts, each with a large lateen sail. The sail was suspended from a dual sectioned yardarm. French sailing galleys were amongst the last vessels to use oars as a prime means of propulsion.

fight and in the following January the last *Bucentaur* was vandalized by French troopers with axes and crowbars. All the gilded upper works and sculptures of the Muses and Virtues were hacked to pieces and the parts were taken to the San Giorgio monastery where they were heaped on a bonfire that burned for three days. The gold was sifted out from the ashes and put in Bonaparte's war chest. The Revolutionary troops had acted like Barbarians but the Venetian society, in an advanced state of decadence, showed no signs of caring. In fact the citizens kept their carnivals and carousals going with such gusto that the occupation police had to issue a decree announcing, in the interest of public order, that citizens found disguised or wearing masks in public places would be arrested!

The hulk of the *Bucentaur* was subsequently renamed *Hydra* and converted into a floating gun battery flying the flag of Austria (which had inherited Venice). It was moored in the Lido pass until 1824. All that now remains of the *Bucentaur* are a few fragments in the Museo Correr at Venice and a piece of the fluted flagpole in the Museo Storico Navale of the Arsenal. Two models, one built at the same time as the last *Bucentaur* was being built, the other after she had been destroyed by the French, bear witness to her exquisite appearance.

A First Rate Ship-of-the-Line: The Victory

As the last gunfire rumbled across the sea and was succeeded by an eery silence, the gunsmoke slowly drifted away from the scene, revealing shattered and blood-stained ships. One, with more than half her masts and rigging shot away, was sailing into history and legend. She was HMS *Victory*. Her admiral, Lord Nelson, was dying but he had just won the most famous of all sea battles: Trafalgar.

The *Victory* was already an old and glorious ship when she fought at Trafalgar. Her building was started in 1759 when Horatio Nelson was only ten months old and she was launched in 1765. At that time England was at peace and the government, to reduce costs, just laid her up in reserve on the River Medway, not very far from the Chatham dockyard where she had been built. The War of American Independence started ten years later. France was unofficially helping the American rebels and open war with England erupted in 1778. The *Victory* was hastily commissioned as the flagship of Admiral Keppel, for the Channel Fleet and she participated in an indecisive action off Ushant the same year. She was then in turn the flagship of Admirals Hardy, Geary, Hyde Parker and Kempenfelt before flying the flag of Admiral Lord Howe. When Spain joined with France against England, the *Victory* was sent on convoy duty to relieve blockaded Gibraltar. There, still under Admiral Lord Howe, she fought at the battle of Cape Spartel. After the peace in 1783 she returned to Portsmouth where she was placed in ordinary.

The peace was short lived. In 1793 England joined the First Coalition against Revolutionary France and the *Victory* was commissioned as the flagship of Admiral Hood, in command of the Mediterranean Fleet: twenty-one ships of the line and fifteen frigates. This fleet and a small expeditionary force held Toulon with the help of French Royalists but it had to evacuate the town and harbour under pressure from the Republican army. One of the Republican officers, a young artillery *capitaine*, distinguished himself on that occasion, earning his first claim to celebrity. It was not his last: *capitaine* Napoleon Bonaparte still had some promotion ahead of him . . .

So did captain Horatio Nelson, who was placed in command, the following year, of a group of men and guns landed from the *Victory* for the successful siege of Calvi in Corsica.

After a brief refit in Portsmouth the *Victory* returned to the Mediterranean under the flag of Admiral Man and in 1795 she took part in the indecisive action off Hyeres, near Toulon, which encouraged Spain to side with France.

Vice-Admiral, Lord Viscount Nelson, Knight of the Bath, K.B., Duke of Bronte (1758–1805), was the most glorious of England's Admirals. He died within hours of the defeat of the combined French and Spanish fleet off Cape Trafalgar in 1805.

The *Victory* returned to Chatham in late 1797 and was paid off and converted to a hospital ship for French prisoners until 1801 when she was docked for an extensive refit which was completed in 1803. Amongst other changes her old-fashioned open air galleries on the stern (used as private

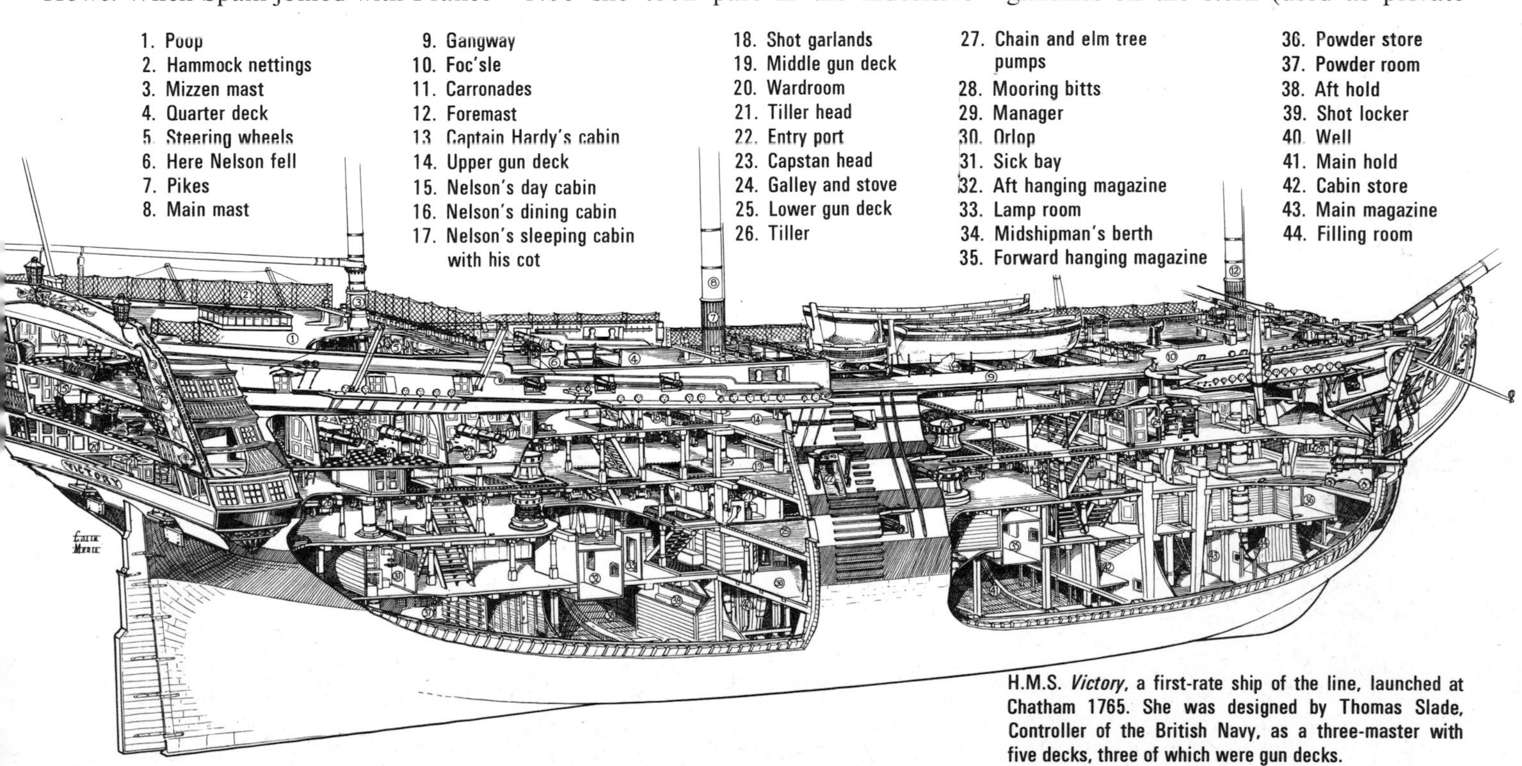

H.M.S. *Victory*, a first-rate ship of the line, launched at Chatham 1765. She was designed by Thomas Slade, Controller of the British Navy, as a three-master with five decks, three of which were gun decks.

walks by the admiral and captain) were replaced by the flat stern that can be seen today; her chains (where the shrouds are fixed to the hull) were moved from below to above the upper gun deck ports and her lower deck was fitted with 32-pounder guns instead of the original heavier but slower-firing 48-pounders. There was no official colour scheme for painting men-of-war and Nelson had her painted to his own style, with black and ochre stripes. The gun port lids, at the level of the ochre stripes, were picked out in black and the style became known as 'Nelson's checkers'. The *Victory* is now preserved as she looked after that refit and as she appeared at Trafalgar.

The *Victory*, despite her age, was still one of the largest ships in the Royal Navy—a first rate ship-of-the-line armed with 104 guns. Her hull is 82 m long and her overall length is 120 m. She is 19 m wide and she has a draught of nearly 7 m. Such ships were never numerous: they were very expensive to build. The oak sides of the *Victory* are up to 72 cm thick and it took about 2,500 oak trees to build her—a small forest. First Rates were also expensive to operate: the *Victory* had a crew of 850 seamen, officers and marines.

The poop deck, the highest deck and behind the mizzen mast, is armed with two 12-pounder guns and with two big stubby guns called carronades. These can only be used at short range but they fire 68-pound balls or 'grape' (shrapnel) and are aptly known as 'smashers'. The captain's quarters are situated just below this deck. Painted white and pale green they are luxurious but still business-like, with guns lashed behind the windows.

Walking down from the poop a visitor will reach the quarter deck, in front of the captain's quarters and extending to the main mast. The double steering wheel (which allows four men to combine their strength to steer the ship) and its steering compasses (in a binnacle holding two compasses either side of a lamp compartment to light them at night) is on this deck, just forward of the mizzen mast. Three 12-pounders are carried on each side of this deck. The quarter deck was the traditional area

H.M.S. *Victory*, a first rate ship-of-the-line, is one of the most famous ships of all time. She was Admiral Lord Nelson's flagship at Trafalgar and, now preserved in dry-dock at Portsmouth (left), still flies an Admiral's flag. She is the oldest commissioned ship in the Royal Navy.

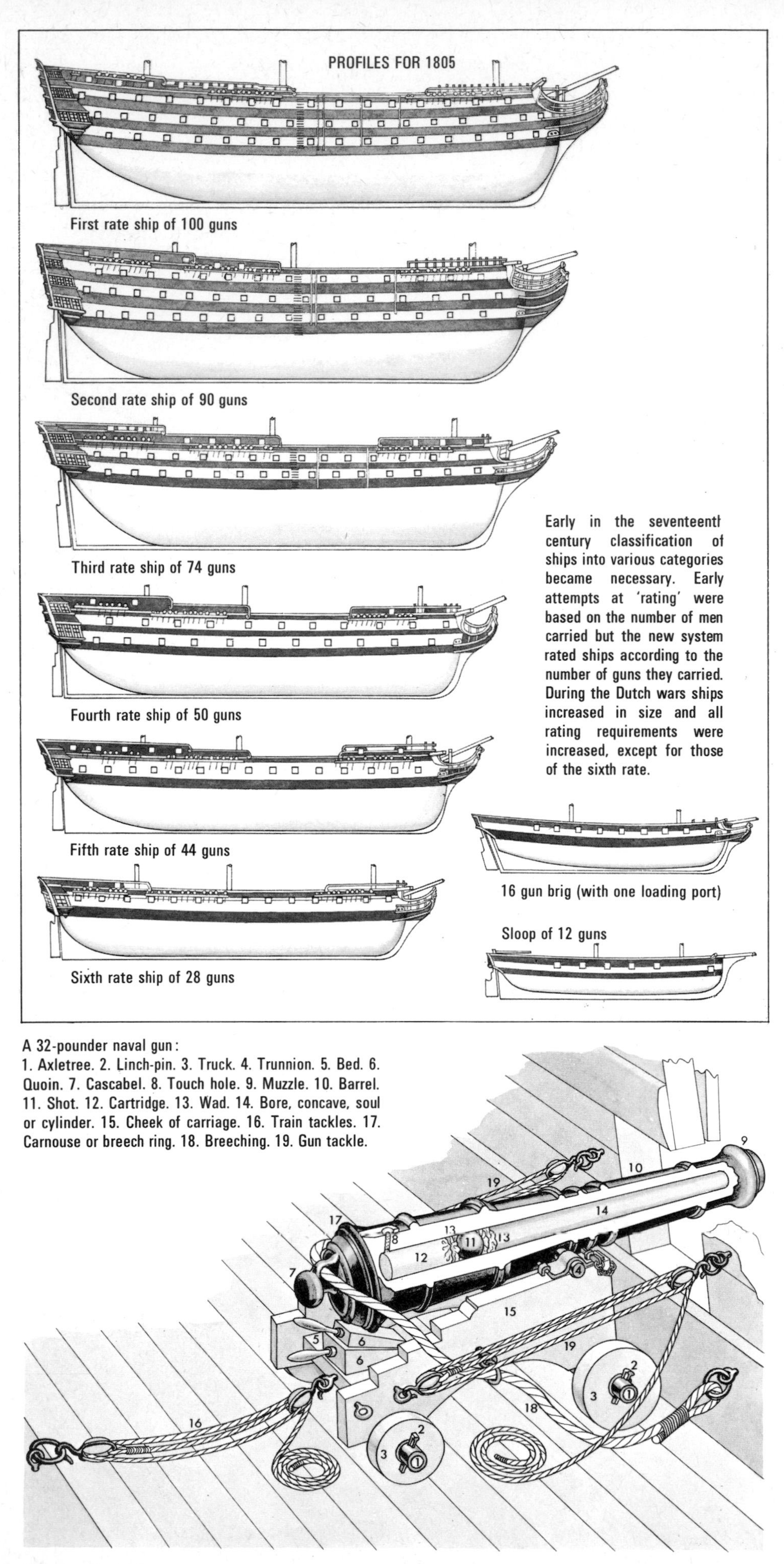

First rate ship of 100 guns

Second rate ship of 90 guns

Third rate ship of 74 guns

Fourth rate ship of 50 guns

Fifth rate ship of 44 guns

Sixth rate ship of 28 guns

16 gun brig (with one loading port)

Sloop of 12 guns

Early in the seventeentl century classification of ships into various categories became necessary. Early attempts at 'rating' were based on the number of men carried but the new system rated ships according to the number of guns they carried. During the Dutch wars ships increased in size and all rating requirements were increased, except for those of the sixth rate.

A 32-pounder naval gun:
1. Axletree. 2. Linch-pin. 3. Truck. 4. Trunnion. 5. Bed. 6. Quoin. 7. Cascabel. 8. Touch hole. 9. Muzzle. 10. Barrel. 11. Shot. 12. Cartridge. 13. Wad. 14. Bore, concave, soul or cylinder. 15. Cheek of carriage. 16. Train tackles. 17. Carnouse or breech ring. 18. Breeching. 19. Gun tackle.

reserved for the officers, and is where Nelson fell mortally wounded by a musket ball fired from the *Redoutable*.

Forward of the quarter deck there is a drop to the upper gun deck below, but two gangways running along the sides of the ship allow a level access to the forecastle which is the *Victory's* upper forward deck and the domain of all the non-commissioned crew. It extends from about half way between the main and fore masts to the head; it is armed with two carronades and it carries the ship's bell in a belfry. The space between the foc'sle and the quarter deck and the gangways is spanned by beams which support the ship's boats and spare spars.

The upper gun deck, beneath the quarter deck and foc'sle level is known as 'upper' because, although guns are carried on higher decks, it is the highest continuous deck to run the length of the ship. On the *Victory* this deck has fifteen 12-pounder guns on each side. The after part of the deck is cut off by a bulkhead (which could be removed when the ship was cleared for action) to form the admiral's quarters, consisting of a dining and day cabin and a sleeping cabin.

The middle gun deck, one deck below, has fifteen 24-pounders on each side. The galley—a big iron stove for boiling the salt meat and dried peas—is on this deck, abaft the fore mast. The area forward of the galley is the sick bay—uncomfortable in a seaway but benefiting at least from the warmth of the galley: there was no other heating in the ship. The upper crown of the fore capstan is on this deck, between the fore and main masts. This capstan extends down to the lower gun deck so that two levels of capstan bars can be fitted, allowing more men to 'heave and pawl'. The main capstan, between the main and mizzen masts, was also two-tiered: 140 men could push on the middle deck bars and a further 120 on the lower deck bars. The after part of the middle deck is partitioned off by removable bulkheads to form the ward-room (the lieutenants' mess), with the lieutenants' cabins opening off it.

The lower deck carries the heaviest battery—thirty 32-pounders. The forward part of the deck has a low timber wall to catch most of the water and mud dripping off the anchor cables as they are brought inboard through the

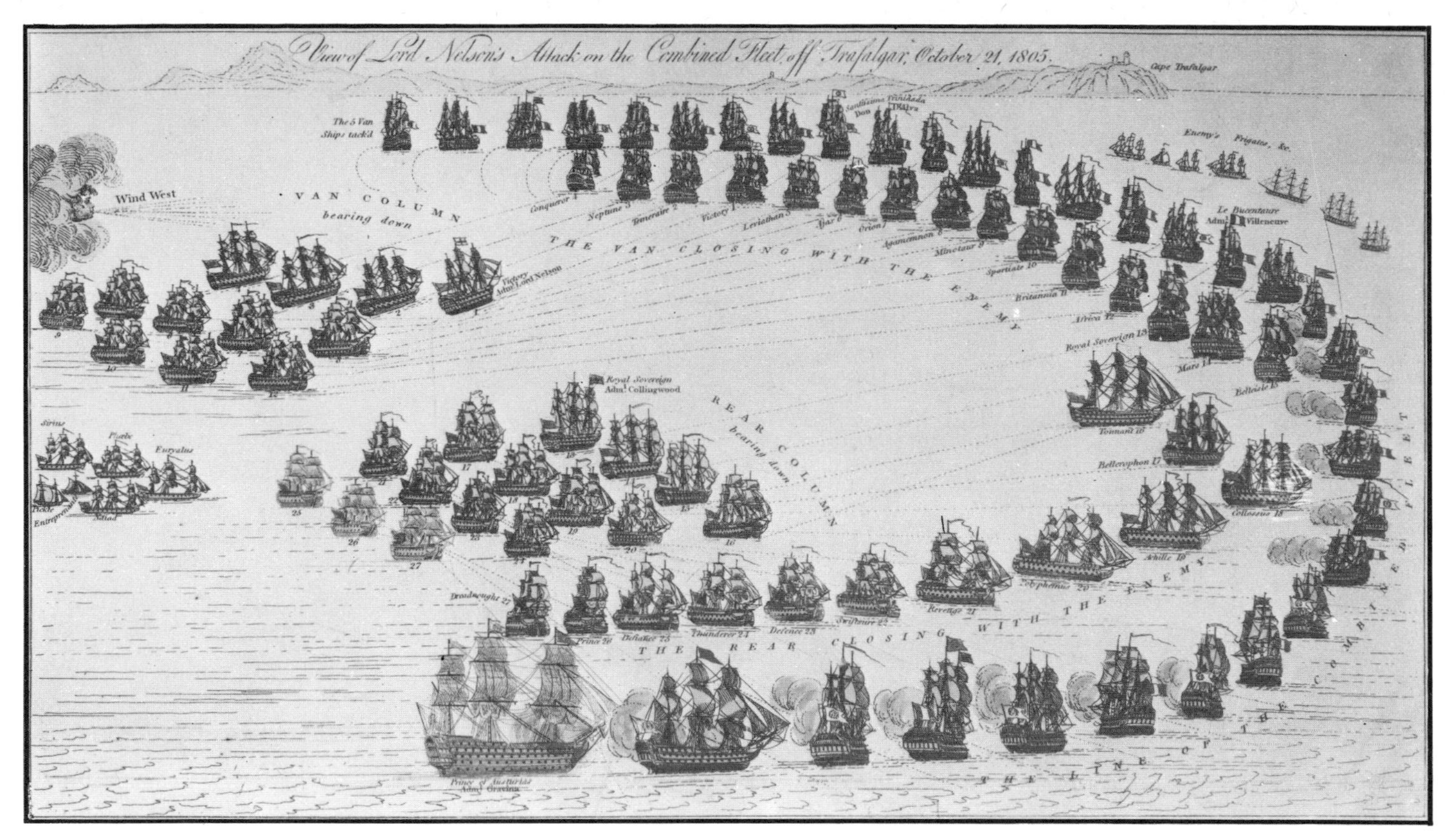

The line of battle for Nelson's attack on the combined fleet off Trafalgar, forming a 'crescent convexing to leeward'. It was Nelson's intention to divide the fleet into three sections of three lines. One division of twelve or fourteen of the fastest two-deck ships was to be kept to windward, or in a position of advantage, and the remainder of the fleet was to be in two lines for immediate attack. In this engagement both Nelson and Collingwood led their respective divisions into action.

hawse pipes. This area was called the manger because the livestock—pigs and goats—were kept there at night; during the day the animals were usually allowed to roam around. The after part of the lower deck, known as the gunroom, was where the young midshipmen messed and slung their hammocks, under the supervision of the gunner (whose other and main duty was to keep the guns in good order). Most of the sailors slung their hammocks in the lower and middle gun decks.

The orlop deck is the next deck below and is below the waterline. It has very little headroom. The bread room where the ship's biscuit is kept, the surgeon's cabin, officers' stores, the two magazines, the after and fore cockpits, the cable tyers, the gunner's stores and the sailmaker's stores are found on this deck. The magazines are rooms where the cartridges are kept ready for the guns. The after cockpit serves as accommodation for the senior midshipmen and during action it was converted into an operating theatre, by dragging the midshipmen's sea chests to the centre to be used as operating tables. The orlop deck is painted red so that the blood and gore would not be so conspicuous. It was in this dark, lantern-lit and blood-stained place that Nelson died. The cable tyer is a big cage-like structure where the anchor cables are coiled and kept.

The hold, below the orlop, is where the food, stores, water, spare shot and powder in kegs are stowed. The holders, men appointed to that part of the ship, very seldom came on deck and hardly ever met their opposites, the topmen, who spent most of their time aloft in the rigging.

The rigging and masts are basically similar to those on the *Boudeuse*. The plain sails consisted of the mizzen (later known as the driver or spanker; these two words had a slightly different meaning in 1800), square sails up to the topgallants, jibs and staysails. In light winds royal yards and sails would be hoisted above the topgallants and studding sails were set to extend the square sails laterally. The tops, as on all men-of-war, were large compared to those on merchantmen, as they were also used as fighting platforms during action, with swivel guns loaded with grape and with marines armed with muskets.

This was how the *Victory* appeared when she was taken over by Nelson in 1803 to command the fleet blockading Villeneuve's fleet in Toulon. After eighteen months, Villeneuve managed to slip through the net but he was hotly pursued by Nelson to the West Indies and back. His fleet was driven to hole itself in at Cadiz and the *Victory* returned to Portsmouth. She left again to join the rest of the British fleet blockading Cadiz on 15 September 1805. Napoleon ordered Villeneuve to get out and, if need be, fight, and the Franco-Spanish fleet met the British off Cape Trafalgar on 21 October 1805.

The *Victory*, leading her column across the Franco-Spanish line, suffered damage so severe that she had to be towed into Gibraltar. After jury repairs she sailed to Portsmouth and Sheerness with Nelson's body in a cask of brandy.

She was refitted at Chatham and recommissioned in 1808 and sent under Admiral de Saumarez to the Baltic and also into Spanish waters. In 1812 she returned to Portsmouth, never to sail again. It was then forty-seven years since her launching and she was put in ordinary once more.

In 1824 she was recommissioned as the stationary flagship for the Portsmouth Command, a role she has been filling to the present day except for the period 1869–89. In 1922 she was put in the drydock where she is today and where she can be visited by the public although she still flies a commissioning pendant and an admiral's flag.

America's First Frigates: USS Constitution

When the American War of Independence was concluded by the Treaty of Versailles in 1783, the new Republic of the United States of America was determined to be a pacific nation. She would have no standing army or navy and would live on her own resources and by peaceful trade overseas. America, however, soon found that it did not pay to be weak. During the first thirty-two years of independence she found her seamen enslaved or ransomed by North African pirates, impressed by the Royal Navy and her ships even seized by her former ally, France. As an American minister said, 'If we mean to have a commerce we must have a naval force to defend it.' So it happened that the United States built a small fleet of powerful frigates, the best known of which is the *Constitution*.

The main threat to the young American navy came from pirates. Her ships were captured by the dozen by Moroccan, Algerian and Tripolitan pirates (the Barbary Corsairs) and their crews were held in slavery and under ransom. At first America was willing to pay up, but giving in to blackmail only caused an escalation of the outrages and demands. The pirates (who only existed because various European powers found it convenient to let them be a nuisance to rival trading nations) finally began to ask for ransom not only in money but also in modern arms and frigates. At last the cry came: 'Millions for defense, not a cent for tribute'.

Congress passed a Bill in 1794 creating the Federal Navy of the United States and authorizing the building of six frigates, though work was to be halted if Algiers (the chief nuisance at the time) became peacefully inclined. The Dey of Algiers, sensing retaliation, did seek peace and only the first three frigates were completed: the *Constellation,* rated at 36 guns, and the *United States* and *Constitution,* both rated at 44 guns. Of these first, historic vessels of the United States Navy, two are still afloat today: the *Constellation* at

The U.S.S. *Constitution* was one of the first three ships built for the newly formed Federal Navy of the United States and was launched in 1797. Larger than other ships of her rate, she carried forty-four powerful guns.

Baltimore and the *Constitution* at Boston. The other three frigates were completed a few years later when the French Revolutionary wars in Europe brought privateers and pirates of all nationalities back to the high seas. These frigates were the *President,* 44, the *Congress* and the *Chesapeake,* 36.

Provisional frigate plans had been drawn before the 1794 Bill and these were finalized when the authorization to build was secured. Many people were consulted and many opinions were incorporated into the plans but the chief architects were Joshua Humphreys and Josiah Fox. Humphreys, a Quaker, was a shipbuilder of Philadelphia and he was well placed as that town was then the capital of the United States. Fox, also a Quaker, from Falmouth in Cornwall, had arrived in the States in 1793, initially for a short stay to visit some relatives. He had been apprenticed to the Master Shipwright at Plymouth Dockyard in England and he had visited many of the European shipyards. With the lack of Americans experienced in naval architecture and shipbuilding and with his superior instruction and qualifications, Fox was readily engaged as clerk in the War Office and as Humphreys' assistant, but his functions—and pay—were far more important than the meaning usually associated with the word 'clerk'.

Since the frigates were to be few in numbers, they had to be as powerful as possible and their upper limit was set at the forty-four gun rating to match the strongest Barbary corsair. They were made very large for their rates. The *Constitution* and the other forty-fours were seven metres longer and a metre wider than the improved British forty-fours and four metres longer and thirty centimetres wider than the French forty-fours (the French ships had fewer guns per unit length of ship than the British who tended to overload their ships). The advantages of greater ship size for the same number of guns are that the gun crews have more room to work in and that the gun deck port sills are higher above the water, allowing the guns to be used in seas that would oblige the smaller frigate to keep her gun ports closed.

One of the major innovations, which greatly increased the fire power of the American frigates, was the flush spardeck which almost made them into miniature two-decked ships-of-the-line. In traditional frigates such as the *Boudeuse* the quarter deck and the foc'sle were separated by the waist where the gun deck below was opened to the sky. From about 1780, gangways (plank walks along the sides of the ship) came into use in frigates, allowing direct access from the quarter deck to the foc'sle, as on HMS *Victory*. On the new American frigates the quarter deck and foc'sle were lengthened and the gangways were enlarged so that a continuous upper deck was formed with only a long narrow well in the centre, used as a hatchway. The spare spars and boats were still carried there, as they could not be stowed elsewhere, and they gave the name 'spardeck' to the new design. The quarter deck and foc'sle had gun ports and bulwarks instead of the usual open rails and the spardeck at the waist had hammock nettings in which rolled hammocks were stowed to provide protection against small arms fire. Spardecks are not the exact equivalent of upper decks on two-decked ships-of-the-line: to put guns along their whole length would overload the frigates, strain their timbers and upset their stability. The waist did not carry guns but the foc'sle and quarter decks were heavily armed.

The *Constitution* is pierced for sixty guns but she could not fill all her gun ports without serious overloading and this was never attempted. The original establishment for the American forty-fours proposed an armament entirely consisting of long guns but by the time of commissioning it was decided to use both long guns and carronades. Carronades were a relatively new type of gun that had been first manufactured at Carron in Scotland in 1779. Short and stubby, they weighed much less than the long or short guns of the same bore and they were thus suited for upper deck batteries. They were easy and fast to load and train and what they lost in range they made up with the weight of metal they fired.

The *Constitution* had a gun deck battery of thirty 24-pounder long guns and she carried sixteen 32-pounder carronades on her quarter deck and six 32-pounder carronades, two 24-pounder long guns and one 16-pounder long gun on her foc'sle. The foc'sle long guns were trained forward to fire at ships being pursued and they were known as bow chasers.

American gunnery was superior to the British. The shots used were slightly larger and heavier, reducing the windage (the difference in diameter between the shot and the gun's bore) and increasing accuracy, and the Americans also used the more accurate long guns instead of the short ones favoured by the English. The advantage of the latter was a faster rate of fire since they were less heavy and easier to handle. The American combination of long guns and a large battery of carronades was to prove a formidable one, allowing effective long range 'softening up' of the target while enabling the ship to remain fairly immune to the return fire before moving in at close range to put the heavy carronades into action.

The *Constitution* is 111 metres overall (only 8 metres shorter than the *Victory*), her hull measures 74 metres; she is 16 metres in the beam and she has a draught of 7 metres. Her displacement is 2,235 tonnes. She was capable of doing 13½ knots. She carried standing royals on all three masts. She originally had a figurehead representing Hercules carrying a raised club.

She was launched on 17 October 1797, after two unsuccessful attempts, the slipway not being steep enough. With the Algerians being 'friendly' (and kept so by offerings of naval stores, including a 32-gun frigate, a brig and two schooners), it would have been thought that the *Constitution* and the other two new frigates would have been put in ordinary but the French Revolutionists were behaving themselves at sea little better than pirates. They were seizing American merchantmen and condemning both the ships and cargoes as 'lawful' prizes often on the flimsy pretext that the cargoes were destined for France's enemies. By 1798 the situation had reached a state of undeclared war, with French privateers operating off the American east coast, from bases in the Caribbean. Not only were the completed frigates commissioned, but the unfinished ones were completed and appropriations were made for new naval units. While the *Constellation* covered herself with glory by capturing the French 36-gun frigate *Insurgente,* off St Kitts, the *Constitution* took only French merchant vessels.

The Bashaw (Pasha) of Tripoli, somewhat envious of the favours given to the Dey, also tried to put pressure on America but in 1802 the Congress authorized President Thomas Jefferson to take whatever steps were necessary to stop the nuisance and the following year an American squadron, led by the *Constitution* commanded by Commodore Preble, sailed for the Mediterranean. This squadron first threatened Tangier, whose Sultan had been authorizing acts of piracy against American ships and then blockaded Tripoli. In 1806 the *Constitution* participated in the bombardment of Tripoli and this pirates' lair was eventually seized by a landed force.

Britain, fighting to the finish against Napoleon, had severe manning problems in her navy and British officers had acquired the habit of stopping American ships on the high seas to search them for British seamen. If found, they were immediately impressed. When the officers were particularly desperate, they did not hesitate to impress as well a few American able seamen. These high-handed actions aroused anti-British feelings in America which crystallized around the slogan 'Free trade and sailors' rights', and war was declared by President James Madison in 1812. The Royal Navy immediately blockaded the East Coast while the *Constitution* in Chesapeake Bay was hastily recruiting a crew. Shortly after putting to sea she fell in with a British squadron and it was a day of slow but hot pursuit as the wind died and all the ships put their boats out to be towed. Captain Isaac Hull of the *Constitution* hauled himself away by kedging—having an anchor dropped ahead of the ship by a boat and hauling in the cable with the capstan while another anchor and cable were rowed out further ahead. To lighten the displacement of the frigate he had to jettison a week's supply of fresh water so he had to put into Boston and slip out again, running a renewed risk of interception. The *Constitution* then went on a cruise off the St Lawrence Gulf where she captured several merchant vessels bound to or from Canada.

On her way home the *Constitution* met HMS *Guerrière* (44 guns), commanded by Captain Dacres. Although rated at the same number of guns, the *Guerrière* only fired a 556-pound broadside to the *Constitution*'s 684 and her scantlings (the thicknesses of her timbers and planks) were also lighter. The disparity however was not all that great and the English—and indeed Captain Dacres himself—were accustomed to win against much greater odds. The usual enemy, however, had been the French—brave but poorly trained and demoralized by years of defeat at sea. The Americans were different and the English had grown complacent. The superior gunnery of the *Constitution*—with well-handled and accurate long guns—shot away the mizzen mast of the *Guerrière* before she could score any significant hits. The mast dragging in the sea slewed her around and made her lose her steerage and the *Constitution* manoeuvered to deliver a couple of raking broadsides which brought down the remaining masts. For a short

The U.S.S. *Constitution* first saw action in 1812 when she ran the blockade of the American East Coast by British ships. During the three day chase all the ships had to put out their boats to be towed, for there was no wind.

Right: The *Constitution* finally escaped by kedging. For this, the kedge anchor was rowed out and dropped ahead of the ship; the ship was then hauled to the anchor by means of the capstan. All available sail was set, including the studding sails, so that the ship was fully prepared to take advantage of any wind.

while the *Guerrière*'s bowsprit fouled the *Constitution*'s mizzen shrouds and the British hoped to board—their last hope—but the sea was too rough and the ships soon separated. The *Constitution,* fearing the arrival of other British ships, ran downwind to repair minor rigging damage and then bore up to the helpless and sinking *Guerrière.* There was nothing left for Dacres to do but to strike his colours. The prisoners were transferred to the *Constitution* and the unsalvageable *Guerrière* was set on fire and blew up.

The *Constitution* returned to Boston and, under the command of Captain Bainbridge, she sailed again, on a South Atlantic cruise. During this she met with and engaged the British frigate *Java* on her way to the East Indies. The story of the *Guerrière* was almost repeated, with the British being much more handicapped by the American's superior gunnery than by their own slightly smaller broadside. The *Java* was a total loss.

The following two years were less eventful. In 1814 the *Constitution* had to return to Boston for structural repairs and when she was ready to leave she was delayed by the blockade. Her new captain, Charles Stewart, finally managed to slip through the net and was at sea when peace was signed at the end of the year. The following February, while north-east of Madeira, the *Constitution* fell in with the British corvette *Cyane* and the sloop of war *Levant* which were also unaware of the peace. Corvettes and sloops are the smallest three-masted men-of-war, smaller than frigates. The combined weight of broadside of the *Cyane* and *Levant* was about equal to the *Constitution*'s, but it was all in short range carronades. Captain Stewart did not allow the English ships within short range, while keeping them within the range of his long guns. The conclusion was a foregone one and it was with prize crews that the small ships, accompanied by the frigate, called at the neutral harbour of Porto Praya in the Portuguese Cape Verde Islands, to lick their wounds. While they were there a British squadron appeared and Captain Stewart made a quick departure, not trusting the British to respect the law of neutrality or the Portuguese to enforce it. The *Levant,* still damaged, had to limp back to Porto Praya where indeed she was retaken by the English . . . and the Portuguese later had to pay compensation to the Americans since by not enforcing their neutrality rights they had caused the loss of the ship. Prizes taken after a peace had been signed were considered valid if the vessels involved were still unaware of the peace.

The apparent immunity of the *Constitution* against the fire of her enemies during the War of 1812 gained her the nickname of 'Old Ironsides' (though like all ships in those days, she was built of wood). After that war she had a varied career in the Mediterranean, the South Pacific and China, and helped to repress the slave trade off the West Coast of Africa. She became a training ship; she carried goods to the World Exhibition of Paris and she became a receiving ship at Portsmouth, New Hampshire. She narrowly missed being made a target ship in 1905 but was fortunately saved and is now preserved at Charlestown, a suburb of Boston, where she can be visited by the public.

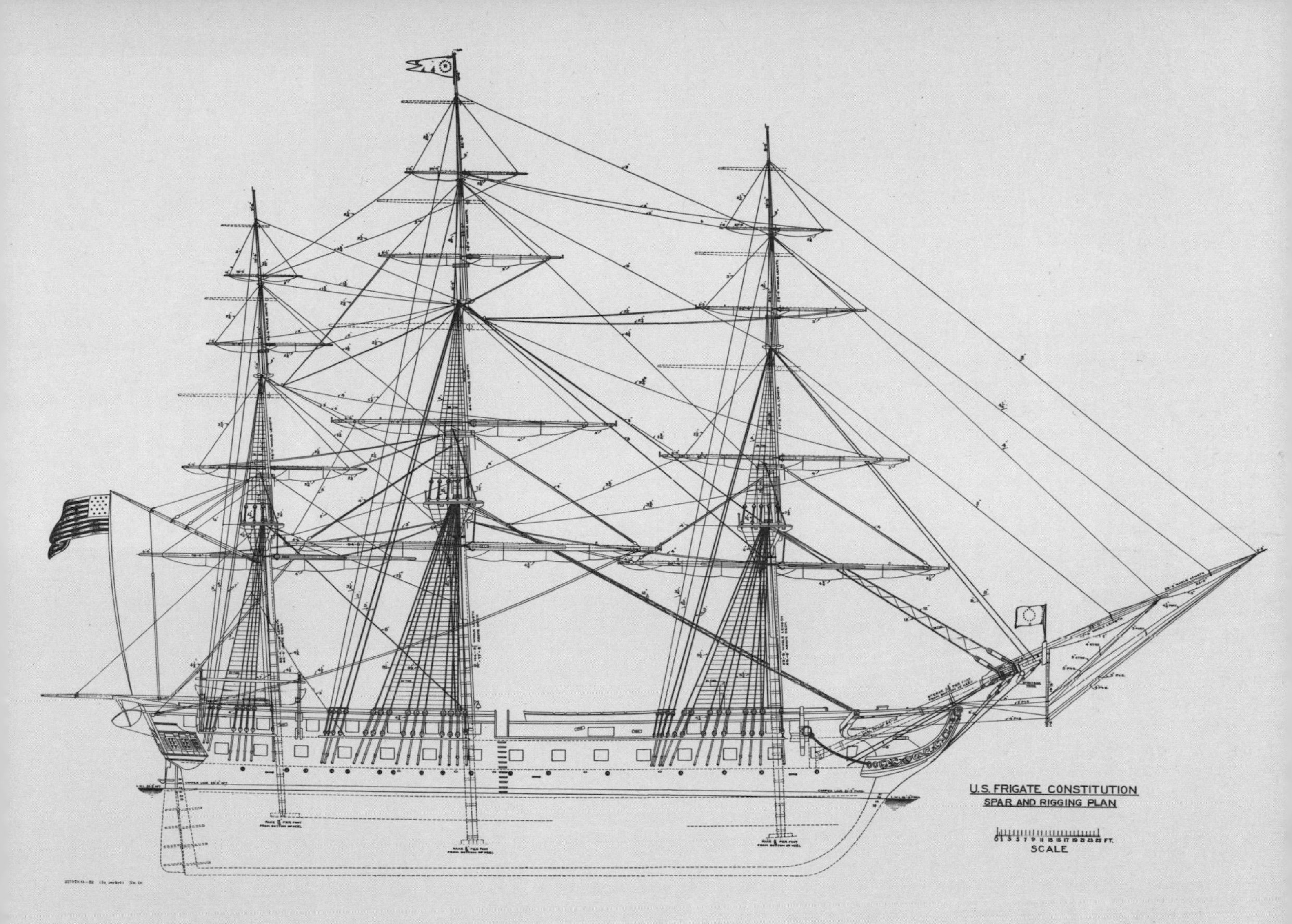

Left: U.S.S. *Constitution* today, preserved at Charleston near Boston. Like the *Victory*, she is still a commissioned ship. In 1976 she underwent major alterations to restore her more closely to her original condition.

Above: The *Constitution*'s masts and rigging were restored in the 1920s, following plans and records of the 1818 period. Although she is known to have carried skysails, these were probably not part of the original plan.

Below: At the beginning of the 1812 War, the spar deck (top) carried two 24-pounder 'bow chasers', twenty-two 32-pounder carronades and an 18-pounder. The gun deck had eighteen long and twelve short 24-pounders.

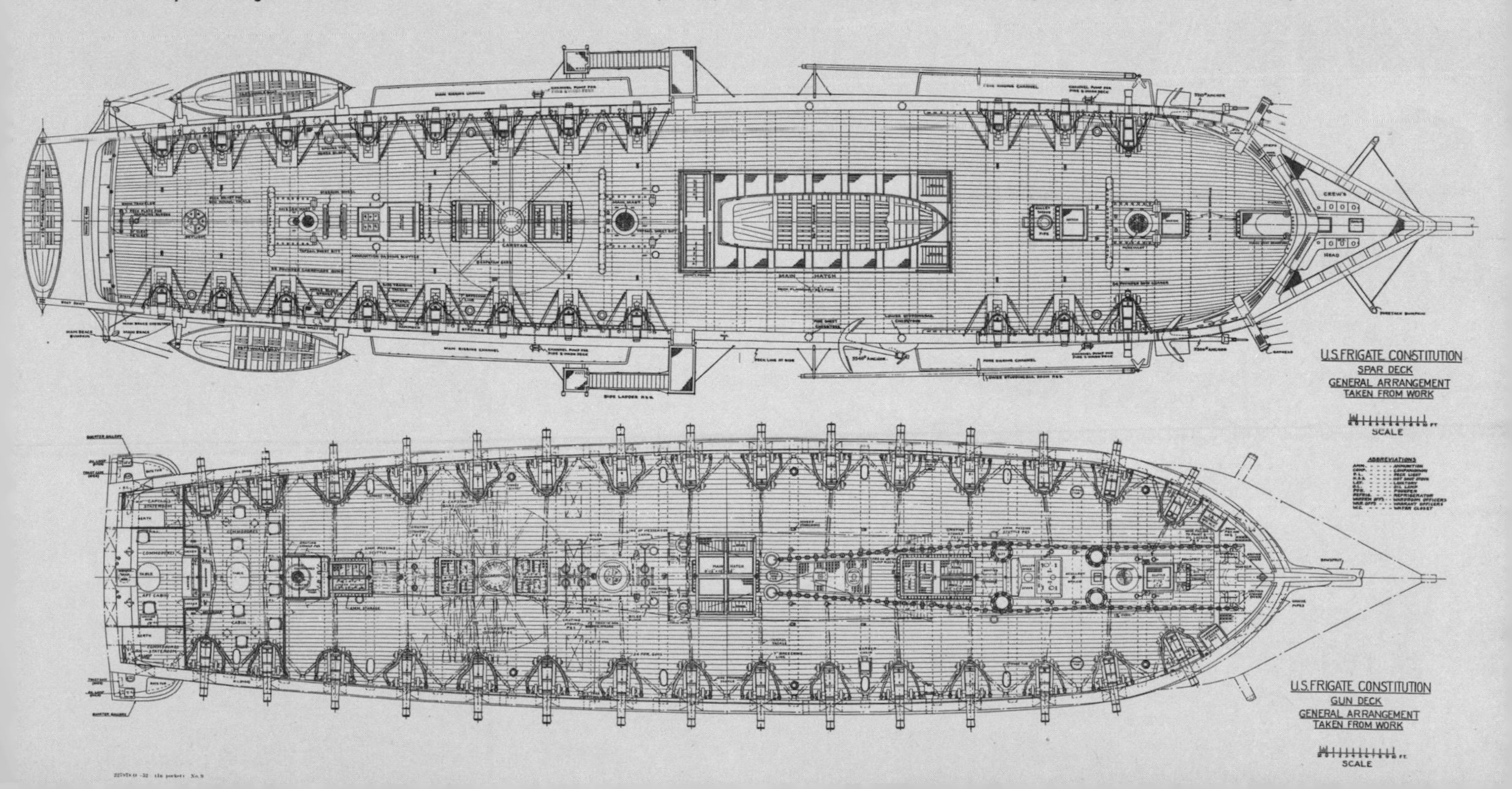

The First Steamships: PS Savannah

From the time man discovered how to use the wind to push ships across the water he yearned to be free of its restrictions: to be able to sail whether there was too much of it or not enough, to be able to make headway even when the wind was blowing from the wrong direction. The invention of the steam engine gave the first and most significant answer to this age-old problem. Practical research into steam started in the late seventeenth century and the first known serious experiment to apply steam power to a boat was conducted in 1737. However, it was not until 1807 that steamboats were shown to be financially viable instead of mere curiosities. The first Atlantic crossing by a steamship was made in 1819 by the PS (paddle-steamer) *Savannah*. In fact the voyage was made almost entirely under sail and it was not until 1838 that the Atlantic was crossed entirely under power—with vast repercussions for the future of shipping.

The first attempt at building a steamboat, in 1737, was made by an Englishman, Jonathan Hulls, but the engine he used was so grossly underpowered that the experiment failed. The first steamboat that really worked was the *Pyroscaphe,* built in France by Claude Jouffroy d'Abbans in 1783. It was followed by other prototypes in the United States and in Scotland. Progress was slow but in 1807 the American Robert Fulton built the first commercially successful steamboat, the *North River Steamboat of Clermont* (usually known simply as the *Clermont*), which operated until 1814 on the Hudson river. The pace of development accelerated when the first coastal passage (which was only a delivery run) was made from New York to Philadelphia by the PS *Phoenix* in 1808. In Europe, the first commercial steam service, on the Clyde, was inaugurated in 1812 by Bell's *Comet.*

Steam power appeared to have come to stay and many steamship companies were created to take advantage of the new technology, particular in the United States. One of these companies, the Savannah Steamship Company, of Savannah, Georgia, purchased a nearly completed ship which it named the *Savannah*. Built at Corlears Hook, New York, by Francis Fickett, she had been launched on 22 August 1818. She had been originally intended for the regular passenger and mail service from New York to Le Havre in France, and she was in every respect a standard sailing packet of her day. However, her new owners, who intended to use her for a passenger and cargo service along the coast of Georgia and neighbouring states, fitted her with a steam engine.

The *Savannah* had a length overall of only 33·5 m, a beam of 7·85 m—11 m over the paddle-wheels—and a draught of 4 m. She measured 325 tonnes gross, 173 tonnes net. It is not often realized how small the great majority of merchant ships were until the 1850s: the *Savannah* had been designed as a passenger ship for the North Atlantic route and, although no longer than many modern sailing yachts, she was much larger than most coasting vessels of her time. In this small hull the passenger accommodation comprised two saloons and berths for thirty-two passengers.

The staterooms and saloons must have been very cramped as the passengers were by no means the only space consumers. The master, his mates and the engineer must have had private cabins and the boatswain, the sailmaker

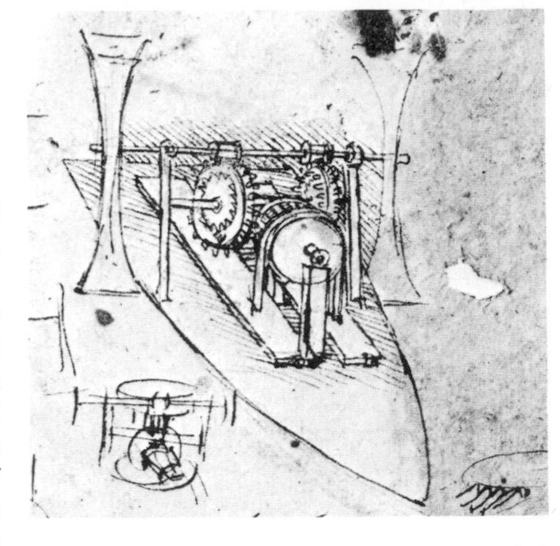

Leonardo da Vinci (1452–1519) sketched plans for several mechanical devices long before they were officially invented. His paddle-boat (above) was never tested. It was not until the development of steam power that paddle-wheels became a practical method of propulsion.

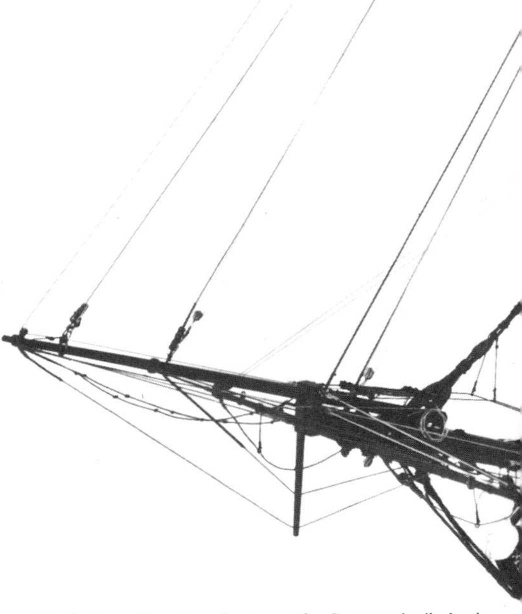

Right: Model of the P.S. *Savannah*. With a length of 33·5m and beam of 7·85m, the *Savannah* was little larger than a modern sailing yacht. On her first transatlantic crossing, steam-driven engines were such a novelty that the smoke pouring from her crooked funnel was mistaken for a fire on board ship.

The first working steamboat was the *Pyroscaphe* (below) built by Claude Jouffroy d'Abbans in 1783 and used on the Saône near Lyons. The 4m diameter paddle-wheels were driven by a steam-cylinder and piston. The first commercially successful steamboat, the *North River Steamboat of Clermont* (left), began a regular service on the Hudson River on 11 August 1807.

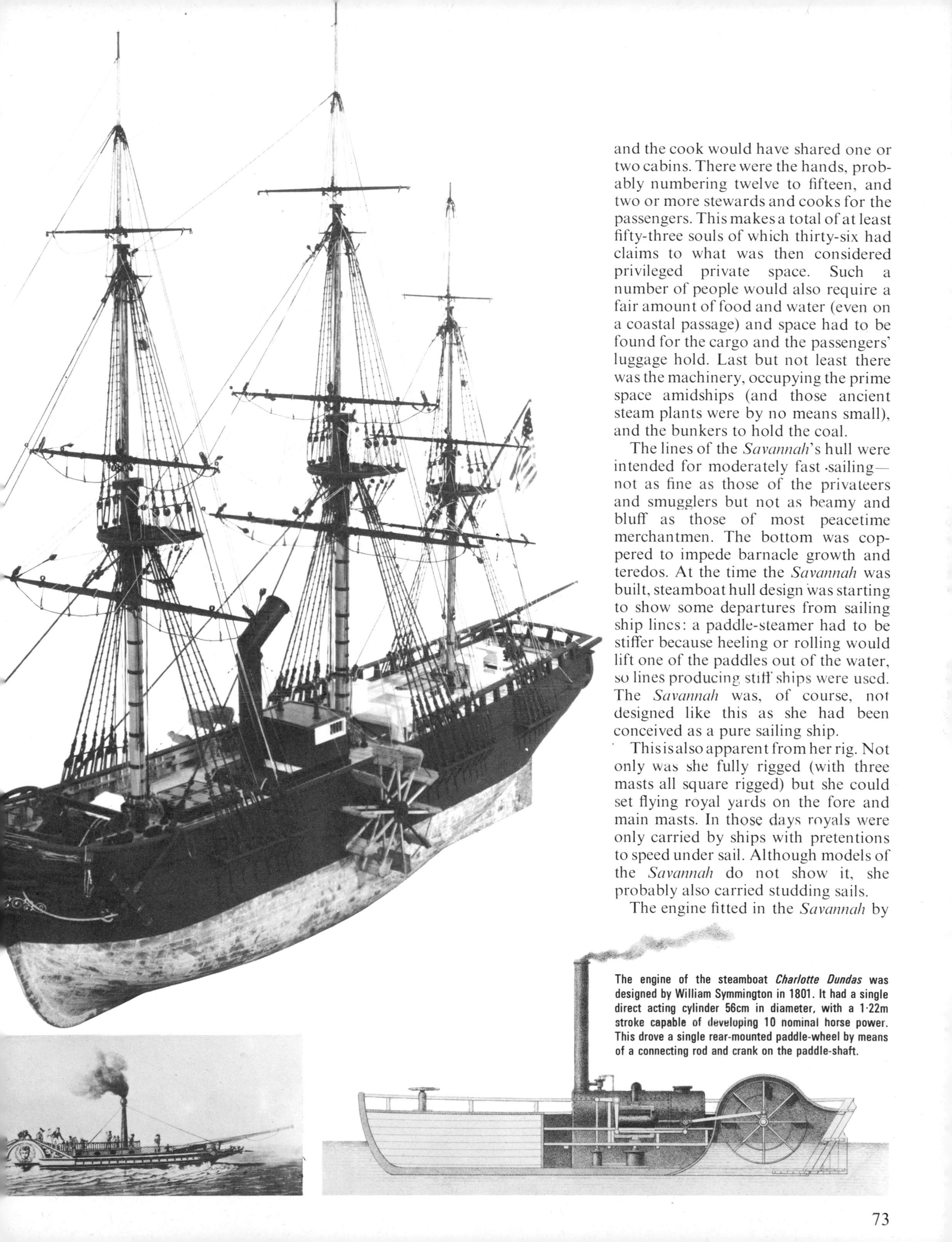

and the cook would have shared one or two cabins. There were the hands, probably numbering twelve to fifteen, and two or more stewards and cooks for the passengers. This makes a total of at least fifty-three souls of which thirty-six had claims to what was then considered privileged private space. Such a number of people would also require a fair amount of food and water (even on a coastal passage) and space had to be found for the cargo and the passengers' luggage hold. Last but not least there was the machinery, occupying the prime space amidships (and those ancient steam plants were by no means small), and the bunkers to hold the coal.

The lines of the *Savannah*'s hull were intended for moderately fast sailing—not as fine as those of the privateers and smugglers but not as beamy and bluff as those of most peacetime merchantmen. The bottom was coppered to impede barnacle growth and teredos. At the time the *Savannah* was built, steamboat hull design was starting to show some departures from sailing ship lines: a paddle-steamer had to be stiffer because heeling or rolling would lift one of the paddles out of the water, so lines producing stiff ships were used. The *Savannah* was, of course, not designed like this as she had been conceived as a pure sailing ship.

This is also apparent from her rig. Not only was she fully rigged (with three masts all square rigged) but she could set flying royal yards on the fore and main masts. In those days royals were only carried by ships with pretentions to speed under sail. Although models of the *Savannah* do not show it, she probably also carried studding sails.

The engine fitted in the *Savannah* by

The engine of the steamboat *Charlotte Dundas* was designed by William Symmington in 1801. It had a single direct acting cylinder 56cm in diameter, with a 1·22m stroke capable of developing 10 nominal horse power. This drove a single rear-mounted paddle-wheel by means of a connecting rod and crank on the paddle-shaft.

The *Savannah* was the first sailing ship with a steam auxiliary to cross the Atlantic. She was originally conceived as a fully rigged sailing ship but was later fitted with a steam engine and paddle-wheels.

the Savannah Steamship Company was very much an auxiliary engine and was not intended as the prime mover. It was built by Stephen Vail at the Speedwell Iron Works near Morristown, New Jersey. It consisted of a single cylinder, 1·026 m diameter with a 1·52 m stroke and it was inclined at 20° to allow direct connection with the paddle-shaft. The steam was supplied at the very low pressure of less than 0·07 kg/cm^2 (1 psi) above atmospheric pressure and the steam was discharged in a jet condenser, without expanding in the cylinder. It was inefficient even by the standards of the day and the coal consumption was enormous. The engine developed a power of 90 indicated h.p. and the speed attained in the best of sea conditions was 4 knots: even if the *Savannah* had been loaded to capacity with coal, she could not have carried enough to cross the Atlantic under power alone.

The steam was supplied by copper boilers with riveted flues built by Daniel Dod, of Elizabeth, New Jersey. The smoke stack had an elbow at the top which could be turned to deflect the soot and sparks from the sails.

The paddle-wheels were 4·65 m diameter and had ten radial arms, held in position by a pair of chains at the outer end. The arms could be folded like a fan by unshackling the chains and it took only twenty minutes to uncouple them and to take them on deck for pure sailing. The paddle floats were 1·37 m long and 0·81 m wide; at cruising speed the wheels turned at 16 r.p.m.

The *Savannah* held her sea trials in New York waters in March 1819 and she proceeded to her home port using her engines for forty-one hours out of the eight and a half day passage. There was a trade depression and it was almost immediately obvious that the ship could not earn her keep in the way her owners had intended. The American market was glutted with good, unwanted ships for sale and the owners of the *Savannah* decided to try to sell her in Europe.

Her master was Moses Rogers who had been in command of the *Phoenix* during the first steam sea-passage in 1808. With no cargo or passengers, the *Savannah* left her home port under power on 24 May 1819 at 5 a.m., with seventy-five tonnes of coal and twenty-five cords of firewood. At 8 a.m. on the same day the paddles were taken on deck and the ship proceeded under sail alone. She had an uneventful Atlantic crossing, only using her engine very occasionally. Steam was still a novelty, and while she was under steam she was reported by other vessels as being on fire. She called at Kinsale in Ireland for recoaling and arrived at Liverpool on 20 June after a

The P.S. *Sirius*, the first ship to cross the Atlantic under steam power alone, arrived at New York harbour on 22 April 1838. The journey had taken 18 days and 10 hours and she had used almost all the coal she was able to carry in her bunkers.

passage of 27 days 11 hours, out of which she had been under steam for a total of about 85 hours. Thus the popular opinion that she was the first vessel to steam across the Atlantic is totally unfounded. At best it can only be said that she was the first steamer to cross the Atlantic although even this is misleading, and it would be more correct to say that she was the first sailing ship with a steam auxiliary to do so.

The *Savannah* spent twenty-five days in Liverpool waiting for prospective buyers but, not finding any, she refuelled and went to Copenhagen, then to Stockholm. The only offer there was made by the King of Sweden, who proposed $100,000 in hemp and iron. This was refused and the *Savannah* proceeded to St. Petersburg in Russia: no-one wanted to buy her there, either. The European venture having failed, she returned to America under sail alone as the price of coal in Europe was considered too expensive. She did, however, cover the last few miles up the Savannah river with her paddles, her stack belching smoke to attract attention.

Attempts to sell the *Savannah* to the US Government failed and she was finally sold at auction in 1820. Her new owners did the wise thing: they stripped out her space- and money-consuming machinery and ran her as a sailing packet between Savannah and New York. She did not last long in her new role for she was wrecked on Long Island during a gale on 5 November 1821.

Although the *Savannah* was typical of the trend in experimenting with steam, she did not represent any technical innovations in that line (on the contrary) and her claim to be the first steamship to cross the Atlantic is, as we have seen, overrated. Nevertheless, she became famous and gave her name to the first merchant navy nuclear ship ever to be built, the NS *Savannah* of 1962.

The first ship to cross the Atlantic under continuous steam power was the PS *Sirius*, built at Leith in 1837 for the London–Cork run. She was 63·5 m long, 714 tonnes gross and she had a 300 nominal h.p. engine. In 1838 she was chartered by the British and American Steam Navigation Company and she left Cork with forty passengers on 4 April, arriving at New York on the 22nd, 18 days and 10 hours out (a mean speed of 6·7 knots), with barely fifteen tonnes of coal left in her bunkers. She was first by only a few hours: in the early hours of the 23rd the PS *Great Western* steamed into New York. She had made the passage in only 15 days and 5 hours (a mean speed of 8·8 knots), and, more significantly, twenty-five per cent of her coal bunkers were untouched.

The *Great Western* was designed by Isambard Brunel specifically for the North Atlantic trade and she was the biggest ship of her day. She was 72 m long and her engine developed a power of 450 nominal h.p. and used about 30 tonnes of coal a day. Although only the second ship to cross the Atlantic under steam, between 1838 and 1846 she made sixty-four crossings, compared to the *Sirius*'s two round trips. Between 1847 and 1857 she ran the service between Southampton and the West Indies before being broken up. It was the *Great Western* that truly established the North Atlantic steam route.

Whaling Ships: The Charles W. Morgan

The New England whaling industry expanded offshore in the mid-eighteenth century and by 1760 tryworks—the blubber-melting apparatus—were being installed on board whaling ships for processing at sea. In the 1840s the New Englanders had about six hundred whaling ships at sea in the Pacific, the Atlantic and the Indian oceans. Despite the primitive means of the hunt they were already depleting stocks of whales and this, combined with the discovery of rock oil by drilling in Pennsylvania in 1858 (which provided a cheap substitute for lamp oil), and with the shipping losses incurred during the Civil War, spelled the end of the great days of whaling. Out of the many thousands of Yankee whaling ships which contributed so much to the history and wealth of the new American nation, only one has been preserved, the *Charles W. Morgan*.

This ship, named after her owner, was launched at New Bedford, Massachusetts, in 1841, the very same year and place Herman Melville had embarked on the whaling ship *Acushnet* for a voyage that was to provide him with the source material for his novel *Moby Dick*. The *Charles W. Morgan* is a typical New England whaling ship. Her principal dimensions are: length overall 51·5 m, length on deck about 35·4 m, beam 8·45 m and she measures 314 gross tons. She represents a type of ship that hardly changed throughout the nineteenth century. Such whalers, at sea for years, were seakindly—capable of riding out the storms—their bows were bluff and buoyant and their tophamper moderate.

The *Charles W. Morgan* has the heavy wooden cranes or davits which are characteristic of all whalers and from which the whaleboats were ready to be lowered at the cry of 'There she blows!' She has davits for two boats on each side, and a couple of spare boats upturned on skids above the deck. The hull is black with a white band with black painted gun ports ('Nelson's chequers') to make the ship look like a powerfully armed frigate. This was intended to deter hostile natives—the Pacific Islanders were not all peaceful in the nineteenth century. However on the first voyage the hull was probably painted all white, a New England whaling custom for maiden voyages.

The tryworks are on deck abaft the fore mast. They are a brick structure with a furnace (fuelled by scraps of previously 'tried' blubber) and two large trypots. Trypots are cauldrons of the type shown in cartoons for cooking explorers, and each has a capacity of about 900 litres. A water box is placed under the furnace sole to prevent the heat from reaching the deck. The poop deck is occupied by the 'roundhouse' which consists of two deck houses, one on either side of the ship, linked by a common roof and housing the galley, the bosun's locker and the companionway to the officers' quarters. The helm is between the two deck houses and is sheltered by the roof span. The helm is of a most unusual design which was typical of New England whalers: the wheel and drum are fixed on the tiller itself and turn with it, the tiller rope leading from the deck round the drum and to the opposite side of the deck. The men's quarters were forward, in the foc'sle, and the space between the men's quarters and the officers' was crammed with stores, provisions and disassembled barrels on the way out and with oil barrels on the way home.

Before the invention of the harpoon gun, whales were hunted from small boats with hand-thrown harpoons, lances, spears and knives. The harpoons were attached to a long line and the whale towed the boat along until it was exhausted and could be killed at close quarters. A steering oar was used to give better control.

The original rig was that of a fully-rigged ship with a standing royal on the main mast and single topsails. The fore royal mast was not used for carrying a royal yard (except on passages) but for the crow's nest—a small platform and two padded hoops at waist level in which the two lookouts would stand scanning the horizon for whale spouts. On Arctic whalers the crow's nest consisted of a deep and narrow barrel which offered better protection against the wind. Later in her life the *Charles W. Morgan* acquired the new style double topsails, by adding an extra yard on her topmasts. This arrangement saved the labour of reefing a deep topsail in heavy weather: the upper topsail was simply furled and the lower was equivalent to a reefed single topsail. Later too, the ship was cut down to a bark rig with a taller spanker, a gaff topsail and no yards on the mizzen mast.

The whaleboats are 9·15 m long and 1·8 m wide and have a retractable centreboard. They carry a collapsible mast and sail (which were only set for long chases or for returning to the ship), three harpoons (always referred

Two famous whaling ships, one fact and one fiction, typify New England whalers of the 1840s: Herman Melville's *Pequod* (left) and the *Charles W. Morgan* (right) which is preserved at Mystic Seaport. The boats from which the whales were harpooned were lowered from heavy wooden davits at the side of the ship.

to as 'irons'), three lances and two tubs in which were coiled respectively 200 and 100 fathoms of whale-line. The boats were manned by five oarsmen and a 'steersman' (who was usually one of the mates) at the tiller. The bow oarsman doubled as the harpooner and was known as the 'boat steerer'.

When a boat approached a whale, the steersman would unship the rudder and replace it by a steering oar (giving more control) and the boat steerer would ship his oar and seize an iron. As soon as the 'fish' was 'fast' (harpooned) the steersman and the boat steerer would swap places and the fish was played like gamefish, sometimes leading to a 'Nantucket sleigh ride', the boat being dragged along at full speed by an enraged whale. When the whale was tired the boat would come right up to it and the steersman would kill it by darting a lance. When the dead whale was alongside the ship, the blubber was peeled off by men working from a stage with sharp flensing irons. The peel of skin or blanket piece was gradually hoisted, in a single piece, by a fourfold tackle leading to the main lower mast head. When the fall was a-block another similar fall was hooked to the lower part of the blanket piece where it was still attached to the carcass and the upper part was cut off and lowered on deck. The operation was repeated until the whale was completely skinned. If it was a sperm whale the head would be opened for scooping out the very fine grade oil found within (case oil) and the stomach would be explored for ambergris, a grey mucilaginous substance highly prized for perfume manufacture. The ivory teeth would be also kept for making carvings known as scrimshaw. If the whale was a whalebone whale the whalebones would be cut out from the mouth. The blanket piece was cut into 'bibles' (chunks the size of a large church bible) and these were sliced into 'bible leaves' which were thrown in the trypots. The rendered oil was scooped out and eventually poured into barrels for stowage.

The *Charles W. Morgan* cost $48,500

to build but her first voyage, which lasted three years, brought back 1,600 barrels of sperm oil, 800 barrels of whale oil and 4·5 tonnes of whalebone valued at $69,591. The master, who was also a part-owner, received $11,000 —a tidy fortune in those days. The crew, as on all whalers, did not receive wages but were on a share basis, having signed on for a given lay or proportion of the profit of the voyage.

From 1841 to 1887 the *Charles W. Morgan* made eleven voyages from New Bedford to the Pacific, one to the Atlantic and one to the Indian Ocean. By 1887 the New England whaling industry was in rapid decline and the ship was homeported at San Francisco, closer to the grounds. From there she made seventeen voyages averaging one a year until 1906, when she returned to New Bedford. She made seven more voyages before she was laid up at Fair Haven, Massachusetts. She had logged more miles and taken more whales (more than 2,500) than any other whaler and she had grossed about $2,000,000.

She is now preserved at Mystic Seaport in Connecticut, restored to her original ship rig and looking ready to go to sea once more in search of whales. If she did so, she would, however, be fortunate to find any. Modern whaling, with its factory ships, fleets of hunters, harpoon guns, sonars and helicopters, has not only destroyed any romance and adventure there might have been in the whaler's calling, but it has also almost exterminated the whales.

The *Harpooner,* a typical eighteenth century whaler, from Whitby. Whalers often followed migrating herds into the Arctic or Antarctic and the *Harpooner's* specially strengthened hull and steeply sloping sides allowed her to rise out of crushing ice onto the ice floes. She was armed with cannon to use against pirates.

Left: A single vertebra from a Greenland Right whale, brought home and used as a butcher's chopping block.

Below, left: An early photograph of the *Charles W. Morgan*. The killed whale has been brought alongside the ship for flensing.

Below: On board, the strips of blubber were cut up before being put into a cutter or chopping machine. The smaller pieces were then placed in large, open boiling pots where the oil was extracted.

The Great Iron Ship: The Great Eastern

The steamship *Great Eastern* was the last ship to be designed by a remarkable nineteenth-century engineer, Isambard Kingdom Brunel, who lived from 1806 to 1859. The son of an emigré French engineer, Brunel was brought up in England in an atmosphere of machine inventions and of engineering projects. When Brunel began work on the *Great Eastern* he had already built two size-record breaking steamships for the Atlantic route, the wooden paddle ship *Great Western* in 1837 and the iron screw ship *Great Britain* in 1834. The *Great Britain* was remarkable in two ways: she had a new method of propulsion, a steam-driven screw, instead of a paddle, and was made not of wood but of iron. It was the first time either had been used in an ocean-going steamer and her success made their future use assured.

The *Great Eastern*, however, was to be six times larger than the *Great Britain* and was designed especially to make the long voyage to the Far East. Her size was dictated by the large amount of coal that had to be carried for a return journey as there were no bunkering facilities in the East.

The Eastern Steamship Company was created to build and operate Brunel's supership and contracts were allocated in 1853 for a total of £377,200. James Watt and Company were to build the screw engines and John Scott Russell was the main contractor, responsible for building the paddle engines and the ship herself.

The *Great Eastern*'s keel was laid down in February 1854 at Milwall in the Isle of Dogs, on the river Thames, and the bad luck that was to follow the ship started early during the building stage. A worker was killed by falling into the hold and another died when a workmate fell on him; a workboy also fell from the scaffolding and was impaled on an iron bar and a visitor had his head flattened by a pile driver. In order to secure the contract by underbidding the other tenders, Russell had not allowed enough money for the work and he went bankrupt early in 1856. For three months all work was stopped on the ship while further funds were sought. Finally, with Brunel busying himself here, there and everywhere, the ship was ready to be launched at the end of October 1857.

The first of the great ships designed by Isambard Kingdom Brunel, the *Great Western* was to confound many of her critics when she arrived in New York in 1838, having crossed the Atlantic in fifteen and a half days. She carried both steam-driven paddle wheels and sails and, although still built of wood, she was immensely strong and far larger than any other steamship then built.

Below: The building of the *Great Eastern* brought with it problems almost as gargantuan as the ship itself. Many times larger than Brunel's previous ships, her size was dictated by the large quantity of coal which was needed for a journey to the Far East. She was so big that she had to be launched sideways.

For technical reasons related to size and weight, the *Great Eastern* had to be launched sideways, a new method devised by Brunel. On 7 November 1857, Miss Hope, the daughter of one of the directors, broke the traditional bottle of champagne, naming the ship *Leviathan*, and the restraining chocks were knocked out as hydraulic presses were applied to the hull. Suddenly the ship rumbled down more than a metre and the brake handle of a chain for controlling its slide flew up, injuring four workmen and killing a fifth. Then the ship refused to move any farther.

It took nearly three months and numerous attempts to drag it centimetre by centimetre to the water's edge but on 30 January 1858 the gigantic hull floated at last. The expense of the launching had pushed up the cost of the ship to £732,000, almost double the original estimate, and she was still far from complete. Brunel's health had been permently impaired by the strain of the work and the Eastern Steamship Company went into liquidation. The ship was towed to Deptford where she laid for a year without any further work being done on her.

A new company, the Great Ship Company, acquired the *Great Eastern*

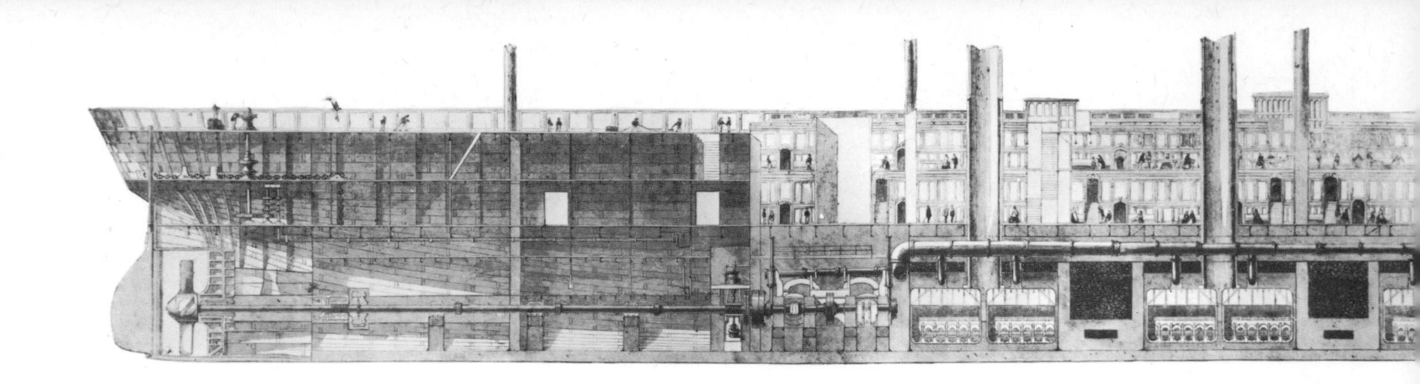

The *Great Eastern* had an overall length of 211m. The iron hull was double skinned and 3 million hand-driven rivets were used in fixing the hull plates. Built to accommodate 4,000 passengers, she had five saloons, the luxurious grand saloon being 19m long. Her cargo capacity was 6,096 tonnes—which was in addition to the 12,000 tonnes of coal required for her own use.

(for this was the name now painted on her bows) and completed her in August 1859. Her characteristics were then:
Length overall: 211 m
Beam: 36 m at the paddle boxes
Loaded draught: 9·2 m
Hull: iron, double-skinned with 25 mm plates below the water line and 19 mm plates above, fixed by 3,000,000 hand-driven rivets. Ten watertight bulkheads plus two longitudinal bulkheads in the boiler and engine rooms.
Tonnage: 18,915 tons gross, 27,859 tonnes displacement. (*Great Eastern*'s tonnage record was not broken until the launching of the liner *Lusitania* in 1907.)
Paddle engines: 1,000 h.p., 4 cylinders with a 188 cm bore and a 4·26 m stroke powered by 4 boilers and activating two 17·1 m diameter wheels with 30 blades 0·92 m deep and 3·96 m wide.
Screw engine: 1,600 h.p., 4 cylinders with a 213 cm bore and a 1·22 m stroke, powered by 6 boilers and driving a 7·3 m propeller with a 1·12 m pitch.
Speed under power: 14 knots
Auxiliary rig: 5,450 square metres of canvas carried by six masts.
Passenger-carrying capacity: 4,000
Cargo capacity: 6,096 tonnes.

Below: The *Great Eastern* was Brunel's last ship. Unlike his successful *Great Western* and *Great Britain* she was never a commercial success and owner after owner lost money on her. The greatest number of passengers she carried was 1,530 and many of her journeys were made half empty.

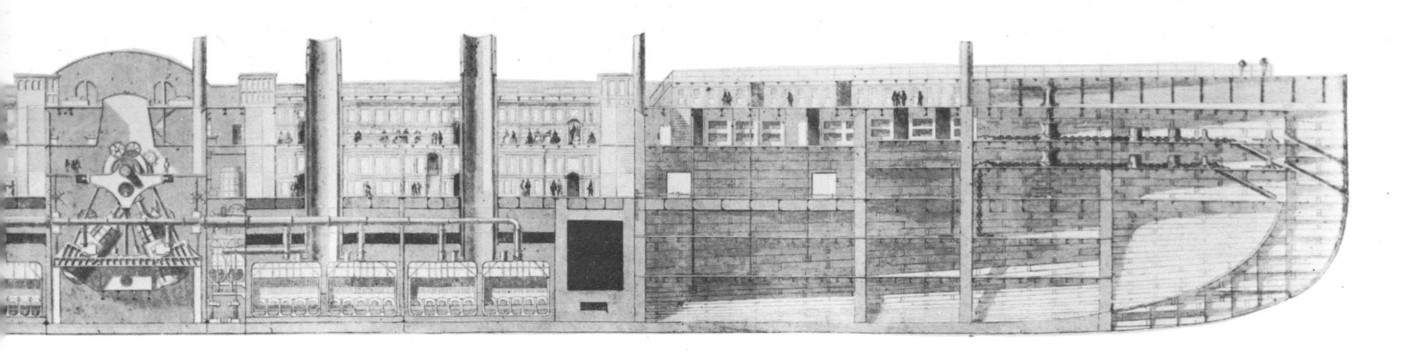

The combination of paddle and screw may seem strange but multiple screws were not then invented and a single screw would have been totally inadequate to propel the ship. As it turned out, the combination gave her great manoeuvrability which was to prove very useful in the future.

The *Great Eastern* was the first of the prestigious ocean liners and was far ahead of her time—which perhaps explains many of the problems that beset her. She had five saloons lit by gas generated in her own gas plant. The luxurious grand saloon was 19 m long, 14·3 m wide and 4·25 m high. There were berths for 4,000 passengers and the first-class cabins had the unheard-of luxury of a bath with running hot and cold water.

Brunel was aboard just before her sea trials, looking into last minute details, when he collapsed with a stroke. The ship left without him and was just off Hastings on 9 September when a tremendous explosion caused by a blocked safety valve erupted through the upper deck. Horribly scalded men crawled out of the boiler room. One of them jumped over the side and was mangled to death

The *Great Eastern* dwarfs traffic and passers-by on the quay-side. It was probably her size that caused most of her problems: passengers preferred the smaller, more reliable packet boats for transatlantic crossings.

The *Great Eastern* had two sets of engines; one for the propulsion of the propeller screw and the other to turn the enormous paddle wheels. The paddle engine was built by John Scott Russell of Millwall, London, under contract. The paddle wheels themselves each measured 17·1m and were made up of 30 radial paddles.

by the paddle wheel; five others were killed on the spot or died in agony a few hours later. Brunel, lying paralysed in his home, suffered a relapse when he heard the news, dying on 15 September.

The *Great Eastern* limped into Weymouth where her boiler room and grand saloon (which had been devastated) were provisionally repaired but the bad luck persisted. The following January (1860) her master, Captain Harrison, his coxswain and a boy were drowned when their gig capsized.

By the time the *Great Eastern* was ready for passenger service, the Great Ship Company did not have enough money left to finance a voyage to Australia and it was decided to try her on the North Atlantic run—for which she had not been designed and was not adapted. She sailed nearly empty on 17 June 1860 but as she arrived at New York ten days later, she received a fourteen gun salute, the first merchant vessel to be honoured in this way. In order to earn a few extra dollars she was opened to the public and in July she was visited by nearly 150,000 people. Two 2-day cruises at ten dollars a head were organized. The first attracted over 2,000 passengers but only 200 berths had been prepared, there was not enough food and the ship was dirty. As a result the second cruise attracted only a hundred passengers. *Great Eastern* returned to England with even fewer passengers and her master suffered a nervous breakdown as soon as he stepped ashore. The ship was a great strain on her masters and she changed them at almost every voyage.

After she had made another money-losing voyage to New York she was chartered by the British government to transport 2,144 troops, 437 women and children and 122 horses to Quebec. This time she crossed the Atlantic in a record-breaking eight and a quarter days but she returned with only 500 passengers.

Her next departure for New York looked promising, with a substantial passenger list. She left Liverpool on 10 September 1861 but three days out she met with a severe storm. An uncoordinated manoeuvre resulted in the rudder shaft shearing off and the helpless ship swung broadside to the seas. The paddles were smashed almost immediately and the propeller had to be stopped because the uncontrolled rudder kept swinging against it. The sails were set but they were immediately blown to ribbons. The storm lasted for three days and the situation was critical; the ship was rolling 45° to each side and the passenger quarters were a scene of utter chaos. The *Great Eastern* eventually limped under jury steering into Cork where the repairs took eight months and cost £60,000.

In May and July 1862 the *Great Eastern* made two transatlantic crossings with reasonable bookings and freight and in August she left for New York with 1,530 paying passengers—her record. But the jinx was still with her: as she neared New York she hit an uncharted reef and tore a 25·5 × 1·2 m hole in her bottom. Had it not been for her double hull construction, she would have sunk like the *Titanic*. Although still watertight she could not sail home without repairs and a special caisson had to be made to fit the hull and enclose the rip. The caisson was then pumped out and temporary plates were riveted in. Four months later she returned to Liverpool, going on to Milford Haven in Wales where proper repairs could be carried out. After another three money-losing crossings to New York she was finally laid up.

In 1865 the *Great Eastern* was chartered by the Atlantic Telegraph Company, as she was the only ship big enough to carry the 2,000 miles of cable necessary for a transatlantic connection. One cable had been previously laid across the Atlantic but it had only functioned for three weeks. The grand saloon and two of the screw boilers were ripped out to make space for the cable tanks and she started her new job on 15 July, from Ireland. After many minor problems, on 2 August, when they were well past the half way mark, the cable parted and vanished into 2,000 fathoms (1,800 m) of water.

The experience was not wasted, however, for the next year she sailed again with better equipment and cable. On 27 July 1866 the Valentia telegraph station in Ireland received a triumphant message from Heart's Content (Newfound-

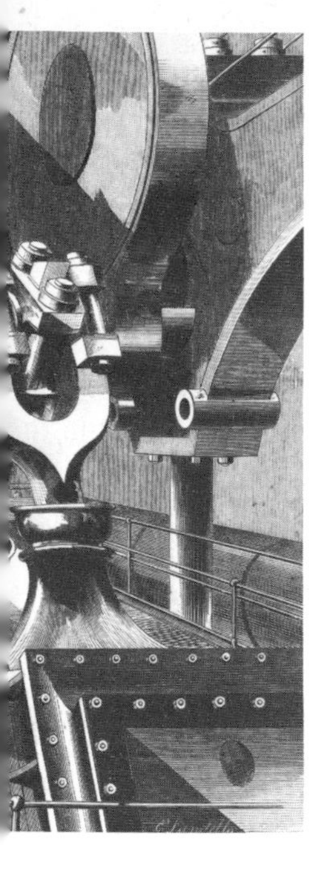

The motive force of the *Great Eastern* was a combination of steam-driven paddles and screws. Despite this, she was built with an auxiliary rig with six masts, and square and fore-and-aft rigging. The total sail surface area measured 5,540 sq.m.

land): success at last. On her way back, the *Great Eastern* also fished up the broken end of the previous year's cable, spliced it and returned to Newfoundland with a second working cable!

The following year the *Great Eastern*'s role changed again. She was chartered by the Société des Affréteurs du Great Eastern, with the backing of the French government, for a special journey from New York to France carrying American visitors to the World Trade Fair in Paris. The ship was reconverted at great cost to a passenger liner but the venture was a financial disaster.

Once more she was laid up, until she was again chartered by the French in 1869 for the laying of a telegraph cable from France to America. After this she carried another cable from England to Bombay and laid it from India towards Suez. In 1870–1 she was engaged in various cable-maintenance jobs and in 1872 laid a fourth transatlantic cable.

Although the *Great Eastern* had been a permanent financial liability to her owners, she had been a successful cable layer but even this was not to continue for very long. In 1874 a specially designed cable layer, the *Faraday* was launched, and the *Great Eastern* became obsolete.

For twelve long years she laid gathering rust at Milford Haven. Then in 1885 she was bought for only £26,000 by Edward de Mattos, who chartered her for one year to the Liverpool clothing and drapery firm of David Lewis to be used as a floating advertising gimmick and fun-fair. At the expiry of the charter, de Mattos tried to use her as a floating museum and for an arts and industry exhibition, but he was not successful. He sold her to the breakers in 1888 for £16,000. They were the last owners to lose money on her: although they sold scrap metal and sundries to the value of £58,000, the ship was so solidly built that it took them two years to dismantle her, at a cost which finally exceeded the profit from their sales.

In September 1861 the *Great Eastern* encountered a severe gale. Because of ill-timed manoeuvring in the midst of the storm the rudder shaft was shorn off, leaving the ship helpless. The storm lasted for three days.

As a passenger vessel the *Great Eastern* was hardly a success but she did succeed in laying the first trans-Atlantic cable. In 1865 her saloons, cabins and holds were replaced by gigantic cable tanks.

The Clipper Ships: The Cutty Sark

Square riggers are beautiful ships and the clippers, characterized by their record-breaking speeds, slim hulls, graceful bows and lofty masts, were the most handsome of them all. As a type of ship they were short-lived; their building spanned only thirty years but they represented the apogee of the sailing ship. Even their owners, hard-nosed and money-minded businessmen, fell in love with them, lavished money on them and were inspired to give them names such as *Sea Witch* or *Flying Cloud*. Today only a single clipper survives from that golden age of sail: the *Cutty Sark*.

The clipper saga started in the United States where clipper ships appeared in response to three stimuli: the expanding tea trade, the Californian gold rush and the repeal of the British Navigation Acts. As a result of the Treaty of Nanking in 1842 many new Chinese ports were opened to foreign trade; tea commerce boomed and high freight premiums were paid to fast ships, as the flavour of tea spoilt during long sea passages. The Fortyniners (the emigrants of the California gold rush of 1849) needed urgent supplies of almost everything, creating an even bigger demand for fast ships than the tea trade, and the clippers reduced the average passage from New York to San Francisco by the Horn from well over 150 days to about 100 days. The repeal of the Navigation Acts which protected British home shipping, meant that American ships could carry tea and other commodities from other countries to England; to compete with the established British shipping companies they needed the edge of speed.

The clipper ship type did not appear unheralded, just because it was needed, but by progressive modifications of traditional plans. The word 'clipper' itself originally only denoted the idea of speed, such as in the 'Baltimore clippers' of the late eighteenth and early nineteenth centuries. These were not clippers in the restricted meaning of the word which appeared in the late 1840s. The direct ancestor of the new clipper type was the packet ship, a civilian luxury goods and passenger vessel derived from the naval frigate. Like frigates, the packet ships had buoyant bluff bows, a main beam placed well forward of amidships and a fine run with concave waterlines near the stern. In the early forties the China ships were still built along these lines and it was then that John Willis Griffiths, an American naval architect, designed the China packet *Rainbow* with modifications of his own to improve speed. He replaced the traditional bluff bows that slow a ship down by a fine entrance bow. This had to be flared so that it would become

The *Cutty Sark* at anchor in Shanghai harbour. She was built to carry cargoes of tea from China to London and, until 1877, she was able to compete successfully with the rapidly developing steamships. Later, with a shortened rig, she entered the Australian wool trade.

By the end of the first half of the nineteenth century, the development of trade in perishable goods called for cargo carriers of great speed. The three-masted *Flying Cloud* was one of the superb clippers built specifically to meet this need. It was with the *Flying Cloud* and other clippers of her type that America achieved her virtual monopoly on certain cargoes until the freight depression in 1857.

Right: The total complement of men on board the *Cutty Sark* was rarely in excess of twenty-eight. Working aloft on the yards of a clipper was both perilous and difficult: one slip could mean certain death, plunging a man into the sea or onto the deck below.

more and more buoyant as it dipped into the sea: the buoyancy was only used when it was needed and would not produce a permanent resistance to forward motion as with bluff bows. To achieve the desired shape Griffiths had to carry the planking further forward, to the beakhead, which thus became part of the stem instead of being a purely ornamental projecting support for the figurehead. Because of the diminished buoyancy of the bows in normal conditions the fore mast was placed further back, increasing the area of the headsails (jibs) which tend to lift the bow, and diminishing the downward leverage of the foresails (the fore mast square sails). The finer entrance also meant moving the main beam to about amidships, and this in turn meant fuller lines aft, doing away with the concave shape of the waterlines near the stern which create eddies and drag.

The *Rainbow* was launched at New York in 1845, the same year as the *Houqua,* another New York ship. The latter was a brig built for the China trade and her designer, Nat Palmer, had by intuition reached the same conclusions as Griffiths, who had tackled the problem in a scientific way. Both ships proved the soundness of the principles of their design, which were then developed further.

The first true clipper was the *Sea Witch,* designed by Griffiths and launched in 1846. The main difference between the half-breed *Rainbow* and the pure-bred *Sea Witch* was that the former, although with a fine bow, still had slightly convex waterlines at the entrance, whereas the latter had hollow waterlines. Such waterlines help improve the flow of the water along the hull. They were the result of a more pronounced flare and Griffiths also dispensed with the clutter of trailboards inherited from the traditional beakhead, producing the first clean clipper bow.

The foremost clipper builder was Donald Mackay, a Nova Scotiaman established in New England. His *Flying Cloud* of 1851 was perhaps the first of the extreme clippers built for all-out speed. By 1855 the heady days of the Gold Rush and of the extreme clippers had already gone but medium clippers were being built in America for English shipowners. The freight depression of 1857 created a slump in orders and American clipper ship building never really recovered before the Civil War ended America's short-lived but glorious pre-eminence in merchant sail. Great Britain was by then designing and building her own clippers for the China Trade, putting her industrial advance to use, with composite construction and all-iron construction following shortly.

One of these clippers was the *Thermopylae,* built at Aberdeen in 1868. On her maiden voyage she sailed from London to Melbourne in sixty-one days (a record under sail which she still holds), before proceeding to China. She was the fastest thing afloat. It was specifically to beat her that 'White Hat' Jock Willis (a white-hatted shipowner and former sea-captain) ordered a new clipper. Her lines were to imitate those of another of his ships, the *Tweed,* which was very fast but too big for the tea trade. The architect of the new ship was Hercules Linton and she was built for £16,150 at Dumbarton in Scotland, by the yard of Scott and Linton.

The new clipper was launched on 23 November 1869, after being christened

The main considerations in building the *Cutty Sark* were speed and cargo carrying capacity and she has all the refinements of a true clipper, though she is slightly fuller in the stern. The vast cargo area was in the hold below the main deck, separated into two levels by a yellow pine 'tween deck. The hatches are located just for'ard of each mast.

The *Cutty Sark* was ship rigged, with three masts, all square rigged. Unlike the extreme clippers of the 1850s she was not oversparred, though at the height of her career her sail area was greater than any other ship in the China trade. Below: In 1896 she was sold to the Portuguese and re-rigged as a barkentine, but was later restored to her original state.

Cutty Sark by Mrs Moodie, the captain's wife. Her strange name means 'short shirt' in Scottish and it refers to the dress of Nannie, the pretty witch in Robert Burns' poem 'Tam O'Shanter'. Tam O'Shanter's story is that he watched Nannie and other witches holding a midnight black magic ceremony. Unfortunately he was spotted and as he galloped away, Nannie, chasing along behind him, managed to catch his horse's tail: the clipper's figurehead shows Nannie with an outstretched arm holding the tail. The name clearly proclaimed that the new ship would outrun her fastest rival.

The overall length of the *Cutty Sark* is 85 m; her hull length is 74 m while her maximum hull width is only 10·95 m. The draught of a cargo ship depends on the weight of her cargo. The *Cutty Sark*'s normal heavy draught is 6 m. She is entirely copper-plated below the waterline to prevent the growth of weeds and barnacles which slow a ship down. The rig of the *Cutty Sark* is that of ship: three masts, all square-rigged. The main mast carries a skysail, and the very top of the main mast, the truck, towers a giddy 45·5 m above the deck. The topgallants, topsails and courses of the main- and fore-masts can be extended by lateral wings, the studding sails. Compared to the extreme clippers of the 1850s which carried skysails on all three masts and sometimes even moonsails above, the *Cutty Sark* was not over-sparred but in her heyday she had a greater sail area (3,045 m^2) than any other ship in the China trade.

The early clippers were entirely wooden but iron sailing ships became common in the 1860s and the *Cutty Sark* shows the increasing influence of iron even in wooden ships. The lower masts and yards and the bowsprit are made of iron; the rest of the spars are made of Oregon pine. The hull has iron frames and deck beams planked with wood, a method known as composite construction. The bulwarks are also made of iron plates.

The fore part of the deck is raised to form a platform known as an anchor deck where the men stand at the 'pump' handles of the windlass to heave the anchor. Still in the bows but under the main deck is the foc'sle, the traditional quarters for the hands. It has four portholes a side and thirty bunks. Many of these were left unoccupied because the total complement never exceeded twenty-eight men and once the ship sailed with only nineteen officers and men. Behind the foc'sle is a watertight bulkhead which prevents the central part of the ship from being flooded in the event of a head-on collision. Similarly there is another collision bulkhead separating the stern section of the ship from the central part.

The deck is teak, the best timber possible for decks—and the most expensive. Behind the fore mast there is a deckhouse, called a Liverpool house because such structures first appeared on ships from that port. Its sides are in panelled and varnished wood and it houses the galley and the accommodation for the bosun, sailmaker, carpenter and cook. A similar deckhouse stands abaft the main mast. This is the half-deck house, where the apprentices—young boys training to become sea officers—lived, and it also shelters the 'donkey', a small steam engine used to load or unload cargo in harbour.

The quarter deck is raised above the level of the main deck and it extends aft of the mizzen mast. In turn it has a smaller deck raised above it, the monkey poop, under which is the cabin, the accommodation for the master and the first officer. When entering this 'officers' country' by the fore entrance there is a narrow passageway with the first officer's cabin and pantry to the right (on the port side of the ship) and the master's cabin to the left. The passageway opens into a yacht-like saloon with woodwork of varnished teak and bird's-eye maple. It has a large table with a lovely brass oil lamp hanging from above and a suspended glass and bottle rack. On each side are comfortable, upholstered sofas and there is even a fire-place. A beautiful teak cabinet holds the silver- and china-wares. Abaft the saloon are the W.C., a bathroom and a ladder leading up to the after part of the quarter deck where the wheel is situated.

The cargo is stowed in the hold, below the main deck. This hold is separated into two levels by a 'tween deck of yellow pine. The hatches are located in front of each mast.

Seen from the outside, the ship looks like a nineteenth-century yacht: all black with only two horizontal gold stripes leading from the gilded scrollwork of the trailboards which flow from the white-painted figurehead, and ending at the gilded scrollwork on the stern which surrounds the words 'CUTTY SARK—LONDON'.

The *Cutty Sark* sailed in the tea trade until 1877. During that time she made good but not brilliant passages and she usually took more time than her rival, the *Thermopylae*. The only time that the two clippers left China together was in 1872. A race was inevitable and bets were flying on the Shanghai waterfront as to which ship would win. It is easy to imagine the mad scramble of the crews swarming up the rigging to cast the sails loose at the start. The *Cutty Sark* had forged some 400 miles ahead of her competitor when her rudder broke off in an Indian Ocean gale.

The clipper *Red Jacket* off Cape Horn, on her way from Australia to Liverpool, August 1854.

Above, left: The American clipper *Three Brothers*, in full sail. In the mid-nineteenth century, fast sailing ships competed successfully with steam. The *Three Brothers* was, in fact, originally built as a steamship—the *Vanderbilt*—but was later converted to sail alone.

Below, left: The *Cutty Sark's* figurehead represents Nannie, the witch who chased Tam O'Shanter, her hair streaming in the wind and her hand reaching out to grasp Tam's horse's tail. The arms and head of the original figurehead were damaged and lost. The present one, shown here, was built up from a block of yellow pine donated by the Canadian Government during the restoration of the ship.

Today, the *Cutty Sark* has been re-rigged to her original appearance. Her lower masts were of rolled iron, and each mast was fitted with double topsails. A sturdy chain was fixed to the lower mast, below the mast top, to assist in supporting the enormous weight of the lower yards. The chain was shackled by an eye on the top of the yard.

During the whole week it took to rig a jury-rudder the gale did not abate and the repairs alone won captain Moodie the admiration of fellow sailors. The *Thermopylae* reached London a week ahead but in corrected time, after subtracting the time lost during the repairs to the rudder, the *Cutty Sark* was the winner. From 1873 onwards the best passages from China were consistently realized by a new iron clipper, the *Hallowe'en*. Iron had previously been thought to spoil the tea.

The Suez canal, which had been opened a few weeks before the launching of the *Cutty Sark*, shortened the journey to the Far East and allowed steamships to become competitive in the China Trade. By 1878 they had driven the magnificent clippers out all together. From 1878 until 1883 the *Cutty Sark* made a living by tramping, that is by carrying odd cargoes to odd places. During that time, in 1880, her rig was shortened: the skysail and studding sails were taken off and the masts and yards were made shorter.

It was under this new look that she entered the Australian wool trade in 1883: her short rig was just right for sailing the worst seas in the world, the famous Roaring Forties of the Southern Ocean which she had to cross on each voyage. In 1885 she was placed under the command of captain Richard Woodget, a superb seaman and a hard driver. It was then that she really came into her own: '*Cutty Sark* first... the rest, nowhere'. Year after year she won the wool race, beating, amongst others, her old 'enemy', the *Thermopylae*. The wool races, like the tea races, were informal competitions, the winners being the ships making the shortest return of the season.

In 1894–95 the *Cutty Sark* sailed from Brisbane to London in 84 days with a record cargo of 5,304 bales of wool. Alas, it was to be her last race and her last voyage under the Red Ensign. She was sold to the Portuguese and renamed *Ferreira* although she was still called 'Pequina Camisola' by her new crew—the Portuguese name for 'Cutty Sark'. In 1916 she was dismasted in a storm and re-rigged in Cape Town as a barkentine, a sad downfall for an ex-China-clipper. She was resold under the Portuguese flag in 1920 and renamed *Maria do Amparo*.

In 1922 this dowdy barkentine was recognized by a British seaman, captain Wilfred Dowman and it is thanks to him that the world's sole remaining clipper has been preserved. He bought her and re-rigged her as a clipper, for use as a training ship. After his death the *Cutty Sark* was given by his widow to the Thames Nautical Training College and in 1953 she was handed over to the Cutty Sark Preservation Society. She is now in a dry dock at Greenwich, open to the public, rigged and painted just as she was in her China days. Relics and souvenirs of the clipper, of her masters and crews and of other proud sailing ships are exhibited in her 'tween deck and lower hold, to remind us of the great days of sail.

The Last Days of Sail: The France II

Square riggers were still being built in the early decades of this century, especially during the pre-war period before 1914. However, from the point of view of sail technology, most of these were static or even regressive. Only two countries, France and Germany, were making improvements and here the square rigger continued to evolve right up to 1914. The Great War naturally stopped all sailing ship building and the freight depression which followed the war finally brought the end of the great sailing ships. A few lingered on until the eve of the Second World War and a few new square-rigged ships were built but these were only sail-training imitations of former glories. Before they were finally replaced by motor vessels, sailing ships had reached a size and efficiency never known before. The final stage of the great ships is epitomized by the five-masted bark *France II*.

Built for the Société Anonyme des Navires Mixtes, she was launched at Bordeaux on 9 November 1911 by the Chantiers de la Gironde. She was the greatest sailing vessel ever to be built, at 5,806 tons gross. In comparison, the *Cutty Sark* measures only 978 tons. Only three other sailing vessels, all built during the same pre-war period, had a gross tonnage in excess of 5,000 tons: the German five-masted bark, the *R. C. Rickmers* (5,248 tons), the American seven-masted schooner *Thomas W. Lawson* (5,218 tons) and the German five-masted fully-rigged ship *Preussen* (5,081 tons). The *Thomas W. Lawson* was the only seven-masted vessel ever built (excluding some Chinese junks) and the *Preussen*'s rig was also unique.

The *France II* was truly impressive. Built entirely in steel, she was 126 m long; she had a beam of 16·90 m and a loaded draught of 7·65 m. She had a very pronounced sheer and walking on her deck towards her bows was said to be like climbing a hill.

She had four square-rigged masts (called fore mast, main mast, middle mast and mizzen mast), each with a course, double topsails and double topgallant sails. She carried nothing above the upper topgallants, and was therefore called a stump-topgallant rig but the trucks of her four masts were higher than the fifteenth storey of a modern building. All four masts were identical: same height, same yards, same sails. This cut down on rig design and manufacturing costs and simplified the spare-parts problem. Furthermore, the masts, yards and sails were identical to those of several other ships of the same company (the *Quevilly*, the *Croisset* and her sister ships), thus leading to further savings and the possibility of quick replacements in the event of a major rigging or sail disaster. The square-rigged masts were made in two parts only: a lower part extending up to the lower topgallant yard and an upper part extending from the upper topsail to the truck, with only one doubling (overlapping), behind the lower topgallant sail. The fifth mast or jigger mast was shorter and made of a single pole.

The bark carried twenty square sails

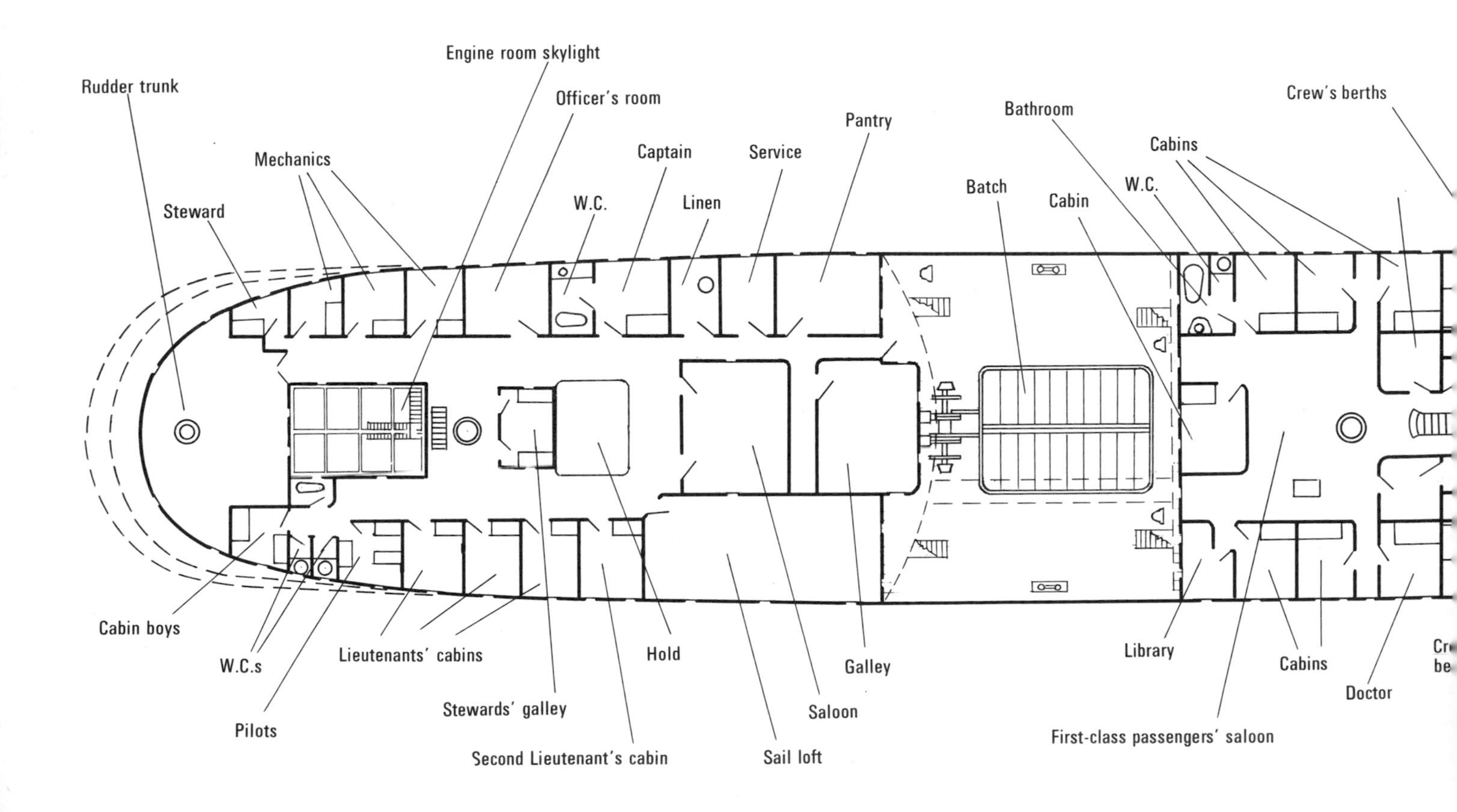

Only three other sailing ships beside the *France II* had a gross tonnage of over 5,000 tons: the German five-masted bark *R.C. Rickmers* (right), the *Preussen*, and the American seven-masted schooner *Thomas W. Lawson* (right, below). The *Thomas W. Lawson* was the only seven-masted sailing ship ever built.

and twelve fore-and-aft sails totalling 6,350 square metres. The weight of the bare masts and yards was 258 tonnes, and the weight of the rigging, including its 871 blocks, was another 198 tonnes. If the running rigging had been put end to end it would have covered a distance of thirty miles (48,198 m). In earlier times all the braces for turning the yards would have been operated by gangs of seamen hauling the tackle falls along the deck but in the big steel ships the work was often eased by brace winches. The *France II* was perhaps the only ship to have a brace winch for every yard, including the topgallants, and four men only could brace at one time all five yards of a mast. There were also winches for the halyards, sheets and clewlines.

The *France II* had a 'three-island' type hull, the main deck being mostly covered by upper decks which extended from side to side: the foc'sle deck, the midship deck and the poop deck. The 'wells' between these structures, where the main deck was exposed to the sky,

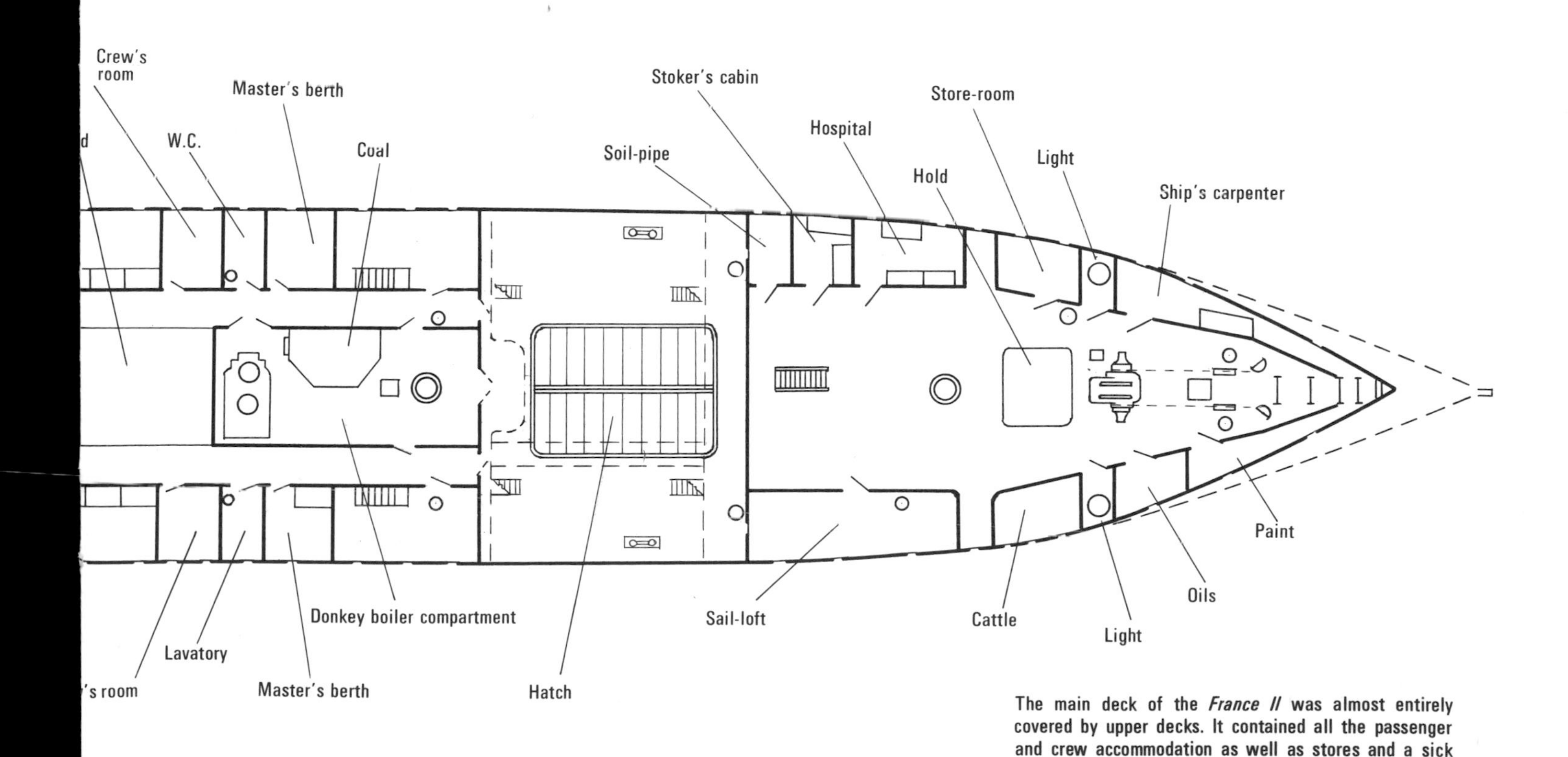

The main deck of the *France II* was almost entirely covered by upper decks. It contained all the passenger and crew accommodation as well as stores and a sick bay. The six first-class passenger cabins were exceptionally large (12sq. m) and were luxuriously furnished.

were quite small and catwalks spanned them so that it was possible to walk from one end of the ship to the other without having to descend to the main deck. All the masts and their gear were located on the islands and there was no need to work on the main deck. This was a safety feature as so many men were swept overboard from the low and exposed main decks of traditional design, particularly on the large steel ships which crashed into the seas instead of riding over them like the older, smaller wooden ships.

The foc'sle deck carried the bowsprit (a steel spar in one piece), No. 1 hatch and the fore mast. The space below it, at main deck level, housed stores and sails, the powered windlass, the greasers' cabins, cattle and livestock pens and coops, and the crew's sick bay, close to the warmth—and the smells—of the manger. No. 2 hatch was located on the fore well-deck.

The midship deck carried the main mast, No. 3 hatch, a passengers' lounge deckhouse and the middle mast. At main deck level, below this island were the donkey engine compartment, the bosun's and crew's quarters and the passengers' accommodation. The *France II* had six first class cabins (and a doctor's cabin) opening on to a spacious and luxurious saloon with a double staircase leading to the passengers' deckhouse. The passenger cabins were unusually large—twelve square metres—and were furnished with a brass bedstead, a bedside table, a double-fronted wardrobe, a chest of drawers,

a settee, a desk and a sink with running hot and cold water. They had two portholes each and three electric lamps. The saloon had a piano, comfortable armchairs and sofas and was decorated with a profusion of potted plants. There was also a library, a photographical darkroom, a bathroom equipped for hydrotherapy, a laundry and a sick bay.

The dining saloon was aft, under the poop deck and could seat twenty-five people. Breakfast consisted of toast and freshly baked *petits pains* and *croissants* with coffee, cocoa or tea. Lunch was a five-course meal (with French pastries twice a week); a light tea was served and the dinner also had five courses. Both main meals included wines, coffee or tea and *digestifs*—cognac or rum. The meats were varied and came either from the livestock pens and coops or from the large reefer (refrigerated) hold. Most of the vegetables were also fresh.

The ship carried more lifeboats than required for the full complement of crew and passengers, and one of them, with an inboard engine, was also intended for excursions in New Caledonia. The standards were as high, if not higher, than on any of the luxury liners. The *clientèle* was not expected to be business travellers or emigrants but wealthy people taking a break, perhaps on the advice of their doctor—if he was not aware of the menus...

No. 4 hatch was on the after well deck. The poop deck carried the mizzen mast, a deckhouse for the steering engine, with an open air bridge and wings above it, No. 5 hatch, the jigger

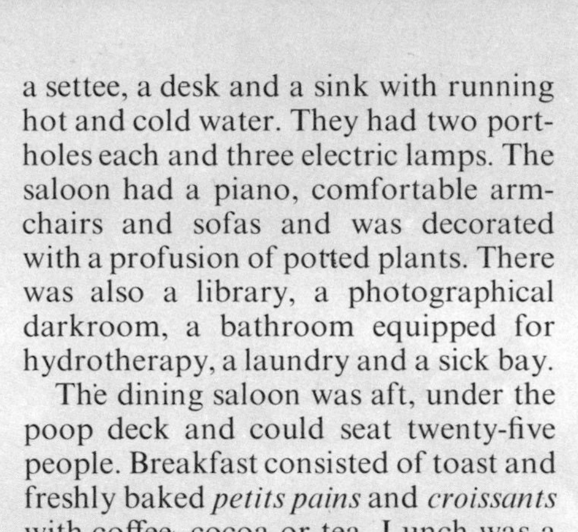

The five-masted bark *France II* was the largest sailing ship ever built—and one of the best sailers. She carried twenty square sails and twelve fore-and-aft sails and although at first she also had a diesel engine, this proved unreliable and she travelled successfully with sail alone. She was primarily a cargo vessel but also carried passengers on occasion: her standards were as high as any of the luxury liners.

The *Preussen* (5,081 tons gross) was launched in 1902. She was unique: a five-masted full rigged ship, with square sails on all her masts.

Below: The *France II* sailed on her maiden voyage in 1913. She survived the war and continued working as a cargo vessel until 1922, when she was wrecked on a coral reef. Her greatest daily run, under sail alone, was 420 miles.

mast, the engine room skylight and the emergency wheelhouse above the rudder. The passengers' dining saloon and the officers' quarters were located at main deck level below this island.

Below the main deck level was the hold, which was divided into sixteen watertight compartments. Steam-driven pumps could cope with large holings; the biggest pump had a capacity of 300 tonnes per hour. The aftermost compartment was not a cargo hold but an engine room: the *France II* was a twin-screw auxiliary bark with two 900 h.p. diesel engines capable of driving her at 10 knots, with the screws turning at 240 r.p.m. The fuel tanks (530 m^3) ensured an autonomy of 11,000 miles (equivalent to two return journeys from Europe to North America) or, in terms of time, an endurance of forty-seven days under power alone. The owners had planned it so that a combination of wind and power would allow an eighty-day journey to New Caledonia, faster than contemporary steam freighters could manage. Diesel engines were not reliable in those days and in 1919 the *France*'s engines were taken out and she became a pure sailer. Without the drag of her propellers when working under sail alone, she made up for the time lost in calms: her passages were just as good without her engines. She naturally kept her several ancillary power plants for the capstans and windlass, cargo-handling gear, pumps and generator (she had a radio and 1,650 electric bulbs). Another modern aspect of the bark was her water ballast tanks which allowed her to sail with her holds empty without the trouble and expense of loading stones for stability-giving ballast. The holds had a capacity of 11,600 m^3.

The *France II* had a crew of forty-five: the master, three mates, an engineer, and his mate, a radio operator, a doctor (only present when there were passengers), a bosun and his mate, a carpenter, twenty-four seamen, a victualling agent, a cook, a baker, two stewards and two boys.

The *France II* sailed on her maiden voyage in late 1913. She went to Glasgow to load coal for Nouméa in New Caledonia where she picked up nickel ore for the return journey. She returned by way of Cape Horn, where she encountered many icebergs and in the South Atlantic, between 50° and 44° latitude, she met with a severe storm which blew out all her sails. The outward bound journey had taken 92 days, the return took 102. She tied up at Rothesay Dock, Glasgow, on 3 August 1914, a few days before the outbreak of the war.

During the war she was armed with two 90 mm guns for self defence and she managed to escape the sad fate of so many square riggers sunk by submarines, raiders or mines. Her narrowest escapes were when she dodged a submarine after being shelled; when she had a fire in the after peak between the ammunition magazine and a hold full of petrol in jerrycans; and when her ballast shifted in a hurricane, throwing her on her beam ends.

At the end of 1916 she was sold by the Société des Navires Mixtes and was managed, with more or less the same crew, by the Compagnie Française de Marine et de Commerce. After her sale she tramped with mixed cargoes to South America and Australia as well as to New Caledonia for nickel. Dakar (Senegal) was then her home port, to avoid the submarine zones closer to Europe. She returned to France in 1919, where she discarded her engines and screws and in 1921, on a journey from New Zealand to London she had runs of over 400 miles a day for three days. Her greatest daily run was 420 miles and she accomplished the complete journey in only 90 days.

On her next voyage, during the night of 11–12 July 1922, she was becalmed off the coast of New Caledonia and, without engines, she drifted helplessly on a coral reef. She could have been salvaged but the cost was too high in that period of slumping freights and she was broken up on the spot.

The Luxury Liners: RMS Queen Mary

In the late 1920s the British Cunard Steamship Company, which had once held the lion's share of the North Atlantic passenger trade, was losing ground to foreign competition. Their three major units, the *Mauretania, Aquitania* and *Berengaria* were all due for replacement and in 1926 the company directors met to discuss plans for the future. Officially they did not set out to build the largest and fastest liners in the world but somehow their solution for the most economical ratio of turnover (i.e. speed) and payload (passenger numbers, i.e. size) called for the building of two liners larger and faster than any previous ship. The two new Royal Mail Ships (RMS) the *Queen Mary* and the *Queen Elizabeth* were to represent the high point in the development of transatlantic liners.

The size of the proposed liners created a major problem: no underwriters were willing to take the enormous insurance risk. This difficulty was only overcome with help from the British government which passed the Cunard (Insurance) Act in December 1930, allowing the State to provide a £1,500,000 coverage —leaving a £2,700,000 balance to be underwritten on the private market. It was also necessary to build a 300 m pier terminal in New York and a special dry-dock in Southampton.

The keel of the first unit was laid down in December 1930 at the yard of John Brown and Company of Clydebank near Glasgow in Scotland, under the yard number 534. But the world economic recession was spreading to Britain and by December 1931 there was no money for further work. Building of the half-completed hull, which had already cost £1,500,000, came to a halt.

The *Britannia*, Cunard's first passenger liner, was built in 1840. It was with compact ships like this that Brunel's money-losing *Great Eastern* attempted unsuccessfully to compete for transatlantic passengers.

However, the building of such a large ship creates a lot of work, from shipyard and engineering companies to upholsterers and tableware manufacturers. When work stopped, 3,500 yard workers and 10,000 workers in subcontracting firms were unemployed. This was a strong argument for obtaining government help and on 27 March 1934 the North Atlantic Shipping (Advances) Act provided Cunard with a loan of £9,500,000 to complete the work, after an interruption of more than two years.

The launching was held on the spring tide of 26 September 1934 in the presence of King George V, Queen Mary and more than 200,000 spectators. The nameboard of Hull 534 was unveiled and the Queen after whom she had been named smashed a bottle of Australian wine on the bows.

The name *Queen Mary* was in fact the result of a misunderstanding: all previous Cunard liners had names ending

Left: The *Queen Mary* was built at the yard of John Brown and Company of Clydebank. She provided work for thousands of men in a period of economic recession and a Government loan was made to enable her to be completed.

Below: She was so much larger than other ships of her time that a special dry dock had to be built at Southampton, and a new terminal at New York. Here she towers over the dockside sheds.

in *-ia* and the name proposed for the new liner was *Victoria*. However this choice needed the royal assent and King George was asked if he would consent to the use of the name of the most illustrious and remarkable woman who had ever been Queen of England.

'That is the greatest compliment that has ever been made to me or my wife,' he replied. 'I will ask her permission when I get home.'

The *Queen Mary* could carry 711 passengers in first class, 680 in cabin (second) class and 577 in tourist (third) class, plus 1,285 officers and crew. The crew included armies of cooks, stewards, bellboys, barmen, bakers, butchers, an orchestra, entertainers, pursers, gymnastic teachers, hairdressers, manicurists, masseurs, shopkeepers, a librarian, detectives, telephone operators, printers, kindergarten nurses, medical staff . . . it was a real town afloat.

There were special cabins for the private servants of first-class passengers and some staterooms had facilities for cooking and serving meals privately. There were two Turkish baths, more than a dozen bars, a swimming pool, a shopping arcade, Catholic and Protestant chapels and a synagogue. There were sixteen levels from the hold to the flying bridge. The main dining room was big enough to hold the first Cunarder, the *Britannia* of 1840, with Columbus's *Santa Maria, Pinta* and *Niña* alongside.

The design and decoration of the passenger areas was typical of the 1930s but in a conservative way, similar to that of Palace hotels of the same period: the passengers were not the type to appreciate *avant-garde* innovations. The style has been described as mild but expensive vulgarity; it did not have the opulence of the Edwardian era but it did have a solid quality which disappeared with the advent of plastic and synthetic materials.

This floating city was housed in a hull of 82,070 tonnes divided by eighteen watertight bulkheads and with a length of 310 m, a beam of 36·2 m and a draught of 12 m. The ship was pushed at 30 knots by four giant screws powered by five sets of boilers driving sixteen single-reduction geared steam turbines. Until the *Queen Elizabeth* was launched in 1940 the *Queen Mary* was the largest ship in the world.

On 27 May 1936 she sailed on her maiden voyage with 1,948 hand-picked passengers. The crossing was a success —and a great social event—and nobody had the bad taste to admit that there were terrible teething problems. It was literally a shakedown cruise. The ship rolled abominably and there were horrible vibrations in the stern; soot from ill-designed stacks covered the decks. A few months later the liner went in for a 'routine maintenance' dry-docking. The great lounge, the smoking room and some first-class staterooms were stripped down to make structural modifications to stiffen the hull, and the propellers were replaced by some of a better design.

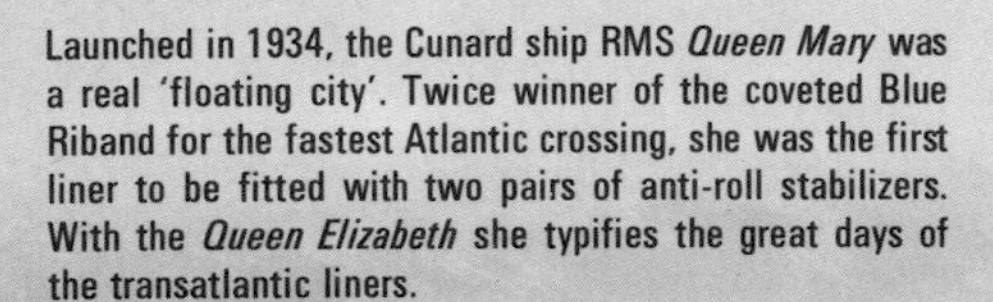

Launched in 1934, the Cunard ship RMS *Queen Mary* was a real 'floating city'. Twice winner of the coveted Blue Riband for the fastest Atlantic crossing, she was the first liner to be fitted with two pairs of anti-roll stabilizers. With the *Queen Elizabeth* she typifies the great days of the transatlantic liners.

In August 1936 the *Queen Mary* won the Blue Riband (the distinction for the fastest Atlantic crossing) from the Norddeutscher Lloyd's *Bremen,* with a time of 3 days 23 hours 57 minutes from Ambrose Light to Bishop's Rock. She lost it the following year to the Compagnie Générale Transatlantique's *Normandie* but won it back in August 1938 with a time for the same run of 3 days 20 hours and 40 minutes.

World War II broke out on 3 September 1939 as the *Queen Mary* was reaching New York. All further crossings were cancelled and she stayed at her New York pier where she was joined by the hastily launched and completed *Queen Elizabeth.* The *Queen Mary,* painted naval-grey, left New York on 21 March 1940 for Sydney where she arrived on 17 April to be converted to accommodate 5,500 troops. For the remainder of that year and throughout 1941, along with the *Queen Elizabeth, Aquitania, Mauretania* and three other non-Cunard liners, she ferried Australian troops up the Red Sea to Suez to fight in North Africa.

When Japan joined the war in December 1941, Australia needed troops for home defence instead of exporting them and the *Queen Mary* ferried American G.I.s from New York to Australia. After that the two *Queens* returned to the North Atlantic run, carrying American and Canadian troops to Belfast or to the Clyde, returning with military personnel for special training in the States and prisoners-of-war for the cotton fields of Alabama or the Canadian camps.

The liners were logistically and strategically administered by the United States and operated by Cunard personnel paid by the British government. Standee bunks—six-tiered folding pipe cots suspended by chains—were fitted throughout the ships, even in the drained swimming pools. By 'hot-bunking' in two or even three shifts, some 10,000 troops could be carried on each journey. In summer, hammocks were slung on

the upper decks allowing 5,000 more troops to be carried: these hammocks were considered first-class accommodation and the men took turns for the privilege of sleeping in them, rather than in the stuffy bunks below decks.

The *Queens* were unescorted during their crossings as they were faster than any hostile craft, but their passage time was lengthened by the need to zig-zag to confuse any lurking U-boat. In fact they never even made contact with an enemy submarine though they were prime strategic targets especially on the three occasions when Winston Churchill made crossings on the *Queen Mary* for summit talks with President Roosevelt.

When the liners came within a hundred miles of Ireland they were met by a screen of escorters and cruisers for the last leg of the journey. It was on such an occasion, on 18 May 1945, that the zig-zagging *Queen Mary* ran down and cut in two the 4,267 tonne, 139 m, anti-aircraft cruiser HMS *Curacao*. Three-hundred and thirty-eight men out of a complement of 439 perished but the liner kept steaming on, under orders not to stop on any account. The damage to the *Queen Mary's* bow was negligible and was not repaired until she had returned to New York.

After the war, from February to May 1946, the *Queen Mary* was used to transport to America some 9,118 European wives of American soldiers (the 'G.I. brides') and their 3,768 children. In September 1946 she finally returned to Southampton for a major clean-up and refit. She was repainted in the Cunard peacetime livery and a proper cinema hall, which had not existed in the original layout, was installed. She resumed regular passenger services across the Atlantic on 31 July 1947.

In 1952 the *Queen Mary* lost the Blue Riband to the brand new American liner *United States* but she remained the travelling public's favourite. The peak year for transoceanic surface passenger numbers was 1957 but already Super Constellation airliners were attracting an appreciable percentage of travellers. From then on, although the overall number of travellers increased, fewer and fewer chose the sea route and the appearance in the early sixties of non-stop jets, the Boeing 707s and the DC8s spelled the end of an era. The *Queens* also had to face competition from the new prestige liner *France* which surpassed the *Queen Elizabeth* in length and was put into service in 1962.

With the building of the *Queen Elizabeth 2* (QE2) in 1968, the old *Queens* were doomed. The *Queen Elizabeth* was sold to a Chinese businessman and was brought to Hong Kong where she was totally destroyed by fire. The *Queen Mary* was bought for $3,400,000 by the city of Long Beach, California. The retirement of the *Queens* heralded the wholesale dispersal of the liner fleets in the late 60s and early 70s and in summer a lonely *QE2* now plies the passenger-deserted lanes of the North Atlantic—but for how much longer?

The last voyage of the *Queen Mary* was a nostalgic 39-day cruise to Long Beach by way of Cape Horn (she was too large for the Panama Canal) with 1,200 passengers who paid from £395 to £3,200 each. It was truly the end of an epoch and the beginning of a legend when the three-funnelled *Queen Mary* tied up for the last time at her dock in Long Beach harbour on 10 December 1967.

She was converted at a cost of more than $40,000,000 into a permanently moored entertainment and convention centre with a hotel, bars, restaurants, convention halls, Jacques Cousteau aquarium and a Museum of the Sea. At first she did very well in her new role but now that the novelty has worn off, and with the present economic climate, her financial security is in doubt.

Inside, the *Queen Mary* was a mass of accommodation and machinery. Steam produced by her five massive boilers drove sixteen single-reduction geared steam turbines which turned four screws. She was equipped to carry over 3,000 passengers and crew in considerable comfort, and had bars, shops, chapels and a Turkish bath as well as the usual dining-rooms and lounges. During the war as many as 5,000 troops were transported, crammed into bunks and hammocks wherever there was space.

The cabin observation lounge and cocktail bar (right) and the corner of the cabin main lounge (below). Decorated in typical 1930s style, the *Queen Mary* combined solid comfort with a sense of luxury.

The *Queen Mary* was for many years the travelling public's favourite ship. She won the Blue Riband for the first time in 1936 and although she lost it in 1937 to the French *Normandie* (right), she regained it in 1938 with a time of 3 days, 20 hours and 40 minutes.

Pocket Battleships: KMS Admiral Graf Spee

When Germany started to rebuild her fleet after the first World War, she was severely limited by the Treaty of Versailles, signed on 28 June 1919. This allowed her to retain only eight obsolete pre-*Dreadnaught* battleships of the *Braunschweig* and *Deutschland* classes. They could only be replaced twenty years after their launching date and replacements could not be larger than 10,000 tonnes, nor could they carry guns heavier than 28 cm. In fact the *Braunschweig,* launched in 1902, was nearly due for replacement but Germany was financially crippled and no new plans were drawn up before 1926.

The problem was to draw the most powerful ship allowed within the letter of the Versailles treaty: the solution was a new class of warships, armoured cruisers with a 28 cm battleship-calibre main battery, which were designed to be 'stronger than anything faster and faster than anything stronger'. Three of these ships, which were nicknamed 'pocket battleships', were built. The best remembered is the KM (Kriegsmarine) *Admiral Graf Spee* which was involved in the River Plate battle of 1939.

Plans were originally made for four ships of this class, known as *Panzerschiffe* (armoured ships) A to D. They were designed for great autonomy and endurance as they were to be usable as raiders—staying at sea for long periods far from supply bases, to harass enemy shipping. To make this possible, they were equipped with diesel engines, although these were then untried on such large vessels. Diesel engines presented no advantage of space and weight over contemporary steam turbine engines but they used considerably less fuel.

The hull weight was reduced by fifteen percent by using electric-arc welded plates instead of rivets—also a first-time technique for large ships. The armour was designed to withstand heavy-cruiser fire (20 cm shells) since this kind of cruiser would be faster than the new *Panzerschiffe*; anything more powerful afloat could be avoided by superior speed. The only exceptions were three British battlecruisers, the *Renown*, the *Repulse* and the *Hood,* which were both faster and more powerful. However, in 1926 Britain was not considered as a potential enemy. France, the country most directly threatened by a rebirth of German naval power, reacted by building two battleships, the *Dunkerque* and the *Strasbourg,* with a speed of 29·5 knots, a displacement of 26,925 tonnes and a main battery of eight 33 cm guns.

The keel of *Panzerschiff* A was laid down on 5 February 1929 at the

The pocket battleship *Admiral Graf Spee* was the third ship of the Panzerschiffe class to be built. She was designed for great autonomy and endurance, with diesel engines, light but strong electric-arc welded plates instead of rivets and effective armour, some 60 to 80 mm thick. Her combination of speed and strength was designed to be 'stronger than anything faster and faster than anything stronger'.

Deutsche Werke at Kiel and this ship, named the *Deutschland*, was launched on 19 May 1931. Work on *Panzerschiff* B began on 25 June 1931 at the Wilhelmshaven dockyard; she was christened *Admiral Scheer* and launched on 1 April 1933, the day the *Deutschland* was commissioned. The *Admiral Scheer* was in turn commissioned on 12 November 1934. The *Deutschland*, first completed of the pocket battleships, measured only nominally 10,000 tonnes: her real standard displacement (without fuel and stores) was 11,888 tonnes and her full load displacement was as much as 16,155 tonnes. *Panzerschiff* C was laid down on 1 October 1932 at Wilhelmshaven and was launched as the *Admiral Graf Spee* on 30 June 1934 and commissioned on 6 January 1936.

The original *Panzerschiff* D of the pocket battleship class was shelved and instead, two new ships were drawn to a different and more powerful design, as the Anglo-German naval agreement of 1935 made it legal to bypass the restrictions of the Treaty of Versailles. These two battleships also became famous, as the *Gneisenau* and the *Scharnhorst*. Two even bigger, 'capital' battleships were built, the *Bismarck* and the *Tirpitz*.

The keel of Panzerschiffe C was laid down on 1 October 1932 and, as the *Admiral Graf Spee*, she was launched on 30 June 1934, at Wilhelmshaven. She had more extensive armour plating than her sister ships, an armoured deck, anti-torpedo bulge and many internal bulkheads to prevent flooding if she were hit.

The KM *Admiral Graf Spee* and KM *Admiral Scheer* were popularly referred to in the German Navy as the *Graf Spee* and the *Scheer* and this is what they will be called here. The *Graf Spee* measured 194·5 m in length, 22·8 m beam and 7·1 m draught; her standard displacement was 12,294 tonnes. Her main armament consisted of six 28 cm guns in two triple turrets with 85 to 140 mm armour plate. These quick-firing guns fired 304 kg shells with a maximum range of 36,000 m. The rest of her armament consisted of eight 15 cm individually-mounted guns with armoured shields, six 10·5 cm and eight 3·7 cm anti-aircraft (AA) guns and eight 53·3 cm torpedo tubes. She also carried an aircraft catapult and two Heinkel-60 spotter planes which were replaced at the beginning of World War II by an Arado-196 seaplane.

The same MAN (Maschinenfabrik Augsburg-Nürnberg) diesel engines that had been specified for the *Deutschland* and the *Scheer* were fitted in the *Graf Spee*. These were double-acting two-stroke 9-cylinder engines placed in two banks of four, each bank driving a propeller shaft. The engines turned at 450 r.p.m. and had Vulcan gear sets which would reduce this to 250 r.p.m. The total power was 56,000 h.p. and the nominal speed was 26 knots although the ship reached 28·5 knots at her speed trials, when she was probably not fully loaded. The operational range was 20,000 miles at a cruising speed of 18 knots, nearly the circumference of the globe and about three times the range of equivalent steam-turbine ships. The diesel engines had other advantages over steam engines: there was no smoke to betray the ship's presence, no steam-hazard during action and a much faster rate of acceleration.

The *Graf Spee* carried a more extensive armour plating than her earlier sisterships. The hull plating was 60 to 80 mm thick, and an armoured deck, an anti-torpedo bulge and many internal bulkheads were also fitted.

In 1938 the *Graf Spee* was the first German ship to be fitted with radar. Its initial range was only 2·7 nautical miles but it was improved to 7·1 before the war. This radar could only give the range: its direction resolution was very poor so the instrument was unsuitable for gunnery control.

The future wartime crew was to consist of 44 officers and 1,080 men, including the radio and intelligence personnel, the plane crews and some merchant navy Naval Reserve officers to take command of prizes.

All three pocket battleships were sent to cruise off Spain during the Spanish Civil War, as part of the International Maritime Non-Intervention Control. After the conclusion of that war even darker clouds were building over Europe and in late August 1939, the *Deutschland* was sent to cruise in the North Atlantic and the *Graf Spee* in the South Atlantic. The *Scheer* was held back for dockyard maintenance.

On 26 September 1939, as the *Graf Spee* was south-west of the Canaries, the order to start operations was received from the German Admiralty: the war had begun.

Official naval strategy was to destroy enemy merchant shipping while avoiding engagement with enemy forces, even if they were inferior. This was because in World War I such engagements, even when successful, had led to the premature curtailment of operations. As we shall see, this pattern was repeated in the *Graf Spee*'s eventual action against

The *Deutschland* (above) and the *Admiral Scheer* (below) were the first of the pocket battleships. Built to meet the limitations of the Treaty of Versailles, which ended the First World War, they formed a new class of warships—armoured cruisers with a powerful 28-cm main battery.

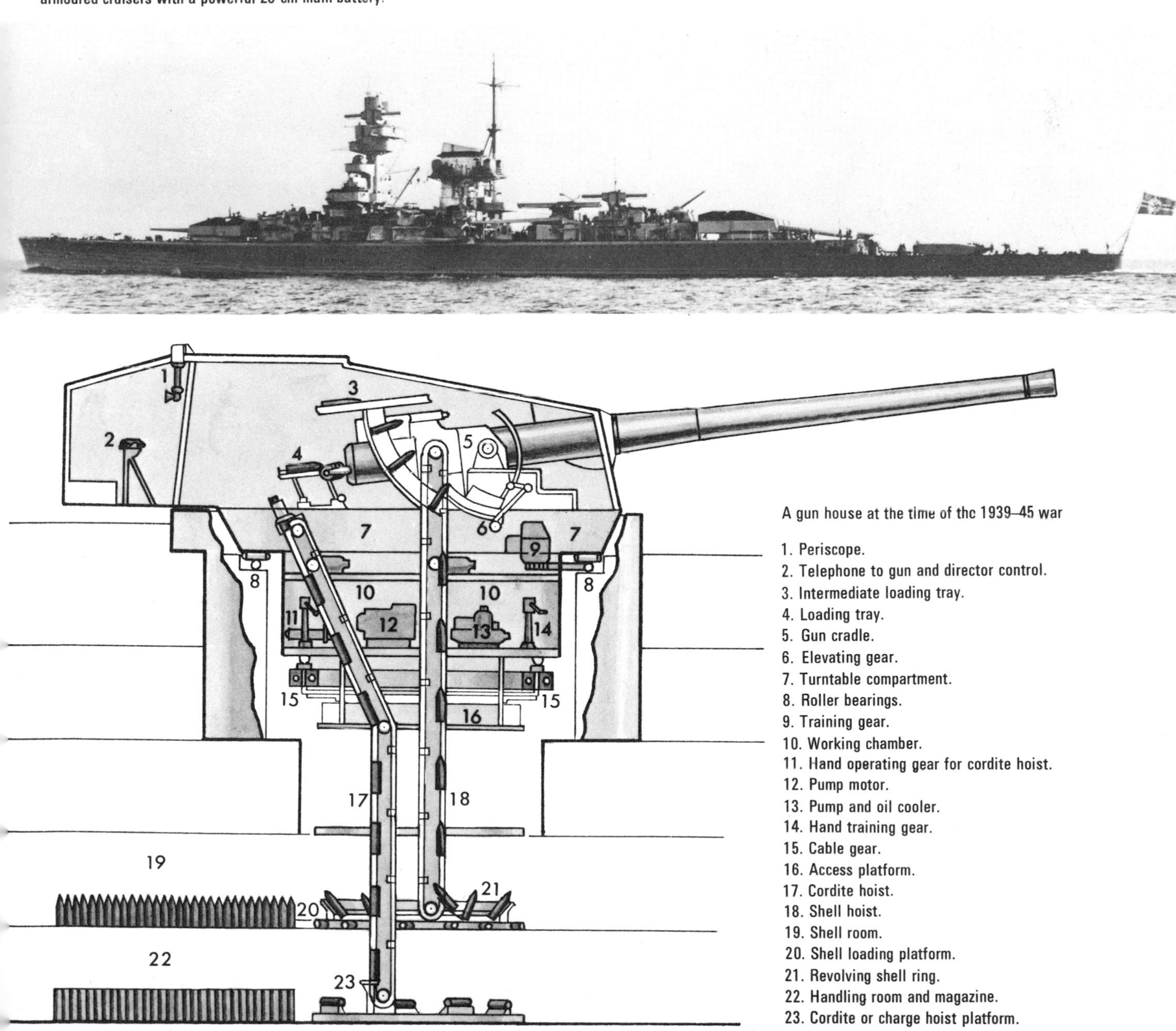

A gun house at the time of the 1939–45 war

1. Periscope.
2. Telephone to gun and director control.
3. Intermediate loading tray.
4. Loading tray.
5. Gun cradle.
6. Elevating gear.
7. Turntable compartment.
8. Roller bearings.
9. Training gear.
10. Working chamber.
11. Hand operating gear for cordite hoist.
12. Pump motor.
13. Pump and oil cooler.
14. Hand training gear.
15. Cable gear.
16. Access platform.
17. Cordite hoist.
18. Shell hoist.
19. Shell room.
20. Shell loading platform.
21. Revolving shell ring.
22. Handling room and magazine.
23. Cordite or charge hoist platform.

Left and below: The *Graf Spee* had an operational range of 20,000 miles and was the first German ship to be fitted with radar. She also carried eight 15cm individually mounted guns, anti-aircraft guns and torpedo tubes. Her strategic purpose at the outbreak of war was to destroy merchant shipping without engaging enemy forces.

a force of lesser warships. On the other hand one cannot help thinking that the heavy armour carried by the pocket battleships was wasted if they had to limit themselves to actions against unprotected merchantmen.

The *Graf Spee*'s first victim was the British SS *Clement*. She was able to send out the alarm to warn other ships and when her crew, landing safely from boats in Brazil, confirmed the attacker's identity, the British Admiralty decided to retain in the area four destroyers which were due to join the Home Fleet.

It was to the *Graf Spee*'s advantage to remain unrecognized until the last moment so that an enemy ship would not have time to give her position or to raise the alarm. *Kapitän zur See* Hans Langsdorff, the forty-five year old captain of the *Graf Spee* modified his ship's appearance by a skilful application of paint patterns to make the central tower look like a tripod mast. Seen bows-on, from a distance, she looked like a French ship. On 5 October, off Cape Verde, the *Graf Spee* came within a mile of the SS *Newton Beach* before swinging to broadside-on and being identified. The *Newton Beach* had only time to send a short SOS without the RRR 'enemy ship' code so that the only ship to pick it up, HMS *Cumberland*, did not break her own radio silence to raise the alarm. The German attack was also so swift that they were able to seize secret British shipping instructions from the radio room. The captured ship was kept as a prison ship to hold the crews of future prizes.

The next prize, the SS *Ashlea* was also captured by surprise and deception on 7 October, without having time to send any call for help. Her crew was transferred to the *Newton Beach* and she was sunk. However, the *Newton Beach* was slow and the following day Langsdorff transferred all the prisoners to his own ship and scuttled her in turn. On 10 October a fourth ship, the SS *Huntsman*, was captured.

A rendezvous with the *Graf Spee*'s supply vessel the Altmark (which was disguised as a Norwegian merchantman) was arranged for 15 October and Langsdorff's mimicry painting was so effective that the *Altmark*'s captain had a bad fright when the *Graf Spee* hove into sight. By this time protected convoys were being formed in the Atlantic and as fighting was to be avoided, the *Graf Spee* was sent to the Indian Ocean. On her way, off Walvis Bay, she sunk the MV *Trevanion* and she narrowly escaped being intercepted by the aircraft carrier HMS *Renown* and the French battleship *Strasbourg*. On 15 November, when the *Graf Spee* was off the Mozambique coast, she sunk the tanker *Africa Shell*, purposely allowing the alarm to be given in order to raise panic across the Indian Ocean. She returned to the Atlantic with a dummy gun turret fitted to imitate the silhouette of a British cruiser.

By now the *Graf Spee*'s engines were long overdue for a dockyard overhaul and for the homeward-bound cruise Langsdorff decided not to avoid engaging enemy ships of inferior fire power, should he meet any. On his way across the South Atlantic he intercepted and sunk the tanker *Doric Star* and the freighter *Tairoa* before meeting again with the *Altmark* to transfer some prisoners. Both the last captures managed to radio their position and from this the British Admiralty wrongly concluded that the *Graf Spee* would be operating off the River Plate. HMS *Ajax*

(Commodore Harwood's flagship), HMNZS *Achilles* and HMS *Exeter* were sent to patrol the area. The *Ajax* was a 1935-built *Leander* class cruiser with a greater speed than the *Graf Spee* but with a main battery of only 15 cm. The *Achilles,* the prototype of her own class, had a similar fire power. The *Exeter,* built in the late twenties, was virtually unarmoured but she had 20 cm guns. All three ships were outgunned by the *Graf Spee*'s 28 cm artillery.

Meanwhile the German ship sunk her last prize, the freighter *Streonshalh*. On board, Langsdorff found documents that made him steam towards the River Plate—where he had no intention of going before. The *Graf Spee* had now sunk nine ships totalling over 50,000 tonnes.

At dawn on 13 December the *Graf Spee* made visual contact with the British squadron. At 0617, as she opened fire, the British ships split up to attack her from different sides—for she had only two turrets of superior fire power. She concentrated her fire on the *Exeter* which received three direct hits within the first half hour. The two light cruisers, feared mainly for their torpedoes, obliged the *Graf Spee* to divert some of her fire and to alter her course repeatedly under a smoke screen. The *Exeter,* with only one barrel left and with a list to port, broke off the engagement at 0715 and the *Ajax* suffered several 28 cm hits, one of which knocked out both after turrets. With only three serviceable guns left and eighty percent of his ammunition used, Harwood, too, broke off the action. However, the *Graf Spee* had also suffered severe damage, particularly a hit in the bows which made her unseaworthy for the intended voyage home; she also had 36 men killed and 59 wounded. Captain Langsdorff decided to call at the neutral harbour of Montevideo for emergency repairs; he was shadowed all the way there by the light cruisers, keeping a respectful distance.

The *Graf Spee* arrived in harbour on the 14th but obtained only a 72 hour permission to stay from the Uruguayan authorities. (Under international law, a warship that is judged seaworthy—though not necessarily fit for battle—may be compelled to leave a neutral harbour.) The only warship the British could summon up at such short notice was HMS *Cumberland* and they delayed the *Graf Spee*'s departure for a while longer by arranging for an allied freighter to leave Montevideo on the 16th: under the laws on neutrality, the Germans could not put to sea within twenty-four hours of an enemy vessel.

Langsdorff had had no time to carry out major repairs so, expecting to meet a superior force on his way out and knowing that he was short of ammunition, he decided to scuttle his ship. At 1820 on 17 October 1939, the *Graf Spee* sailed out from Montevideo on her last voyage with only forty-one men aboard. The rest of the crew followed in the German freighter *Tacoma.* The *Graf Spee* anchored in international waters, her skeleton crew transferred to the *Tacoma* and she was blown up at sunset.

The *Tacoma* landed the German sailors in Buenos Aires where they were interned for the rest of the war. In the night of 20–1 December, Hans Langsdorff dressed himself in full uniform, knelt on his ship's battle ensign and shot himself, courageously forestalling any allegations that he had avoided further action through cowardice.

The fates of other ships mentioned in this chapter deserve to be mentioned. In 1941 the *Ajax* was sent to the Mediterranean, where she sunk several Italian ships and was involved in the battle of Matapan and in a diversion to the battle of Taranto. She survived the war and was scrapped in 1949. The *Achilles* was transferred in 1948 to the Indian Navy and, renamed *Delhi,* she is still in commission as a training cruiser. The *Exeter* was not so fortunate—she was involved in the Japanese naval invasion of the Dutch East Indies and suffered severe damage on 27 February 1942 during the Java Sea battle. As she was limping towards Australia on 1 March she met with a Japanese squadron and was sunk. On the German side, the *Altmark* was boarded in a Norwegian fjord on 16 February 1940 by the destroyer HMS *Cossack*; the *Scheer* was destroyed by the RAF while in dry dock at Kiel, on 9 April 1945 and on 16 April the *Deutschland* (by then renamed *Lutzow* to avoid damage to morale should she be lost) was also sunk by the RAF near Swinemünde.

Following her engagement with the British Squadron—*Ajax, Achilles* and *Exeter*—the *Graf Spee* was compelled to flee to the neutral harbour of Montevideo. As sufficient time was not available to carry out the necessary major repairs, she was blown up by her captain at sunset on 17 October 1939.

The Liberty Ships

It is no accident that this is the only chapter to be named after a class of ships instead of after an individual ship: to have chosen a particular Liberty ship would have missed their main point—that they were mass produced to meet an urgent need for economical merchant tonnage. The Liberty ships were all built to the same plan for speed of production, and they played a vital role during World War II as emergency strategic transports. Between 1941 and 1945 the United States built no fewer than 2,710.

The Liberty ship was first conceived in Britain when the British Admiralty decided to simplify the plans of a tramp steamer, the *Dorington Court,* as part of a programme for the building of emergency wartime merchant ships. The first such ship was the *Empire Liberty* built, like the *Dorington Court,* at the Sunderland yard of J. L. Thompson and Sons. But the British had to go to the United States to order the quantities they needed and the Americans simplified the plans further, proposing a welded hull instead of a riveted one. Sixty such ships —which were all given names starting with *Ocean*—were delivered to Britain between late 1941 and November 1942. Britain also ordered 116 similar ships (partly riveted, mainly welded) from Canada; these were given names starting with *Fort.*

When the United States realized that their status was likely to change from neutral to belligerent, they decided to build their own emergency fleet and adapted the Ocean design with further simplifications. President Roosevelt, announcing the decision on the radio in February 1941, described these ships as 'dreadful looking objects' but Admiral Emory Scott Land, Chairman of the US Maritime Commission was more aware of the psychological aspects of the programme. He coined the expression 'Liberty Fleet', inspired by the names of the *Empire Liberty* and of the *Ocean Liberty,* the second Ocean launched. From this the ships became known as Liberty ships.

The adaptation of the Ocean design included fewer double-curved plates requiring skilled labour, a new rudder design and the grouping of all the crew accommodation in the deck and bridge structure, which was placed slightly aft of amidships.

The Liberty ship was a 135 m long, 38·4 m draught dry goods cargo vessel with a displacement of 10,658 tonnes. The gross tonnage (which is a measure of the space available for the cargo) was, at 7,176 tons, slightly superior to that of the *Empire Liberty* (7,157 tons). Gun platforms were fitted on the bows and on the poop and were usually armed with a 10 cm gun.

The engine room was placed under the deck structure. The engine was the same as that on the *Empire Liberty,* and on Oceans, Forts and Parks of the same class. (The Parks were Canadian-built ships identical to the Forts, but intended for Canadian use.) It was a triple expansion steam engine of 2,500 indicated horse power designed by the North Eastern Marine Engineering Company of Wallsend-on-Tyne. It powered a single screw at 72 r.p.m., giving a speed of 11 knots. The North Eastern engines were eventually produced by no less than seventeen builders in the United States and Canada and the parts were so standardized that Canadian parts could be fitted on American assemblies and vice versa, according to temporary regional surpluses and shortages.

On the *Empire Liberty,* the Oceans and some of the Forts steam was supplied (at 17·5 kg/cm^2 or 250 psi) by three single-ended cylindrical coal-fired Scotch boilers. Britain preferred the readily available coal to imported oil but the Liberties, the Parks and the remainder of the Forts were powered by two oil-fired, water-tube boilers.

Modified Liberty ships were also designed and built for special purposes: there were sixty-three Liberty tankers of 10,845 tonnes deadweight, twenty-four Liberty colliers, thirty-six boxed aircraft transports, eight Army tank carriers and six Liberty hospital ships.

The major Liberty ship builder was Henry J. Kaiser (1882–1967). As Isambard K. Brunel, who designed the *Great Eastern,* is the archetype of the Victorian engineers, so Kaiser is the original twentieth century American entrepreneur. When he entered into partnership with Todd shipyards for the Ocean building programme, he had no previous experience of shipbuilding but he had exceptional managerial and organizational talents coupled with engineering imagination. He was the proponent of the all-welded ship, of mass production techniques and of hull prefabrication. No doubt many traditional shipbuilders smiled when they heard this newcomer talking of 'front' and 'back ends' of boats, but one can imagine their expressions when Kaiser assembled and launched the Liberty ship *Robert E. Peary* in four days fifteen and a half hours.

Some 30,000 components went into

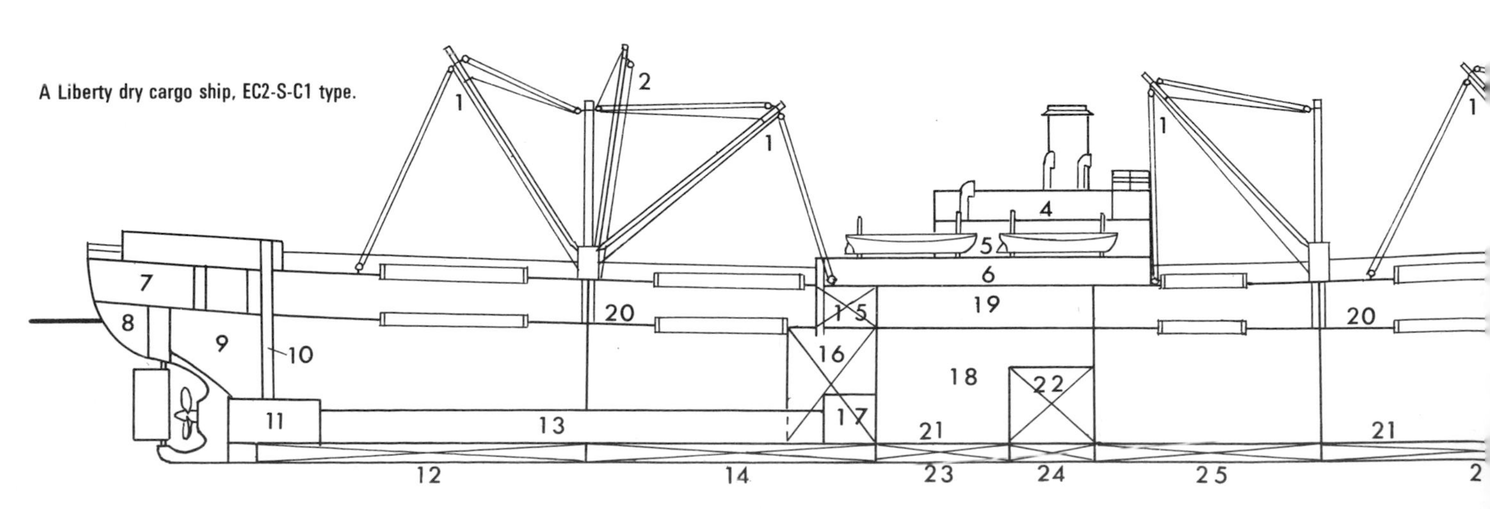

A Liberty dry cargo ship, EC2-S-C1 type.

The *Patrick Henry,* first of the Liberty ships, was launched on 27 September 1941, some ten weeks before the United States entered the war. She was built by the Bethlehem Steel Corporation and, after being finally laid up in 1958, was sold back to her makers for scrap.

Above: The *William S. Halstead* was built at the Fairfield Yard of the Bethlehem Steel Corporation in 1943 and operated by the U.S. during the war. In 1951 she was sold for commercial use and renamed first *Ocean Sea,* then *Ocean Lotte.*

Below: Victory ships were fast cargo vessels, built to an improved Liberty ship design. They were slightly larger and were powered by a steam turbine instead of a reciprocating engine. The *Pacific Victory* was built in 1945, and, now flying the Liberian flag, still operates under her original name.

the building of a Liberty ship but as much prefabrication as possible was done before the parts were sent to the slipways where the ships were assembled. The deck structure could be prefabricated complete with wiring and pipe connections and dropped in position over a completed hull. Double-bottom sections with pre-fitted piping, stern-frame assemblies and bow units were also delivered ready-made to the slips. There were factories in thirty-two US States making Liberty ship components and part assemblies.

The design of the Liberty ships may have been sound but the same could not always be said of their construction. The speed at which they were assembled and the relatively new technology of welding resulted in a fair amount of structural failures. Some Liberties broke in two, sometimes with heavy loss of life; others dropped their propeller. Nevertheless, by and large, they were tough ships. Many were awarded 'Gallant Ship' plaques, the *Samuel Parker,* for example, which spent six months in the Mediterranean in 1943 in front line duty, and the *Stephen Hopkins* which sunk the German raider *Stier*: she was, however, so severely damaged in the encounter that she, too, was sunk.

Many Liberties were lease-lended by the United States to her allies during the war. In addition to the early Oceans and Forts, Great Britain received some two hundred Liberties, all with names beginning with *Sam*—not after Uncle Sam but from the initial letters of 'Structure Aft of AMidships'. In 1947 the United States asked for the return of these ships, though some remained under the lessees' flags, and were eventually bought outright. Great Britain purchased 106 Liberties, Italy and Greece one hundred each, France seventy-five, Norway twenty-four and China eighteen. The remainder were either operated by American companies or were 'mothballed' as part of the National Defense Reserve Fleet. Those which had been lent to the Soviet Union, however, were never returned.

After the war, these economical and practical ships were very popular, especially as there was a shortage of other ships. As they grew older some were sold to the merchant navies of smaller nations—where some are still working today—while many others were scrapped, particularly in the mid and late sixties.

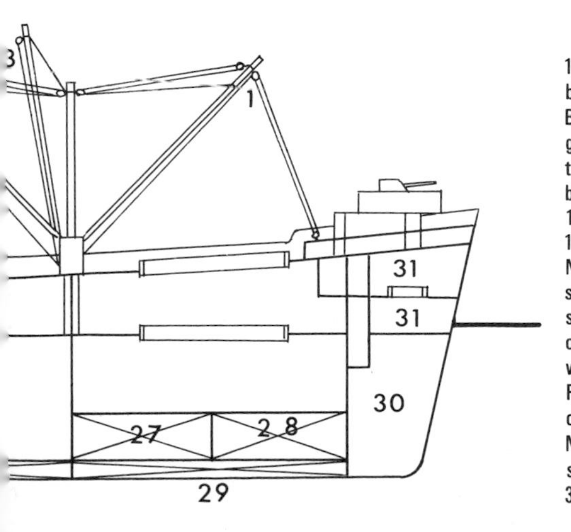

1. 5 tonne boom port and starboard. 2. 30 or 15 tonne boom centre line. 3. 50 or 30 tonne boom centre line. 4. Bridge deck. 5. Boat deck. 6. Upper deck. 7. Steering gear compartment. 8. Void space. 9. After peak. 10. Shaft tunnel escape trunk. 11 Tunnel recess. 12. Fuel oil or ballast tank No. 6 port and starboard. 13. Shaft tunnel. 14. Fuel oil or ballast tank No. 5 port and starboard. 15. Fresh water tanks port and starboard. 16. Deep tank No. 3 port and starboard. 17. Thrust recess. 18. Machinery space. 19. Refrigerated rooms and storerooms port and starboard. 20. Second deck. 21. Inner bottom. 22. Fuel oil settling tank port and starboard. 23. Reserve feed water tank No. 4. 24. Void space port and starboard. 25. Fuel oil or ballast tank No. 3 port and starboard. 26. Fuel oil or ballast tank No. 2 port and starboard. 27. Deep tank No. 2 port and starboard. 28. Deep tank No. 1 port and starboard. 29. Fuel oil or ballast tank No. 1. 30. Fore peak. 31. Stores.

Liberty ships were British in conception but adapted and produced in the United States. Fulfilling a vital need for emergency strategic transports during the war, they were mass produced on a vast scale. Modified liberty ships were also purpose-built as tankers, colliers and hospital ships. Some are still in use today.

Nuclear Power: USS Enterprise

During the First World War a new weapon was used for the first time: the aircraft. The naval authorities immediately realized its potential as an observation or attack instrument at sea and even before the war was over some cruisers had had their upper decks cleared of most superstructures and gun turrets to be converted into sea-going landing and take-off strips: the aircraft carrier was born. Just over twenty years later, when the Second World War broke out, the aircraft carrier had developed into a purpose-built ship of great strategic value.

Almost every major action in the Pacific involved aircraft carriers, and of the many such ships fighting there, one became particularly famous: the USS *Enterprise*, familiarly known as *'The Big E'*. She earned twenty battle stars, more than any other ship of the United States Navy. When she was broken up for scrap in 1958, it was natural that her name should be given to the first nuclear-powered carrier, the keel of which had been laid down a few months previously.

In modern strategy, carriers are essential to a surface fleet. They provide it with air cover, with long range anti-submarine aircraft protection and with an air attack capability against enemy shore or sea targets. At the same time the carrier is dependent on a screen of small ships to protect it against various types of threats. Whereas the submarine, particularly the nuclear strategic type, can cruise alone, the carrier is inherently a fleet ship.

Although the *Enterprise* (CVAN 65) has inherited her name from *'The Big E'* (CV6) of 1938, there is an intermediate generation between the two ships. The 'Forrestal' class, which came into commission in 1955 with the USS *Forrestal*, was the first post-war American carrier class, incorporating the experience of the Second World War and of the Korean War and some British inventions such as the angled flight deck, steam catapults, mirror landing system and armoured flight deck.

When she was commissioned in 1961, the *Enterprise* was the second nuclear surface ship; she had been preceded by only a few months by the nuclear cruiser *Long Beach*. For over ten years, until the carrier USS *Nimitz* (CVAN 68) was commissioned in 1974, the *Enterprise* was the largest warship ever to be built.

The principal dimensions of the *Enterprise* are:
Displacement: 76,915 tonnes, 90,428 tonnes at full load.
Length overall: 341·3 m (more than five times the length of HMS *Victory*).
Length at waterline: 317·0 m
Beam: 40·5 m.
Flight deck width: 78·3 m. (HMS *Victory* could sit across this deck with space to spare.)
Area of flight deck: 18,000 m².
Draught: 10·8 m.
Depth from flight deck to keel: 28·75 m (equivalent to a ten-storey block of flats; measured to the top of the mast, the height from the keel would be that of a twenty-five storey building).

The ship's complement is 5,502 men: 162 ship's officers, 2,940 enlisted men and 2,400 air wing personnel. The size of the ship and her complement is best shown by a few figures: more than 16,000 meals are served each day, her distilling plants could provide fresh water for 1,400 households; she has more than 1,800 telephones; and her electricity generating capacity would be sufficient for a town of 2,000,000 inhabitants.

The width of the flight deck is considerably larger than the beam of the hull proper. In fact the deck-edge overhangs house the four elevators which carry the aircraft from the hangar deck below to the flight deck, the island structure, the catapult controls and the missile sponsons. There are four steam catapults which take their steam from the reactors. They are capable of accelerating a 36-tonne aircraft (the heaviest type on board) to 260 km/h in 60 m, and they can be adjusted for each weight and type of aircraft. Two of the 'cats' launch over the bows and the other two over the fore end of the angled deck. With all the 'cats' in operation, it is possible to launch an aircraft every fifteen seconds.

The angled deck is the landing deck and has four arresting wires capable of halting heavy planes in a few metres. If a plane's tail hook or landing gear has been damaged, a nylon net can be erected across the deck to catch the aircraft with only minor damage. The elevators measure about 370 m²; three are to starboard and one is on the port quarter, allowing aircraft to be lifted and lowered simultaneously.

The island structure rests outside the hull, supported by a sponson. The big

white square-looking 'billboards' are a 360° fixed array radar antenna system which not only scans the horizon faster than a rotating antenna but also give a three-dimensional picture and an increased range. Above this radar array is the flag bridge where the admiral and his flag officers supervise the fleet and air wing movements and those of the enemy, with the help of advanced electronic and computer monitoring systems which include the Naval Tactical Data System (NTDS) and the Integrated Operational Intelligence System (IOIS). The NTDS can simultaneously analyse multiple enemy threats, propose counter-measures in microseconds and, through radio links with other ship- or airborne systems, it allows the control of a task force as if it were a single ship. The IOIS provides a continuous analysis and updating of intelligence gathered by reconnaissance aircraft, other ships and outside intelligence sources. There is also a direct link with the Pentagon.

The navigation bridge is situated above the flag bridge and it, too, has an impressive array of electronics. A continuous digital position display is provided by automatic satellite navigation and computer processing. The accuracy is such that if the satellite aerial were moved from one side of the island to

The U.S.S. *Enterprise* (left) has been developed to make full use of aircraft in naval warfare in the nuclear age. The massive tower (above) houses the computerized weapon and monitoring systems and the huge white screen fascias contain her 360° fixed array radar system antennae. The area of the flight deck (below) measures 18,000sq.m and is angled so that the deck edge overhangs the hull proper. She carries up to a hundred aircraft, which are launched from four steam catapults, each capable of launching aircraft of up to 36 tonnes.

the other, the difference in position would be recorded. Above the navigation bridge is the control tower.

The thimble-shaped dome and the mast support radar and radio aerials such as the Electronic Countermeasure (ECM) aerials which ring the dome, and radar aerials for search, navigation, and low-flying aircraft and missile detection. The main ship-borne defence is provided by two Basic Point Defense Missile Systems (BPDMS) with Sea Sparrow missiles.

About ninety-five aircraft of different types are carried, the ratios of which vary according to the mission: fighters (such as Phantom IIs), attack aircraft (such as Corsairs and Intruders), reconnaissance aircraft (such as Vigilantes), electronic countermeasure aircraft (such as Skywarriors), in-flight refuellers, early-warning radar, communications and search and rescue aircraft.

When they are not in use or on display, the aircraft are kept on the hangar deck, just below the flight deck. This hangar deck, with a 6·25 m headroom, is remarkably spacious, as it runs almost the entire length of the ship. The crew accommodation, computer rooms, back-up control rooms, magazines and machinery space are below this deck.

Nuclear power was first used at sea in

The U.S.S. *Enterprise*, commissioned in 1961, was the second nuclear powered surface ship. She has eight reactors which give her a speed of 35 knots. When fully operational she is capable of launching one aircraft every fifteen seconds, and she carries two Basic Point Defense Missile Systems, with Sea Sparrow missiles.

USS Nimitz (CVAN68) is now the world's largest warship. Like the *USS Enterprise* she is powered by nuclear reactors. These are of an improved design and only two supply all the power she needs.

1955, with the submarine USS *Nautilus*. The advantages of nuclear power are multiple. The range of endurance of the ship is limited almost solely by the endurance of the crew. The first set of uranium cores on the *Enterprise* was replaced after three years and 207,000 miles while the third, current set can power the ship (and provide fresh water and electricity) for ten to thirteen years. Cores are now being developed which could last an aircraft carrier her full operational life of thirty years. The endurance advantage of nuclear power in carriers is somewhat tempered by the fact that they still depend on a mainly conventional fleet which needs either naval bases relatively near at hand or secure sea lanes for fuel-carrying tankers. Nuclear power also saves space. The absence of boiler room bunkers allows more space for aircraft fuel bunkers and magazines and because there are no stacks, the ship can be sealed against nuclear fallout, combat gases and biological agents. Finally, nuclear power allows quasi-instantaneous variations of the power output, giving the ship a high manoeuvrability.

The *Enterprise* has eight reactors providing more than 200,000 h.p. and capable of pushing the 90,000 tonne ship at 35 knots. The reactors are water-cooled under pressure, and steam for the turbines and generators is made in heat exchangers as the water in contact with the cores is radioactive and must remain in closed-circuit. The turbines actuate four five-bladed propellers with a 6·4 m diameter and a weight of 33 tonnes. There are four rudders, one astern of each propeller.

The design of the *Enterprise* started in 1950 and Congress appropriated funds for its building in 1957. The keel was laid down on 4 February 1958 at the Newport News Shipbuilding and Dry Dock Company of Newport News in Virginia. The ship was launched on 24 September 1960 and commissioned on 25 November 1961.

In 1962 she was sent to the Quarantine station off Cuba during the Cuban Crisis, when the Soviets were dissuaded from landing nuclear missiles in Cuba. In 1964 she sailed with the nuclear cruiser *Long Beach* and the nuclear frigate *Bainbridge* on Operation Sea Orbit—a 30,500 mile, sixty-five day circumnavigation without replenishment of any kind. She was drydocked at Newport News for overhauling and recoring (with fresh uranium) from October 1964 until the following February. Late in 1965 she was on station off Vietnam, starting her first tour of duty in those waters. She did a second tour of duty in the Far East from December 1966 to July 1967. She returned home once more, but on 23 January 1968, the North Koreans seized the US intelligence ship *Pueblo* on the high seas and the *Enterprise* was sent off the North Korean coast. Later she returned to Yankee Station in the Gulf of Tonkin, leaving for home in June 1968. Just after she had left Hawaii for her fourth combat tour in January 1969, a rocket exploded accidentally on the flight deck. There was a fire and the subsequent explosions of ammunition killed twenty-eight crewmen and destroyed fifteen aircraft. The *Enterprise* resumed her mission in March after repairs at Pearl Harbor. After this combat tour she returned to Newport News for her second overhaul and recoring in 1969–70. In 1971 she was on her last Vietnam combat tour and since then she has been in various seas, only occasionally making a show of force, never in action.

In 1974 she was joined in the US Navy by another, slightly larger, nuclear carrier, the USS *Nimitz* (CVAN 68, 92,867 tonnes full load displacement) which has only two reactors, of improved design. A second 'Nimitz' class carrier, the *Dwight D. Eisenhower* (CVAN 69) was commissioned early in 1976 and a third, the *Carl Vinson* (CVN 70) was laid down in 1971.

The World's Largest Ships: Globtik Tokyo

Modern technological civilization is based on oil. It is oil that provides much of the world's electricity, oil from which most of the plastics are made, oil that is the raw material for countless other synthetic chemicals, from detergents to medicinal drugs, oil that moves cars—and most ships. Oil not only moves goods and ships in an unprecedented world maritime trade but it represents itself an appreciable part of the trade and it has led to a new type of ship unknown only a century ago—the tanker. Tankers are now the largest ships ever built and in this race to gigantism, the first ship to reach half a million tonnes was the *Globtik Tokyo*.

The sailing ship *Elizabeth Watts* imported the first cargo of Pennsylvania oil to London just over a century ago. This cargo was stowed in 1,329 barrels and totalled only 200 tonnes. For many years barrels were the standard packaging but because of their shape they wasted a lot of space in the ships' holds and they were eventually replaced by rectangular metal cans protected in wooden cases. The answer to the increasing trade, however, was to ship oil in bulk, in tanks. The first tankers had separate tanks built in their holds and the next step in tanker development, the one leading to the modern concept of tanker, was to use the hull itself as the tank. The first such tanker, *Glückauf* (2,307 gross tons), was built at Newcastle in 1886 for the German-American Oil Company; she was a coal steamer with auxiliary sails.

The invention of the internal combustion engine and the motor car and the use of oil as raw material for the chemical industry led to a steady increase of the trade, with the need to build bigger ships.

Between the two World Wars, tankers ranged from 8,000 to 17,000 tonnes deadweight (tdw). The size of these tankers was the result of factors including not only the economic requirements of the shippers and importers but the output and storage capacity of the refineries at the port of origin (the trade was then primarily one of refined products) and the size limitations of the waterways, such as the Suez Canal and the Shatt al Arab.

It was only in the late 1940s that economic and political factors led to the building of refineries in the importing countries, and the sea trade changed from product to crude oil carrying, which demanded larger tankers. The Suez Canal, through which the major part of European imports had to pass, was widened and deepened to 13·8 m. In the early 50s there were many 'super' tankers of about 30,000 tdw. An appreciable jump in size was represented by the West German-built *Tina Onassis* of 45,750 tdw, launched in 1953.

Japan was rapidly expanding her manufacturing industries and was importing increasing amounts of crude oil from the Middle East without having to tailor her tankers to the dimensions of the Suez Canal and she soon built 100,000 tdw tankers. In plain economical terms, the larger the tanker, the less the costs in transport per tonne of oil: neither the fuel consumption nor the manning requirements increase proportionally to the size. The upper limit in size was only governed by the state of the shipbuilding industry and the size of the shipyards.

The nationalization and temporary closure of the Suez Canal in 1956 showed that Europe, too, needed some 100,000 tdw tankers if oil was to be carried economically from the Persian Gulf, by way of the Cape. In 1965 Vickers' yard at Barrow built the first European 100,000 tdw class tanker, the 111,420 tdw *British Admiral*, for the BP Tanker Company, but by that time

Floating a supertanker, the 378,000 tonne *Nissei Maru* Giant tankers were first constructed in Japan in the early 1960s at the shipyard of Ishikawajima-Harima Heavy Industries, the company which built the *Globtik Tokyo*. Every aspect, from the huge tank capacities to the vast quantities of paint used, is of phenomenal proportions.

the Japanese were already engaged in building 150,000 and even 200,000 tdw vessels such as the *Tokyo Maru* (151,250 tdw) and the *Idemitsu Maru* (210,000 tdw). The long closure of the Suez Canal which followed the Arab-Israeli war of 1967 made supertankers mandatory for Europe.

It was in 1967 that Mr Ravi Tikkoo, a former Indian Navy officer, formed the London-based Globtik Tankers Ltd, a family concern where 99 per cent of the shares were owned by himself and the balance by his wife. The company acquired its first ship, the *Globtik Sun,* in 1968 and its second, the *Globtik Mercury* the following year. In 1968 Mr Tikkoo worked out that the most economical very large crude carrier (VLCC) size would be between 450,000 and 500,000 tdw. This represented in practical terms a huge size jump and the plans to go ahead were greeted in shipping circles with scepticism.

Mr Tikkoo nevertheless ordered two such ships to be built at the Kure (Japan) yard of Ishikawajima-Harima Heavy Industries and the first one, the *Globtik Tokyo,* was laid down in April 1972, launched the following October and delivered on 20 February 1973. She was followed on 31 October 1973 by her sistership, the *Globtik London.* Although not operating to or from Britain, both ships fly the Red Ensign.

The *Globtik Tokyo* cost about £23

million to build. She is 483,404 tdw and was the largest ship in the world until the launching of the *Globtik London*. Both ships have a tank capacity of 580 million litres; the overall length is 378·85 m, nearly a quarter of a mile, or approximately the length of six jumbo jets nose to tail. The beam is 62 m and the loaded draught is 28·20 m. The height from the keel to the top of the radar mast is 75 m—the height of a twenty-three-storey building—and that to the top of the wheelhouse is 57 m—a seventeen-storey building. The deck area—20,668 m²—is big enough for seventy-nine tennis courts, and mopeds are used by the crew to move around.

The hull has a rectangular, flat-bottomed section, with shapes only introduced at the bow and stern. The bow is of the bulb type, a modern design which improves the flow of water and decreases resistance. The welds used in the building of the *Globtik Tokyo* total a length of over 683 miles, more than the north-south dimension of France. Paint was also used in phenomenal quantities: 400 tonnes. The rudder weighs 250 tonnes and has an area large enough to park forty-seven small passenger cars side by side. Despite the single-screw propulsion, the *Globtik Tokyo* has a turning circle of less than three times her length. The two anchors weigh 29 tonnes each.

The tanker is powered by steam turbines geared to a single shaft developing 45,000 s.h.p. The five-bladed propeller is 9·25 m in diameter and weighs 61 tonnes. The normal service speed is sixteen knots. By setting the propeller in reverse gear, the ship can be stopped within three miles. Machinery control is automated and watched by two engineers in an air-conditioned and sound-insulated control room.

During ballast passages it is common tanker practice to clean out the tanks and the flushing out of oil residues has created considerable environmental damage. The practice is now forbidden within fifty miles (if not more) of coastlines. The *Globtik Tokyo* has automatic fixed tank cleaning equipment and the soiled water is collected in two

The supertanker *Globtik Tokyo* was the first ship to reach the half million tonne class and is now the second largest ship in the world. Her massive tanks, carrying 580 million litres of oil, can be pumped out in only nineteen hours, and her decks are so large that the crew use mopeds.

1885 *Palgrave*. 3,238 tonnes. Length 98·2m. Beam 14·9m.

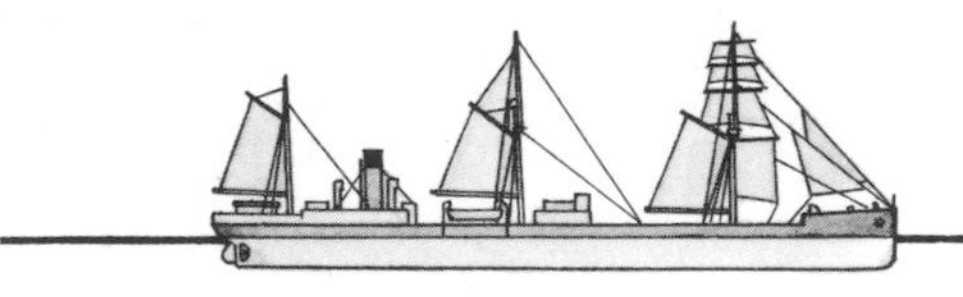

1886 *Glückauf*. 2,307 gross tons. Length 91·5m. Beam 11·3m.

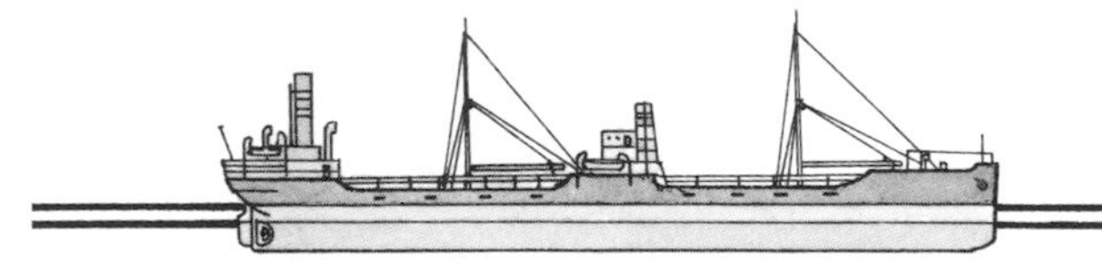

1912 *British Marshal*. 6,031 tdw. Length 108·8m. Beam 14.6m.

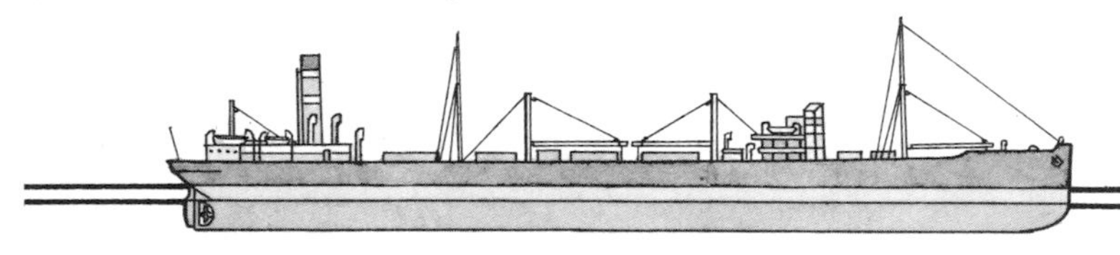

1914 *San Jeronimo*. 15,578 tdw. Length 164·5m. Beam 20·2m.

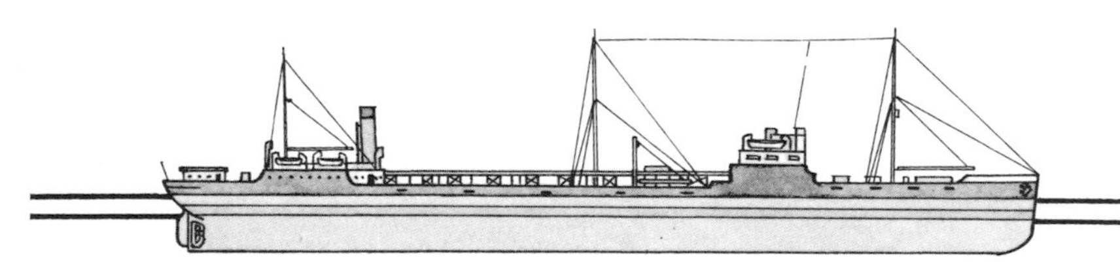

1921 *William Rockefeller*. 22,600 tdw. Length 174·5m. Beam 22·8m.

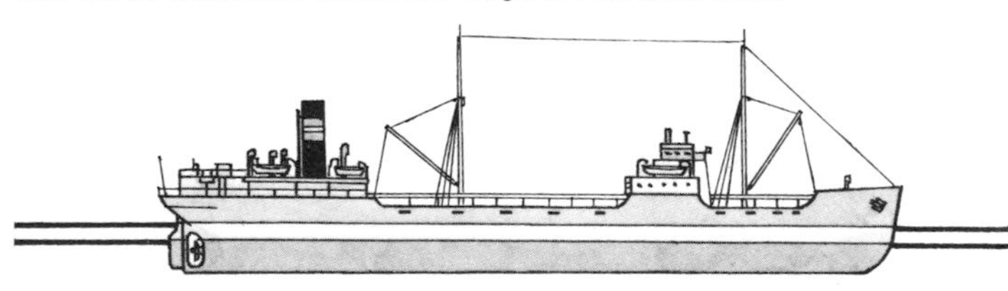

1922 *British General*. 10,150 tdw. Length 134·1m. Beam 17·3m.

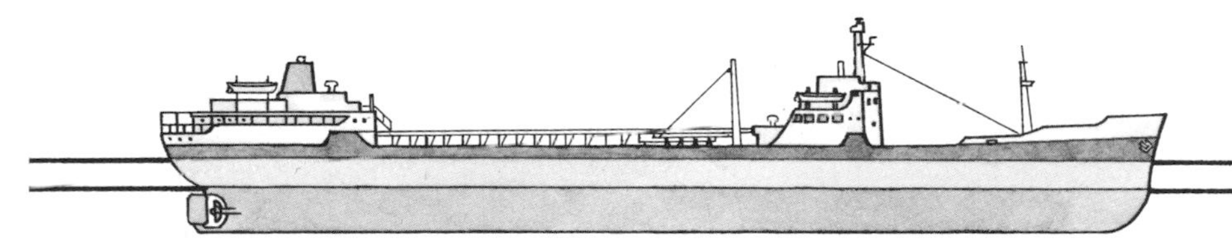

1956 *Cities Service Norfolk*. 32,825 tdw. Length 201·4m. Beam 27·4m.

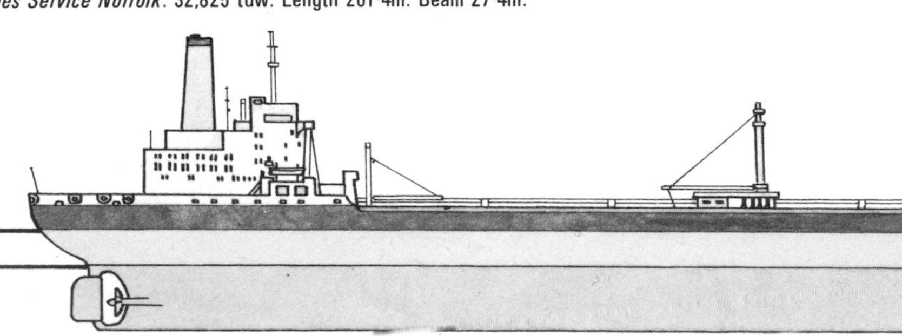

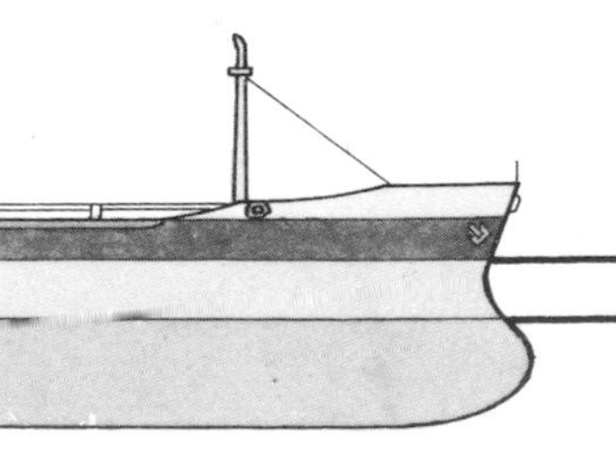

1968 *Murex*. 208,800 tdw. Length 325·2m. Beam 47·2m.

slop tanks where the oil and water are separated so that only purified water is discharged at sea.

The mixture of hydrocarbons and air is highly explosive and modern tankers are fitted with inert gas systems to flush out atmospheric air in the tanks. On the *Globtik Tokyo* the boiler uptake gases (consisting of nitrogen, carbon dioxide and carbon monoxide) are cooled, filtered and fed into the tanks. Even during the cleaning and after it, the controlled atmosphere must be kept: the tanks are so big as to have their own 'weather' with discharges of static electricity which have resulted in a series of disasters. In 1969 the Shell tanker *Marpessa* blew up and within the same month the 208,560 tdw *Mactra* and the 219,000 tdw *King Haakon VII* were severely damaged by similar explosions. Despite all precautions the danger is still there and in late 1975 the most expensive shipping insurance loss to date occurred when the 223,963 tdw ore/oil carrier, *Berge Istra*, with a cargo of iron ore blew up, leaving only two survivors to be picked up three weeks later. Presumably oil residues in the tanks were the cause.

Over the last ninety years, as the demand for oil has grown, the size of the ships which carry it has increased dramatically. The earliest oil carriers, such as the *Palgarve*, carried their cargo in cases. The prototype of the modern tanker was the S.S. *Glückauf*. The upper limit in size seems now to be governed only by the state of the shipbuilding industry and the size of the world's shipyards.

The internal construction of an early bulk oil carrier, built by Sir William Armstrong Mitchell and Company in 1891. There is little essential difference in the construction of this tanker and the earlier S.S. *Glückauf*. The oil was carried next to the hull. A single longitudinal bulkhead separated the cargo space into two levels, each divided into compartments by transverse bulkheads. Her dimensions were: 3,000 gross register tons. Length 96·3m. Beam 11·5m.

For manoeuvring in confined waters the *Globtik Tokyo* is equipped with a Doppler Sonar Docking System (based on the Doppler effect on underwater sound waves), which determines the movements of the ship within a metre; it is linked to automatic speed and rudder controls. In open waters a Navy Navigation Satellite System is used, similar to that on the USS *Enterprise*. There is also an anti-collision device.

The crew, which is UK-based, is only 38-strong, including the master. All the accommodation is air-conditioned and there is a swimming pool and many other recreational amenities to relieve the tedium of tanker passages from the end of a desert pipeline to the jetty of an oil refinery and back in quick and monotonous rotation. Generous leave is granted after a series of voyages and the crew is periodically relieved by aeroplane. The senior officers may take their wives to sea with them.

The *Globtik Tokyo* run goes from the Kirre refinery in southern Japan to Kharg island, off Bushire, Iran, in the Persian Gulf, by way of the Malacca Strait, the shortest route. The voyage, done in ballast, takes sixteen days at 17 knots. The return journey has to follow a longer route because the loaded draught is too deep for the Malacca Strait: it passes through the Lombok Strait, between the islands of Lombok and Bali, and through the Macassar Strait; this journey takes twenty-one days. The cargo is pumped out in nineteen hours and the ship is ready to leave again within twenty-four hours of arrival.

The *Globtik London* is identical to the *Globtik Tokyo* except for minor internal modifications which add 535 deadweight tonnes, making her the largest ship in the world, at 483,939 tdw. This title may soon be lost to the twin-screw sister ships *Batilus* and *Bellaya*, 550,698 tdw, which are being completed by the Chantiers de l'Atlantique at St Nazaire, France, for the Société Maritime Shell. The Globtik Tanker Company is reported to have made inquiries in Japan about a 700,000 tdw giant but with the current slump in oil demand and much of the world's tanker tonnage lying idle, it is likely that there will be a pause in supertanker construction. However the possibility of seeing million-tonne tankers is not so remote, as they cut down the transport costs on each barrel of oil. The Harland & Wolff yard in Belfast has even announced that it could build 1·75 million-tonne tankers. Such large ships will need new draught-reducing designs (by increasing the beam) or they will be extremely restricted in their destinations. Even so, special deep-draught terminals, miles offshore are being contemplated.

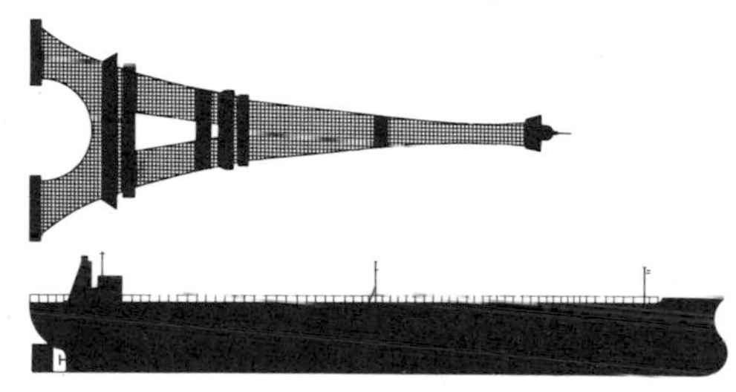

The Eiffel Tower (314·8m high) shown to scale with a 477,000 tonne tanker planned for Globtik Tankers Ltd.

Left, below: The bulb type bow of the *Globtik Tokyo* has been designed to improve the flow of water and reduce resistance. The total building cost was approximately £23 million and she is nearly a quarter of a mile in length.

Below: The *Globtik London* under construction. She is identical to her sister ship, *Globtik Tokyo*, except for some slight modifications internally which add a further 543 tdw. At 491,705 tdw she is the largest ship in the world.

Glossary

Parts of sails and rigging, different hull shapes and different types of rigs are defined and illustrated in the Introduction (pp. 10–20). Here are some sailing terms which a novice may find unfamiliar.

Abaft: Toward the stern of a vessel.
Aft: Near the stern of a ship.
Ballast: Iron or stone or other heavy material placed in the bottom of a ship's hold to keep it stable. (Coarse gravel known as shingle ballast is also used.)
Bilge: The bottom of a ship's hull. The ship would rest on the bilge if it ran aground.
Beak-head: A name given to a ship's head when its forecastle is square or oblong; common in all wooden warships.
Bonnet: An extra piece of sail attached to the bottom of a fore-and-aft sail to give additional sail area—usually taken off in bad weather.
Bowsprit: A large and sturdy spar projecting from the bows of a vessel.
Bulwarks: The woodwork, around and above the deck, fastened to timberheads and stanchions.
Carvel: Planking laid edge to edge.
Class: Ships built to the same overall specifications are said to be of the same class; they take their name from the original ship of that particular design.
Clinker: A form of planking with each plank overlapping the one below.
Cutwater: The foremost part of a ship's prow.
Davit: Beams of timber or iron, with blocks or sheaves at the ends, projecting out over the side or stern of a vessel for hoisting up boats.
Decks: The platforms or "floors" of a ship varying with type or size of the ship; e.g. gun deck; main deck, running the full length of the ship; mess deck, a lower deck where the men eat; poop deck, a small deck at the aftermost end of the ship; quarter-deck, a smaller deck over the half-deck, covering half the length of the ship; spar-deck, a light upper deck; orlop deck, the lowest deck covering the hold.
Draught: The depth of water between the waterline and the bottom of the hull which allows the vessel to float.
Fore: Used to describe the forward part of a vessel i.e. fore-mast etc, as opposed to things aft.
Forecastle: The part of the upper deck which is forward of the fore-mast.
Forward: Towards the fore-part of the ship.
Fore-and-Aft: From end to end or throughout the length of the whole ship.
Frigate: A light fast warship carrying its main armament on one deck.
Gunports: Holes in the side of a vessel through which the guns are fired.
Hogged: The condition of a vessel when it is made to droop at each end under strain thus causing the centre to rise.
Jib: Triangular sail carried forward of the foremast.
Keel: The lowest and main timber of a ship, running fore-and-aft, on which the whole frame is supported.
Knee: A crooked piece of timber, having two arms, used to connect the beams of a ship with her timbers or sides.
Larboard: The left side of a ship when facing forward.
Leech: Border or edge of a sail, either perpendicular or sloping.
Leeward: Opposite direction to which the wind blows—the lee side.
Luff: To put the helm towards the leeside. Also forward leech of fore-and-aft sails.
Man-o-War: An armed ship.
Mast: Long round piece of timber standing upright from the keel, or deck. Of one or several pieces according to the nature of the mast i.e. main-mast fore-mast etc.
Moonsail: A small sail above a skysail sometimes carried in light winds.
Poop: The deck raised above the aftermost part of a spar deck.
Port: Used instead of larboard, the left side of a ship facing forward.
Ports: Openings in the side of a vessel through which to point cannon as in gunports. Also portholes, small window openings as on a liner or other contemporary ships.
Rates: Classification of warships based mainly on the number of guns carried. Rates prior to the seventeenth century were classified according to the number of men carried.
Ratlines: Lines running horizontally across the shrouds, similar to rungs of a ladder, to step upon when going aloft.
Sails: Usually named from the mast to which they are attached e.g. mainsail, foresail, spritsail. *See also* pp. 16–17.
Seakindly: A good sailer.
Sheave: The grooved wheel of a block upon which a rope runs.
Ship-of-the-line: Ship carrying fifty or more guns considered to be suitable to fight in the line of battle.
Skysail: A light sail sometimes carried above the royals.
Spar: General term to describe masts, yards etc.
Sprit: Spar, set diagonally, extending fore-and-aft sail.
Starboard: The right side of a ship, facing forward.
Stays: Large ropes for supporting the mast, leading from the top of one mast to another or to some other part of the ship. Named according to direction of attachment, backstays, fore-and-aft stays.
Strake: A continuous line of planking along the side of a ship.
Studding sails: Light sails extended on booms rigged out for that purpose, outside the square sails.
Tack: To alter the course of a ship from one 'board' to another i.e. starboard to larboard. The course of a ship slanting to windward.
Tonnage: Total number of tonnes registered or carried. Gross tonnage: total capacity calculated in volumetric tons of 100 cubic feet (non-metric measurement internationally accepted). Deadweight: total contents of ship including cargo, fuel, passengers, crew etc., with the exception of boiler water, measured in metric tonnes. Displacement tonnage: used to define the weight of a naval vessel, and relates to the weight of the volume of water displaced by a vessel under normal seagoing conditions.
Transom: Beam or timber extended across the stern-post of a ship, to which it is bolted.
Wale: Strong planks in a vessel's sides extending the whole length fore-and-aft, to strengthen or reinforce.
Windward: Lying towards the wind.
Yard: Long piece of timber, slightly tapering towards the ends, hung at the centre from a mast, upon which the square sails are spread.

Index

Figures in italics refer to illustrations.

A ship of 74 guns, 1805, from a contemporary engraving by T. Milton.

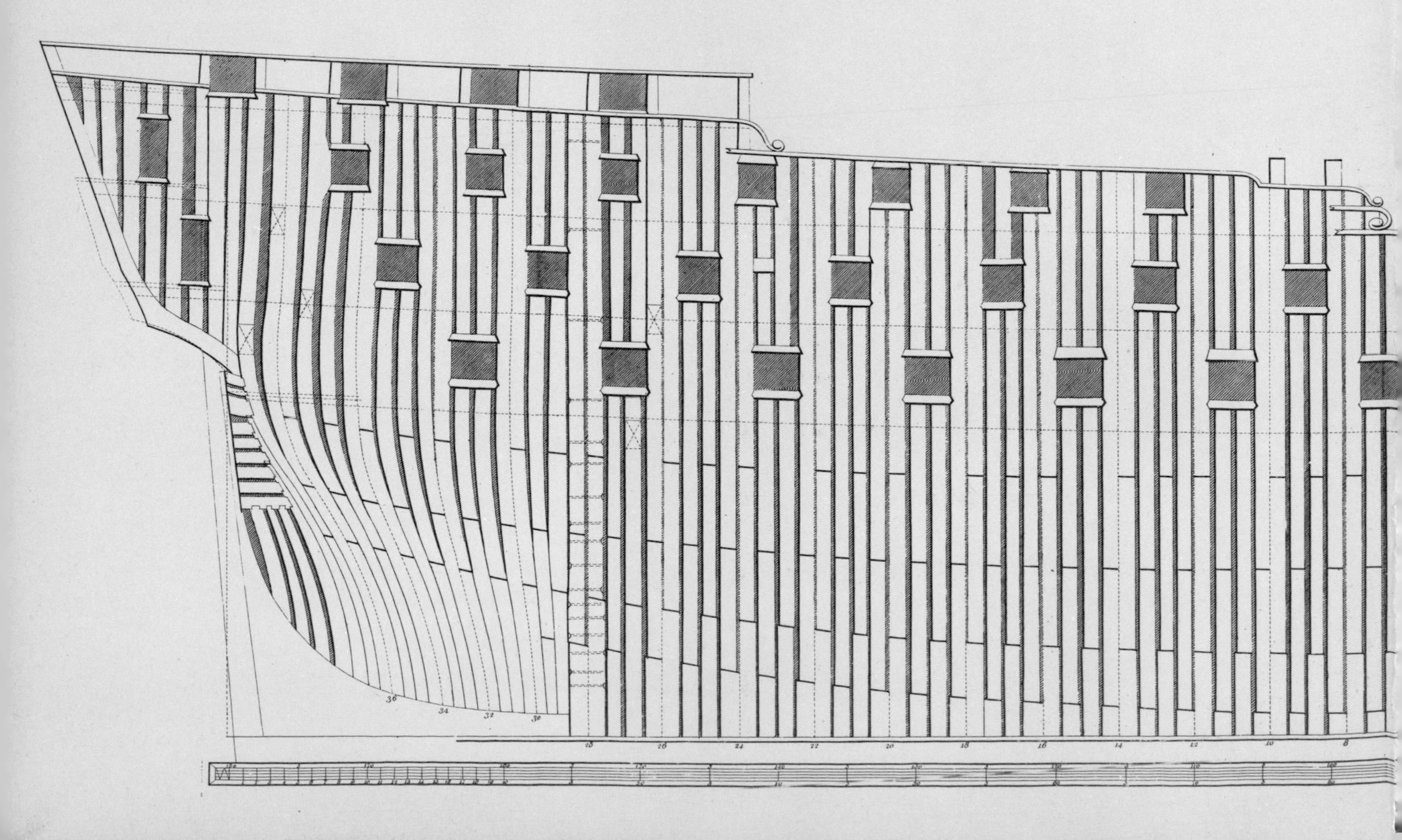